A Deal's A Deal

A Deal's A Deal

GARY TAYLOR

Chandos Publishing
Oxford · England

Chandos Publishing (Oxford) Limited
TBAC Business Centre
Avenue 4
Station Lane
Witney
Oxford OX28 4BN
UK
Tel: +44 (0) 1993 848726 Fax: +44 (0) 1865 884448
Email: info@chandospublishing.com
www.chandospublishing.com

First published in Great Britain in 2008

ISBN:
978 1 84334 431 5 (paperback)
1 84334 431 9 (paperback)

British Library Cataloguing-in-Publication Data.
A catalogue record for this book is available from the British Library.

Typeset by Domex e-Data Pvt. Ltd.
Printed in the UK and USA.

To Melinda and Glyn, a big thanks for all the editorial help, advice and professional direction. But most of all I thank you for believing I could achieve my goal within the stressful lives we all lead. Without you it would not have been possible.

Also, Travel West Midlands, after thirty-one years, you will never know how much you contributed.

Finally, I would like to thank my wife Nicky and four daughters, Holly, Katie, Chloe and Ellie. For your patience on those long evenings, when my eyes were diverted from my family to a notepad and computer screen.

Contents

Lisa Dean

On the outside Lisa Dean looked like any other fifteen year-old schoolgirl: happy-go-lucky attitude, blonde hair and blue eyes, more mature physically than most at that age, but very much a child at heart. Inside, however, were secrets that couldn't be told. Secrets that would destroy her whole existence. Secrets that would destroy her family. As an only child she was doted on, but as she grew it was as if the novelty of a beautiful young child in the house had worn off. Walking home from school on that sunny Friday afternoon, all she could think about was what the weekend had in store for her.

'Lisa,' came a shout from some distance behind her, 'wait for me.' Her friend Gurjinder, a young Asian girl living in the same block of flats raced up behind her, her long plaited hair trailing behind her. Coming from a third-generation Asian family, she had a western attitude to life. 'What are you doing tonight? Fancy going to the pictures? Some of the other girls will be meeting up at the shopping centre – maybe we could get something to eat and see a film?'

'I'd love to, Jinder, only my mum asked me to help her with some stuff round the house.'

'You never come out any more, Lisa. Have I upset you or something? If I have, I'm sorry. Can we talk about it?'

'It's not you, honest. I just have that much on my mind at the moment. I don't seem to find the time.'

'You should have more fun girl. I'm going to enjoy myself while I'm young.'

They turned into Cherry Tree Crescent, a typical inner city street, full of kids with nothing to do but cause mischief. As they approached the flats Lisa seemed to be slowing down in a daydream. 'If you slow down any more you'll stop,' said Jinder.

'What?' said Lisa, distantly.

'My God girl, what's with you?' Jinder shook her head; Lisa's thoughts were obviously miles away. 'Listen, Lisa, anything you need to talk about, I'm here you know.'

'Thanks, Jinder. This is something I have to sort out myself. But I do appreciate it; you're a good friend. I'll see you at school on Monday.'

As Gurjinder approached the lifts, Lisa headed straight for the stairs. She had learnt not to use the lift after spending six hours on a Sunday afternoon stuck in there with an old lady after some of the local juvenile delinquents urinated on the control panel.

She arrived on the eighth floor breathing quite heavily. She had run up the stairs many times before, but she still found it tiring. Flat 32. She stood looking at the front door contemplating whether to go in or head off back down the stairs. As she placed the key in the lock, through the glass she could see the shape of her mother approaching the door. Before she could turn the key the door opened. Standing before her was her mother, Carol Dean, a very attractive, though slightly overweight, forty year-old. You could see where Lisa got her good looks from: blonde hair, now dulled by age, but sparkling blue eyes that seemed to have stood the test of time. The lines on her face showed the weight of stress in her life. 'If she knew the whole story it would kill her,' thought Lisa.

'Did you have a good day, dear?' Carol enquired, with a pleased-to-see-you expression on her face.

'Just boring old school,' replied Lisa.

'Don't be like that. If you want to make anything of yourself you need to get good grades.'

'Some hope of getting out of this place,' Lisa murmured as she walked past her mother, down the hall and into the living room. Carol closed the door and followed her.

'When your dad gets home we'll all sit down and have a nice meal. We can get a take-away if you like.'

'I'm not hungry,' said Lisa, 'I'm going to have a lie down.'

'You feeling OK?'

'Yeah,' sighed Lisa, 'just need to close my eyes for a little while.'

Lying on her bed, within seconds she drifted off to sleep, safe in her own little world.

She woke with a start. It was still light. She wondered how long she had been asleep for; her mother hadn't called her for tea. Extending her arms she stretched and yawned simultaneously before rolling off the bed onto her feet. She walked into the bathroom and looked at her face in the mirror before rubbing the sleep from her eyes. Walking down the hall and into the living room she noticed the clock on the mantelpiece: 7:30.

Her mother was sitting on the sofa reading one of the free local newspapers.

'Where's dad?' asked Lisa. A blank expression on her mother's face said it all. 'He's gone straight to the pub hasn't he?' said Lisa.

'I don't know,' snapped her mother, the tone of her voice confirming Lisa's question.

'Don't have a go at me,' Lisa snapped, equally agitated by the situation.

'I'm not, it's just I was hoping to have a nice family night in, just like in the old days.'

'I suppose we'll just have to make it the two of us then, won't we?' said Lisa feeling almost sorry for her mother. Carol stood up and opened her arms as if to beckon Lisa to her. Lisa responded and they hugged each other, both realising that this show of emotion was long overdue.

They went into the kitchen and prepared a meal of spaghetti bolognaise. It was Lisa's favourite meal and her mother thought a little bit of pampering might just cheer her up. After their meal they settled down to a quiet night in. There was nothing on the television either of them particularly wanted to watch; it was just nice to relax on the sofa. Carol opened a cheap bottle of wine and over the next couple of hours it was slowly drunk.

A scratching noise caught their attention – they looked at each other, realising simultaneously what it was. Lisa's father was trying to put his front door key in the lock; he'd had so much to drink the chances of that happening were very slim. Carol got up from the sofa, slowly, almost unwillingly, she walked down the hall to the front door. Through the glass panel she could see the silhouette of her husband. Alex Dean was a small but powerfully built man. At the age of forty-five he was still in remarkably good physical shape. Considering the amount of drink he had consumed over the last ten years or so, it was a miracle that he was still alive. He had worked in a factory all his working life, with no ambition or inclination to try and remove himself from that environment. When Lisa had started school he had changed dramatically, binge drinking at weekends, then slowly increasing until he was drinking virtually every day of the week. When Carol complained he would become angry, saying that he worked hard for a living so was entitled to some enjoyment, oblivious to the reality that it was at the expense of his family.

Carol opened the door; he could hardly stand. Leaning against the doorframe he looked pitiful. 'Where have you been till now, Alex?' asked Carol, a look of distaste on her face.

'I think that's pretty obvious don't you?' he slurred at her.

'You know what I mean. Come on in, I'll get you something to eat.'

'Already eaten,' said Alex.

'I'll make you some coffee then,' replied Carol.

He staggered down the hall, slamming into the display unit and the picture frames fell off, clattering to the floor. Lisa continued to watch the television, hoping he would ignore her, but she was not so lucky.

'And how is my beautiful daughter?' enquired Alex, his voice slurring heavily.

'Fine,' answered Lisa, trying to limit the conversation. When he was this drunk he could become violent at the drop of a hat. Lisa got up to get a drink from the kitchen. As she passed him he grabbed her and pulled her close, the smell of alcohol making her nauseous. His hands slid down her back onto her bottom. Immediately she pulled away pushing him off. 'Ooh, touchy aren't we,' he said. Staggering over to the sofa, he collapsed in a heap. With a loud sigh, then a yawn, he started to fall into a drunken sleep.

Carol came in with coffee. 'Typical,' she said, 'I don't know why I bother.'

'I'm off to bed,' said Lisa.

'OK,' sighed Carol, 'I think I'm going to leave him there and let him sleep it off. Night love, **see** you in the morning.'

Lisa headed for the bathroom, cleaned her teeth and changed into a pair of boyish-looking pyjamas. She climbed into bed and lay there thinking about her father. Why did he have to drink so? If only he had not been a drinker, none of this would be happening. She slowly drifted off to sleep, wondering what else was in store for her that weekend.

Lisa suddenly woke; she had the feeling that she was not alone. The hairs on the back of her neck were standing up. She could hear breathing, and the sudden smell of alcohol alerted her senses even more to the presence in the room. Her body was rigid with fear. She sensed that someone was sitting on the side of the bed directly behind her. She knew it was her father; this was not the first time he had come into her room at the dead of night. He slid his hand under the bed cover. She wanted to scream but it was as if she had been gagged; no sound came from her mouth. He moved his hand down her side onto her bottom. Her muscles tensed in fear of what was about to happen. Her father climbed into the bed and whispered, 'Don't make a noise and I won't hurt you.' As his hands started to move over her body Lisa thought that she would vomit at any second. He placed his hand between her legs and she tensed her thighs closely together hoping it would deter him.

He moved up her body, squeezing her breasts, pressing his aroused body against her. CLICK. The sound of a switch stopped him instantly; it was the sound of her mother's bedside lamp being turned on. 'Don't make a sound,' he hissed. He quietly got out of the bed and quickly moved to the bedroom door. Carol got out of bed, walked across the hall and went into the bathroom, closing the door behind her. On the sound of the door closing, Alex tiptoed down the hall into the living room, lay down on the settee and closed his eyes. He heard water running as Carol washed her hands, then the sound of the bathroom door opening. She walked into the living room and stood looking down at him.

'Drunken git,' she said under her breath, then shook him vigorously; Alex immediately sat up.

'What's wrong, what's wrong?' Alex repeated himself.

'Nothing,' said Carol. 'It's half two in the morning and you have to be in work at seven.' She pulled him to his feet and he staggered, still partly inebriated, to the bedroom. He threw his clothes off and crawled into bed. Carol turned off the light and fell back to sleep.

Lisa was still very much awake, tears running down her face. What was she going to do? It was only a matter of time before he raped her. Who could she confide in? She had to do something. She wiped the tears from her eyes and lay desperate for sleep but terrified of his return. She drifted into a fitful sleep, waking at the slightest noise or movement in the flat.

When Lisa woke it was daylight and the flat was silent. Her father worked most Saturday mornings but her mother was usually at home. She pulled on her dressing gown and went into the living room; a note taped to the television said GONE SHOPPING BACK BEFORE LUNCH, MUM. She glanced at the clock: ten o'clock. 'God,' she thought, 'I never sleep this late.' She went into the kitchen, pressed the button on the side of the kettle and put two slices of bread in the toaster. After breakfast she washed and dressed, her mind still going over and over what had happened in the early hours of the morning. The flat felt like a prison and she had to get out. 'Wonder what Jinder's doing today?' she thought. She got her key off the hook, grabbed her coat and headed out the front door and down the stairs.

Jinder lived two floors below at Flat 21, with her parents and two younger sisters. Like Lisa's flat, there were only two bedrooms and they were very cramped. Jinder's family had been promised a council house ever since her youngest sister was born; that was over two years ago now. Lisa got to the front door and rang the bell. She heard a shout from inside, 'I'll get it.' Lisa recognised Jinder's voice. The door opened.

'Lisa,' said Jinder, 'what have I done to deserve a visit from you?' Lisa's face dropped. 'I'm only joking, come in. I'll tell you about last night.'

Jinder's mother was standing in front of the television ironing a huge pile of clothes.

'Morning, Mrs Patel,' said Lisa, bravely producing a large smile.

'Hello, Lisa. I haven't seen you in ages. Have you been OK?'

'Fine, thanks. I've just had a lot on with school and all that,' said Lisa.

'Would you like a drink or something to eat?' Mrs Patel was the type of person who would give you the last penny in her pocket if she thought you needed it. 'I've just had breakfast, but thank you anyway,' she replied.

'Come on, Lisa, we can go in my room,' said Jinder. They went down the hall to the room Jinder shared with her sister, Gurpreati, who was playing on the floor with her dolls.

'Preati, out,' ordered Jinder.

'Do I have to?' pleaded Gurpreati. Jinder held the door open without speaking. The seven year-old picked up her dolls and, with her chin on her chest, made her way to the living room. 'That's got rid of her,' said Jinder.

'You're awful to your sisters, you are. Wish I had a brother or sister,' said Lisa.

'What's happening anyway?' asked Jinder.

'Can you come out for a bit?' asked Lisa, 'I need to talk to you.'

'Talk away girl, I'm all ears,' replied Jinder, looking excited.

'I can't talk here. Honest, I have to be sure nobody else can hear what I have to say.'

'God, this sounds important. I'll get my coat.' They went into the hallway. 'Going out for a bit, mum,' shouted Jinder.

'OK,' called her mother, 'but be back before two o'clock. Your father will be back then and he'll want his dinner. Be good.'

As they left the flat, Jinder went straight to the lift. 'See you downstairs,' said Lisa.

'Nothing ever changes with you, does it, Lisa? Come on. I'll walk down with you.'

They went down the stairs and out of the flats, turning right onto Cherry Tree Crescent. The park was about half a mile down the road. As they walked, Jinder told Lisa about the previous evening's events, but Lisa's mind was elsewhere. She grinned and nodded at the right times, but heard little of what Jinder said.

At the park they went straight to the children's play area. There were no small children there; the area was strewn with broken glass bottles, and had ceased to be an attraction for families with children long ago. It was now a focus for teenagers making a nuisance of themselves. The council had made promises of various initiatives, but nothing had ever materialised. They sat on the two swings that remained in working order.

'Go on then,' said Jinder excitedly, 'Give me all the sordid details.'

'If I tell you something, will you promise not to tell another soul?'

'God, this sounds like it's going to be good,' Jinder eagerly replied, 'OK, OK, I promise.'

Lisa looked down at the floor trying to think of the right words to use.

'There's only one way to say this, Jinder,' said Lisa, flatly.

'Go on then, go on,' pleaded Jinder, rattling the metal chains of the swing, barely able to contain herself.

'My dad's messing with me.'

Silence. Lisa's gaze remained fixed on the ground. Jinder's jaw nearly hit the floor. Still silence. It seemed like an eternity.

'Jesus Christ, Lisa,' whispered Jinder, 'Do you mean what I think you mean?'

'Yes.' Lisa's reply was barely audible.

'How long has this been going on?' asked Jinder, excited anticipation now blasted away by the sudden shock and concern for her friend.

'On and off for months.'

'You have to tell, Lisa.'

'What about my mum?' said Lisa.

'What about you, more like? If you keep this a secret it's going to get worse. I'll come with you; we'll talk to your mum.' Jinder knew by Lisa's body language that this was serious and they needed help.

'No Jinder, you promised not to tell anyone unless I say.' The sound of panic in Lisa's voice worried Jinder even more.

'Yeah, but I never thought it was going to be this bad. This isn't going to go away, Lisa. You have to sort it out.'

'I will, I just need time to think.' Lisa knew Jinder was right, but how to sort it was a real problem. Whichever way it came out, it was going to change her life forever.

They got off the swings and started walking back towards the park gates. Lisa was already wondering if she had done the right thing by confiding in Jinder. Right or wrong, she felt that a huge weight had been lifted from her shoulders.

'Do you fancy coming to our house for dinner this afternoon? Mum would love to have you round,' asked Jinder.

'No, I have to get back, my mum said she would be home for dinnertime. She'll have brought something in with her. Thanks for the offer though, you're a good friend Jinder.'

'So are you Lisa, that's why I'm so worried about you.'

'I'll be OK, don't worry, I'll sort it out.' Jinder didn't know whether to hug her or shout at her in an attempt to make her do something about it.

They walked back to the flats. As they entered, Jinder did not consider the lift, she just followed Lisa up the stairs, trying to give her any comforting words she could before she reached her floor.

'You must be really fit using these stairs all the time – I'm shattered,' gasped Jinder.

'You get used to it,' replied Lisa.

'Listen Lisa, any time you need me I'm only two floors away, day or night, you got that?'

'Yeah, I know. See ya, and thanks for listening.'

As Lisa carried on up the stairs, she felt as if she had confessed to something awful and been forgiven. It was strange; she almost felt guilty for what had been happening to her. She opened the front door and from the living room her mother shouted, 'That you, Lisa?'

'Yeah,' she called back.

'Dinner's nearly ready. Your dad will be home soon.' The mention of her father made her feel sick in her stomach. She went into the living room.

'Are you all right? You look as if you've seen a ghost.'

'I've just run up all the stairs. It's tiring,' said Lisa.

'We're going down the club tonight – one of your dad's work mates retires at the end of the month and they're putting a surprise do on for him. Fancy coming?'

'Nah, I'm not keen on that club. It's boring, there's no young people go there, and I can't sit through the bingo. Anyway, Jinder said she'd come up later to watch telly.'

'OK, but the offer's there if you fancy it.'

The front door opened; it was her father home from work. Before even reaching the living room he said, 'What a morning I've had. It's non-stop at that place. Too much work and not enough staff. We keep telling them but they won't take anybody else on.'

Lisa was unable to look at him or acknowledge him.

'Are we all going out tonight then? Should be a good night. Old Geoff hasn't got a clue about the party,' said Alex. He acted as if nothing had ever happened. Was he that drunk that he was unable to remember what he had done?

'Lisa's not coming, dear,' said Carol.

'Why not?' he asked, looking puzzled.

'Jinder's coming over. They're having a girls' night in.'

'You're going to miss a good 'un – don't say I never told you so. I'm going to get a wash.'

'Don't be long,' chirped Carol, 'dinner's nearly ready.'

By seven o'clock Lisa's parents were ready for their evening out. Saturday night was the only time they ever socialised together. Carol was not a big drinker, but on Saturday nights at the club she would let her hair down and, every now and then, have one too many. She was the type of person who would just curl up in the corner and go to sleep. Alex, on the other hand, was quite the opposite. Always the life and soul of the party, in his friends' eyes he could do no wrong.

Later that evening the party was a great success and Alex's friend, Geoff, was taken completely by surprise. The send-off his friends and family had prepared for him was far more than he had ever expected. Beer flowed, and as the evening wore on, Alex and Carol got more and more drunk. To say that Carol was letting her hair down would have been an understatement. Alex, a more practised drinker, jokingly pleaded with the crowd to excuse her, 'She don't get out that often,' he quipped, to rapturous laughter.

Lisa lay on the sofa with no intention of asking Jinder to come up. It had taken her all her courage to talk about her father that afternoon and she did not want to go through the whole thing again, not just yet. As the evening wore on, Lisa decided to have an early night. There was nothing on the television, so a good book seemed the better option. She brushed her teeth, changed into her pyjamas, poured a glass of milk and climbed into bed.

At the club, the party was in full swing, Carol had already had her fair share of drinks and was beginning to slow down. Alex, on the other hand, was just getting started. By midnight, the party was slowing down and people were saying their goodbyes and generally heading off home. Carol sat on a bar stool looking very worse for wear. Alex came over, 'Come on ducks, lets get you off home,' he said, his voice slurring. He pulled her to her feet and they both staggered across the room, Alex making gestures to his friends about Carol's condition as they left.

As they approached Cherry Tree Crescent the night air had well and truly got to both of them. Each relied on the other to stay upright. They pushed open the main entrance to the flats, the doors crashing against the walls. Suddenly, a car alarm sounded, then a dog started barking.

'Bollocks,' said Alex.

'Sssshh,' slurred Carol in an attempt to eliminate the noise they were making. They got into the lift, the quantity of alcohol they had drunk disguising the smell of urine. The lift stopped at the seventh floor and they staggered out, too drunk to realise that this was one floor below their flat. It didn't help that all the front doors in the block looked the same, only the numbers gave them any identity. Alex was attempting to put his key in the door of number 22 when the lights came on in the flat.

'Piss off,' came a voice from inside, 'I'm phoning the police.' Alex suddenly came to his senses and realised it was the wrong flat.

'Shit! Quick,' he hissed at Carol, 'Back in the lift.' Fortunately, the doors had not closed. Giggling like children, they stumbled back into the lift and went up one more floor. They arrived at the flat and, after two or three attempts, Alex managed to open the front door. The flat was in darkness. He felt along the wall for the light switch and clicked it on. Carol followed him down the hall and into the living room, turning the lights on as they went.

'I'm going to bed,' said Carol, putting her jacket on a chair and making her way unsteadily down the hall to the bedroom.

'I'm going to have a nightcap before I turn in. Won't be long,' replied Alex. But Alex had other things on his mind; he poured himself a scotch and sat down on the sofa waiting for Carol to fall into a deep sleep. After about twenty minutes Alex got up and went to the bedroom. Carol was flat out, snoring loudly. Alex stripped down to his boxer shorts and went into the bathroom. Lisa had been in bed for about three hours and was in a deep sleep. She did not hear the door open or feel the bedclothes move as he slid into the bed beside her. With a start, she was conscious of his hand across her mouth, preparing to muffle her screams. In a split second, her senses were totally alert.

'I've waited so long for this,' he said under his breath. She was petrified. This was it; he wasn't going to stop this time. Should she fight or accept the inevitable? At least if she stayed still he might not harm her physically. She couldn't just lie there; she started to push at his shoulders but he was so strong she could not move him; she remembered the glass on the bedside cabinet. Her hand flared out in an attempt to arm herself but in the darkness she hit the glass, sending it to the floor. With his spare hand he pulled at the buttons on her pyjama jacket; one by one they popped open, exposing her naked upper body. He pulled at her pyjama trousers; little by little he pushed them down, her body now rigid with fear. She started to sob, his clammy hand still across her mouth. The tears rolled down her face but he did not stop, it was as if it excited him even more. One leg came out of her pyjama bottoms and he immediately forced her legs apart, fully aroused he plunged himself into her body; the pain was excruciating. Her nails dug into the top of his shoulders as he forced himself into her. With his spare hand he grabbed her throat and she released her hands from his body. Fearing for her life, she realised that the only way to survive this attack was not to resist. He seemed to go on for an eternity; her state of mind became trance-like. Finally, he stopped and rolled off her. Without uttering a single word he left the room. She lay in the darkness, eyes transfixed on the ceiling, trying to believe that it had not really happened. Uncontrollably, she cried; hot, burning tears rolling down her face. Turning onto her side she pulled her knees up to her chest and remained frozen in the same position for the remainder of the night.

Lisa woke just before eight o'clock; how she had slept at all she did not know. She felt dirty with the vile smell of stale sweat and alcohol surrounding her body. She got out of bed, pulled on her dressing gown and went into the bathroom. Locking the door behind her she began to run a bath. What had happened just hours before had made up her mind; she had to tell her mother and, whatever the outcome, he had to be stopped. Climbing into the bath she attempted to cleanse herself of his odour, feeling it ingrained in her skin. But it would take more than just a bath to cleanse her mind of this horrendous experience.

She heard movement in the flat. Somebody was out of bed. Hoping it was her mother but not sure, she tried to be as quiet as possible; she didn't want to attract any attention, just in case it was him. After about fifteen minutes she heard the front door open and close. She quickly climbed out of the bath and dried her body. Still feeling dirty, more mentally than physically, she opened the door and peered down the hall towards the living room. It looked very still and quiet. Her mother's bedroom door was ajar. Peering through the gap she could see her mother, still in bed, sleeping soundly. Lisa went into the kitchen put the kettle on and sat down at the table. She started to think about how to tell her mother that her father had raped her. It seemed like an impossible task, but it had to be done and done today.

About an hour later, Lisa had dressed and was watching television. Her mother came out of the bedroom tying her dressing gown belt. Her eyes told the story of the previous evening's indulgence. Picking up the remote control she turned down the television volume.

'My God, I feel terrible and my head's pounding. Did you have a good night?'

'No, I was raped by my father.'

No reply. Her mother had gone into the kitchen. Lisa got up and followed her.

'Did you hear me?' asked Lisa. Her mother stood facing the kitchen sink, her hands in a bowl of water washing some cups. Still no reply. Lisa stood to the side of her mother looking at her face, tears rolling down her cheeks.

'You did hear me, didn't you?' She hadn't expected this reaction from her mother. Carol picked up the tea towel and started to dry her hands. She moved over to the kitchen table and sat down heavily.

'Are you going to say something?' said Lisa, almost whispering.

'I don't know what to say, I thought it would stop,' replied Carol quietly. Lisa's eyes widened – a very large penny had just dropped; she knew he was molesting her.

'You knew,' Lisa replied, totally enraged, 'YOU KNEW? YOU'RE MY MOTHER FOR GOD'S SAKE! YOU'RE SUPPOSED TO LOOK AFTER ME!' Suddenly Lisa felt physically sick. She ran to the bathroom. Falling to her knees beside the toilet she vomited and retched until her stomach was in spasm. Cupping her hands, she swilled her mouth then dried her face. She went to her bedroom, slamming the door behind her. Sitting on the bed she felt totally dejected and alone; the only person she could turn to was also betraying her with her silence. Lisa knew there was only one thing to do: she had to look after herself, she had to leave and it had to be today. Pulling her holdall off the top of the wardrobe, she filled it with underwear, t-shirts, jeans – things that would still look good after two weeks in a suitcase. 'Money,' she thought. Her father had a small metal box under his bed and he always kept money in it, she had seen him take cash out of it when he went to the club. Her mother had gone into the bathroom; this was her chance. She tiptoed down the hall into their bedroom, pulled out the box and opened it. Medical card, wage slips. 'Yes,' she thought, there was a plastic wallet containing about fifty pounds in cash. She took it and put everything else back exactly where it was. There was no turning back now. Quietly, she went back to her room, pulled on a denim jacket, stuffed the money into her pocket then grabbed the holdall. Her mother was still in the bathroom. Briskly, Lisa walked down the hall to the front door, stopped and took one last look at the flat, then quietly closed the door behind her.

Going down the stairs she thought 'Jinder, I have to tell her I'm leaving, she's the only one that cares.' Knocking at Jinder's door, she could see her silhouette approaching. Jinder opened the door. 'Hi Lisa, come in.'

'No,' Lisa replied. 'I can't stop, I just wanted to tell you I'm leaving.'

'What do you mean?' asked Jinder.

'I'm going away.'

'I don't understand. What's happened, Lisa?'

Tears spilled over as Lisa tried in vain to control her emotions. 'Last night,' she paused, 'he raped me.'

'That's it. I'm going to get mum,' said Jinder, with a look of fury on her face.

'No, no, please don't, I've got it sorted. I'm leaving and I just wanted you to know. When I'm settled I'll give you a call. I just wanted you to know I was safe.'

'You're fifteen years old, Lisa, they'll come looking for you.'

'I know, but they've got to find me first and anyway, I'll be sixteen soon.'

'God, Lisa. Do you know what you're doing?'

'Yes, I finally think I do. But you haven't seen me, OK? I'll keep in touch, I promise.'

They hugged each other tightly, then Lisa headed off down the stairs. As she got near the bottom she slowed, her father was out of the flat and she had to avoid him at all costs. Checking her pockets for change, she found just enough to get her into town on the bus. She waited at the bus stop for what seemed like an eternity; as it was Sunday there were fewer buses running. After about forty-five minutes a bus came, its destination said 'Town Centre.' 'That'll do,' she thought. She sat on the bus, her mind racing. What was she going to do? Where was she going to go? She really was on her own. The bus pulled in at the terminus. A sign in front of the bus in big letters said STATION. Following the sign she thought 'I'll go to London. They won't find me there.' The revolving destination signs in the station were all blank as she stood looking up. Suddenly they started to spin – NEW STREET – was it an omen? New Street, new start. She went over to the ticket office.

'Single to New Street, please.' She didn't even know where it was.

'You'll have to be quick, it's just pulling out, platform two, three pound fifty please.'

She gave the clerk a ten-pound note, took the ticket, scooped up the change and dashed down the passageway. The guard was closing the last couple of doors. She ran to the door he was just about to close.

'Quickly, please,' he called. As she climbed breathlessly into the train, the guard passed Lisa her bag. The carriage was nearly empty. She stuffed her bag onto the overhead rack before dropping onto a seat by the window as the train moved off.

'Good riddance,' she sneered, then leant her head back against the seat.

'What's in store for me now?' she thought. It could not possibly be any worse than what she had just left.

2

New start

Lisa sat looking out of the window, watching the world go by. After about an hour and a half the view became increasingly industrial, then the train slowed down. Over the speaker she heard, 'Approaching Birmingham New Street.' As the train passed through the tunnels the scene through the window became gloomy, almost depressing.

'Well, it's not quite London,' she thought, 'but it's still a major city.'

She knew it would be difficult to find anyone who did not want to be found. The train rolled into the station and came to a halt. Lisa grabbed her bag, leaned out of the window and opened the door. She had never been to Birmingham and was quite excited. Leaving the platform she went up the stairs and into the main station.

'Drink,' she thought. There was a coffee shop near the main entrance, upmarket, but she went inside anyway.

'Coffee please.' The girl behind the counter looked her up and down, making her feel uneasy. Lisa knew that if she was to survive on her own, she had to stand up for herself.

'Is there a problem?' asked Lisa.

'No.' The girl suddenly became sheepish. Lisa paid for her drink and sat down, feeling good that she had not let the girl belittle her. She now had to find somewhere to spend the night. She was not going to stay on the streets. She knew she had enough money to book into a hotel, but also knew that she needed to budget carefully. Anyway, hotel staff might question her age and call the police. She sipped her coffee, gazing at nothing, thinking 'What am I going to do?'

After about half an hour of contemplating her next move she got up and headed towards the station exit sign. Although it was Sunday, it was very busy. Walking through a large shopping centre she came to a ramp and noticed the road sign 'New Street.' She thought it must be the main shopping area of the city. It was bustling with people, some handing out leaflets and magazines. Most of the shops were closed; she wondered what business so many people would have in the city centre on Sunday lunchtime. As she walked round the town trying to get her bearings, she noticed some busy restaurants and pubs, accounting for the number of people around the centre and the sociable atmosphere. Trying not to stay still for too long, as she did not want to draw attention to herself, she kept walking. After some time going round and round, she found a small park with an impressive old church. It looked so relaxing; the weather was fine and she had been walking for a couple of hours. Sitting down on one of the benches she started attracting the pigeons, and within a few minutes there were about fifty birds around her feet. 'Talk about not drawing attention to yourself,' she thought.

A middle-aged man approached and, as he passed, clapped his hands, the startled pigeons engulfing the surrounding area with wings fluttering in panic. 'That's why they call it Pigeon Park you know,' said the man, with a big cheesy grin on his face.

'Idiot,' said Lisa under her breath. She got up and continued across the park, feeling as if everyone in the surrounding area was looking at her. All the walking had made her hungry and her stomach was rumbling. On the edge of the park she noticed a pizza parlour. She was not a fussy eater and anything would do when she was hungry. She went in and sat down; when the waitress came over she ordered a medium cheese and tomato pizza, a portion of garlic bread and a large Coke.

'That'll fill the gap,' she thought. When the food arrived she took her time, not relishing the thought of another two-hour walk. She had been at the table for almost two hours and thought that it was time to go, before being asked to leave; the bill had been placed on the table a good half-hour previously. The waitress came over to collect the money.

'You wouldn't know where there are any B&Bs or small hotels close by would you?' enquired Lisa. The waitress was no more than a couple of years older than Lisa.

'Hagley Road,' she replied, knowledgably, 'that's your best bet.'

'Where's that?' Lisa asked politely.

'You new in town then?'

'Yeah, just passing through, though I might stay a night.'

'Tell you what, I'm finished in about half an hour. I have to catch the bus down that way. I'll show you if you want,' said the waitress.

'That would be great, thanks,' replied Lisa, genuinely pleased. Sure enough, half an hour later the waitress came over with her coat on.

'You ready?'

'Yeah, replied Lisa.

'My name's Sam, short for Samantha, but no one calls me that except my mum.'

'I'm Lisa, pleased to meet you.'

'So what you doing in Brum?' Sam was curious about the girl.

'I'm on my way to my sister's in London. I've never been to Birmingham so I thought I'd take a look on the way down.'

'You haven't missed much, believe me,' replied Sam, with a tone that implied dullness. 'Fancy going for a drink on the way?' she added, overestimating Lisa's age. Lisa thought about it for a few seconds then replied, 'Yeah, why not?'

Sam looked about seventeen or eighteen, very attractive, about five foot five inches tall with black hair, olive skin and piercing green eyes that you couldn't help looking at. As they walked across the town, Lisa noticed the amount of attention they were getting from boys walking by, but not realising that most of the attention was for her. It was Lisa's first time in a pub alone. Just like any other fifteen year-old, she was more concerned with what her date of birth should be if she was asked, rather than what she would be drinking. The Acorn was a quiet little place, friendly enough, but her age was not mentioned, even if she looked a little young.

'There are loads of places to stop on the Hagley Road,' said Sam, 'B&Bs are probably a little cheaper than the hotels.'

'Guess I'll look for a B&B then,' replied Lisa.

For the next couple of hours they talked generally, getting to know each other, but Lisa was careful with what she said, constantly keeping her guard up. She told Sam that she was seventeen, which Sam accepted.

'Tell you what,' said Sam, 'why don't you stop at my place tonight? My mum and dad won't mind, there's plenty of room. I'll tell them you work at the pizzeria – it's only for one night after all.'

'Are you sure?' replied Lisa, trying not to be overexcited, but inside feeling pleased.

'Yeah I'm sure, it'll be fine, and you'll be able to have a proper drink at my local, instead of that fizzy water.' Lisa smiled at her; inside she wanted to shout 'YES' but managed to control the emotion.

Back at Cherry Tree Crescent all was not well. There had been an uncomfortable silence all day. Carol was beside herself with worry. All Alex could think about was what was going to happen if it became public knowledge that he had abused his daughter. Carol broke the silence.

'What are we going to do, Alex?'

'She'll be back, if not tonight then tomorrow, you see,' replied Alex.

'If it hadn't been for you none of this would've happened.'

Alex was becoming agitated. He stood up and paced around the living room, anxiously rubbing his hands together.

'Why Alex? Why?' pleaded Carol, involuntarily raising her voice a few decibels. She turned towards her husband and recognised the mood he was moving into, his aggression starting to boil over.

'Shut up,' he shouted, 'If you had been more of a wife to me, it would never have happened in the first place.'

Carol stood up. 'Are you saying it's my fault that you molest our daughter, you bastard?' Alex spun round and with the back of his hand, hit Carol high on the cheek, knocking her clean over the back of the sofa. He had shown her aggression before but had never struck her. She got to her knees, her cheek and eye already swelling at an alarming rate. She backed against the wall in shock and fear. He looked at her, realising that he had now gone too far. He turned, walked down the hall and out of the front door. Carol sat on the sofa and cried. She had no choice; she knew she had to go to the police.

Lisa and Sam left The Acorn at about a quarter to eight.

'It's only about twenty minutes on the bus, then a short walk to my house,' said Sam.

'Are you sure your mum's not going to mind?' asked Lisa, apprehensively.

'Honest, Lisa, she'll be pleased to meet you, you'll see.' They got off the bus and started walking; it was literally a five-minute walk. Sam's house was a typical suburban three-bedroomed semi, mortgaged up to the hilt, but an achievement her working-class father was proud of. Sam opened the door.

'Come in Lisa. Mum,' shouted Sam, announcing her arrival.

'I'm in the kitchen,' came the reply. Lisa put her bag down in the hall. Looking around she was amazed at the decoration. It was like a show home on a new estate and far removed from the council flat she had left only twelve hours previously. They went into the kitchen.

'Mum, I've got someone to meet you.'

Sam's mother turned from the sink, drying her hands with a tea towel. Margaret Maguire was a very thin, frail woman, very kind; you couldn't meet a nicer person.

'Hello, I'm Margaret. Pleased to meet you.'

'Hello, I'm Lisa,' she replied.

'Lisa's a workmate of mine. She's off to London tomorrow. I said she could stop the night so we can go out for a drink before she goes.'

'Of course she can, dear, any time, you know that. Got something nice going on in London, Lisa?' asked Margaret.

'Just visiting my sister. Haven't seen her since she moved down there.'

'Come on, Lisa,' said Sam, 'we can go up to my room and get ready to go out.' They both headed off towards the stairs. Lisa was glad to get away in case her mother asked more awkward questions. Sam's mother shouted after them, 'I'll make you both something to eat, don't be too long.' Lisa pulled on a clean t-shirt and jeans; Sam had a wash and dressed in similar clothing, making Lisa feel more comfortable. After thirty minutes or so they went downstairs to find that Margaret had made chicken salad sandwiches. Lisa was not very hungry but she didn't want to offend so she ate some. Anyway, she didn't know where her next meal was coming from. Half an hour later they set off for Sam's local pub.

The Red Lion was a typical local where everyone knew everyone else's business and many of Sam's friends drank there. Within an hour Lisa was made to feel that it was her local too. Everyone wanted to talk to her, especially Sam's male friends. She wondered if they would feel the same if they knew she was only fifteen. Lisa had a couple of halves of lager. They were constantly offered drinks, which Sam accepted, but Lisa mostly refused; she had to keep her head together. By eleven o'clock last orders had been called and the pub was slowly clearing out. They said their goodbyes and set off back to Sam's house. When they arrived the house was in darkness. Lisa tried to help Sam into the house, without alerting Sam's parents; Sam had had plenty to drink. They moved as quietly as possible, given Sam's condition. Lisa directed her up the stairs to her room. Sam kicked off her shoes, lay on the bed and instantly fell into an alcohol-induced sleep. Lisa went into the spare room, undressed and slid into the bed, for the first time feeling safe in her bed. Even though she was in a strange house with people she had only met hours before, she felt no threat. She closed her eyes and fell into a deep sleep.

The following morning Lisa woke at about eight o'clock, hearing movement downstairs. She could not remember having such a relaxed and refreshing night's sleep. After washing and dressing she went downstairs to the kitchen. Sam's parents were sitting at the kitchen table. 'Morning, Mrs Maguire,' said Lisa

'Morning, Lisa,' came the reply. 'What would you like for breakfast?'

'Don't worry about me, Mrs Maguire, but a slice of toast would be nice, thank you.'

'I'm Phil,' said the man sitting at the table, 'Sam's dad.'

'Hello. Pleased to meet you,' said Lisa. Phil Maguire was a typical forty-something chap, receding hair, moustache, constantly battling with a middle-age spread, but happy with his lot.

'There you go, dear.' Four or five pieces of toast and a large mug of tea were placed in front of her.

'Gosh, Mrs Maguire, I couldn't eat all that,' said Lisa.

'Nonsense, you have a long journey today and you need something inside you,' said Mrs Maguire firmly. Lisa was not used to being pampered but thought she could easily become used to it.

'What time's your train, Lisa?' enquired Mr Maguire.

'I haven't booked a ticket, I was just going to go the station on spec.'

'You shouldn't have too much trouble; there are trains about every hour or so. I have to go into town later so I can drop you at the station.'

'It doesn't matter, honest, you've all done enough for me already,' replied Lisa.

'It's no trouble, I have to be in for about half eleven. Gives you a couple of hours to get yourself sorted,' said Mr Maguire.

'Thanks, that will be great.'

With that, Sam came in to the kitchen

'Ooh my head,' said Sam.

'Too much to drink last night, dear,' replied her mother. 'Sit down, I'll get you some breakfast.'

Shortly after eleven o'clock Lisa said goodbye and climbed into the car. The traffic was very heavy all the way into the city and especially so around the entrance to the station.

'I'll have to drop you by the entrance, if that's OK?'

'That'll be fine. I can't thank you enough,' replied Lisa.

'Here we are. Next time you're in town come and see us, OK?'

'I will,' replied Lisa, 'thanks for everything. Bye.' Lisa climbed out the car, gave him a wave and started to walk towards the main entrance to the station. Mr Maguire watched her go into the station and then drove off. Lisa went back to the same coffee shop she had been to just the day before, ordered a coffee and sat down. Her first day alone had started so well, but now she was back where she had started.

Carol had decided it was time to call the police. She called the operator, asked for the number of the local police station and dialled. The phone rang for thirty seconds or so before a voice said, 'Cromwell Lane Police Station, can I help you?' Carol went quiet; the voice came on again, 'Hello, can I help you?'

'Yes, my name's Carol Dean. I'd like to report a missing person.'

'Right, madam. Let me take some details.' Carol gave the officer Lisa's details.

'Your fifteen year-old daughter has been missing for over twenty-four hours and you have just reported it,' stated the officer. Carol clammed up. 'We will have somebody round to you within the hour.'

'Thank you,' said Carol quietly and put down the receiver. Within half an hour two officers arrived.

'Mrs Dean?'

Carol nodded.

'PC Truman and WPC Evitts from Cromwell Lane Police Station,' said one of the officers. Carol invited them in. They went into the living room and sat down on the sofa. Truman took out his notebook and a pencil.

'OK, your daughter, Lisa, has been missing for twenty-four hours. So that means she went out sometime yesterday morning. Do you have an exact time?'

'About nine-thirty,' said Carol, 'We had a bit of a row and she slipped out when I was in the bathroom.'

'Did she take anything with her?'

'Yes, she took some clothes in a holdall.'

'So it looks like we have a runaway on our hands. Has she done this before?'

'No, never. We have our arguments but she's never done anything like this.'

'Is Mr Dean about?' asked Truman, wondering where the presumably worried father was.

'He'll be back soon – he went for a walk round the estate to see if he could find her.' Carol was already covering for Alex; the only place he would be now was waiting for the working men's club to open.

'Have you got a recent photo of Lisa we can have, Mrs Dean?' asked Evitts.

Carol gave them a passport-sized photograph which Lisa had taken with Jinder from a booth in the shopping centre.

'Pretty girl,' observed Truman.

'She certainly is,' replied Carol.

'Any boyfriend?' he asked.

'Not that I'm aware of – she's never bought one home.'

'The other girl in the photo, Mrs Dean?'

'That's her friend Jinder. She lives two floors down, Flat 21.'

'Have you been down to see if they have seen her?'

'No, I never thought,' said Carol. The two officers glanced at each other.

'OK, I think that's the first place we have to check. Don't worry Mrs Dean, you wouldn't believe how many kids get a bee in their bonnet at this kind of age, especially young teenage girls. Usually they are back within a short while with their tails between their legs. One more thing, Lisa isn't on any medication or got any medical conditions we need to know about has she?'

'No,' replied Carol.

'When your husband gets back, give me a call on the station number. I'll need to have a chat with him ASAP. If she turns up or you get any information that might help, let us know straight away. I'll get the ball rolling. It's important you stay here in case she tries to contact you.' The officers stood up.

'Try not to worry, Mrs Dean, we'll do every thing we can to find her.' They walked to the door, followed by Carol. 'We'll be back later this afternoon. Bye for now.' Carol closed the door behind them.

'Did you see the marks on her face?' asked Truman.

'Yeah, looks like we've a few domestic issues here. Complicates matters a little,' said Evitts, 'Can't wait to meet the father. I've got a feeling we'll get a few answers there.' The officers headed towards the stairs, knowing better than to use the lifts; the local kids were highly amused at seeing police officers stuck in them. They approached Flat 21; younger children on the stairs had seen them and were shouting the usual names and making the usual noises up the stairwell. The officers paid no attention. They knocked on the door. Jinder's mother came to the door and looked through the glass, a feeling of dread taking hold of her as she opened the door.

'Sorry to disturb you, madam. We are investigating the disappearance of a young girl in the flats, and we believe your daughter is a close friend of hers; Lisa Dean.'

'Oh my word, Jinder, quick, come here.'

Jinder came to the door. 'What's wrong?'

'Lisa's gone missing.'

Jinder did her best to look surprised.

'Do you mind if we come in for few minutes?'

Mrs Patel ushered the officers to the living room, 'Please sit down. Can I get you a drink?' Mrs Patel was being as hospitable as ever.

'We're fine, thank you. We just need to have a chat with Jinder, if that's OK? Try to establish the last time she was seen.'

'Of course. Jinder, tell them everything you can,' said Mrs Patel.

'Not a lot I can tell you really. Last time I saw her was Saturday. She dropped in for a chat. She seemed OK. She never said she was upset.'

'Are you sure?' asked Evitts, 'Only she gets up on Sunday morning, packs a holdall with a few clothes and walks out. Something's upset her. If we can find out what that is, I think we'll find her.'

'Lisa always keeps things to herself. I try to get her out more but she just says she's busy.'

'What about her boyfriend?' asked Truman.

'Didn't know she had one,' said Jinder, with a startled look on her face. Truman was trying to put words into her mouth, but it wasn't working. She was probably telling the truth.

'If she tries to contact you, you must get in touch with us straight away. You can leave a message at Cromwell Lane Station any time, twenty-four hours a day, just say it's for PC Truman or WPC Evitts. Right, we won't keep you, thanks for your help.'

'Any time,' said Mrs Patel.

They stood up and walked towards the door. The officers walked down the remaining six flights of stairs, ignoring the abuse from the local kids. Truman had a worried look on his face. 'First things first, we check all the local hospitals. If this kid doesn't want to be found she is going to take some finding. She could be anywhere by now. I think we have to move quickly with this one, or she's going to disappear. Most of these kids just want some attention, but I have a bad feeling about this one and I hope I'm wrong.' Truman checked around the car; you had to stay switched on in this neighbourhood where the kids did some really stupid things. When he was happy, they both got in and drove off.

Lisa was in Pigeon Park, sitting on the same bench by the old church. She knew that if the police were trying to find her, they would be looking for a girl with blonde hair. She walked around the shops until she found a chemist. She chose a mousy brown hair colour that would not look too unusual against her complexion. She bought the hair dye, a toothbrush, toothpaste and some cheap make-up. She had to try and make herself look that little bit older. In just two months' time she would be sixteen and then legally able to leave home without being searched for. She waited at the same bus stop that she had been at the previous evening. When the bus arrived she took the same journey down Hagley Road, passing the large, expensive hotels on both sides of the road. Gradually, there seemed to be more guest houses than hotels. She got off the bus and randomly picked one out. The name plaque on the wall said Cedar Croft Guest House. A small slide-in sign below stated that there were vacancies. Lisa tried the door. It was locked, so she rang the bell. A smartly dressed middle-aged man opened the door.

'Hello, can I help you?'

'Yes, I see you have vacancies. I need a room for a couple of nights,' said Lisa. She could feel herself shaking, but tried her best to portray herself as very confident and mature, hoping that she would not give away her real age.

'Certainly, madam,' came the reply. 'Please come in. Just the two nights?

'Yes, I'm on a course in the city centre.'

'Will you be paying via a company account?'

'No, cash if that's OK?'

'That will be fine, madam.'

'That will be ten pounds per night; evening meal is an extra two pounds fifty, if you would like that also.'

'Yes, please,' replied Lisa.

'If you would kindly sign the guest book, I'll show you to your room.' Lisa signed the book under the name Miss Suzanne Grove; it was a school friend's name that just came into her head.

'If you would like to follow me, Miss Grove.' They went up one flight of stairs. 'All the rooms are en-suite and there are tea and coffee-making facilities. Here we are, room number four.' He opened the door, removed the key and handed it to her.

'I hope everything's to your satisfaction. Any problems, just ring the bell on the desk at reception. Breakfast is from seven till nine-thirty and the evening meal is six till eight-thirty. Enjoy your stay.' As he left the room, Lisa thanked him and closed the door. Very nice, she thought. She put her holdall on the bed and checked the en-suite; it was small but had everything she needed. She went back into the bedroom and emptied her holdall onto the bed. Picking up the hair dye, she read the instructions: leave on for up to thirty minutes. Right, she thought. It had been two days since she had cleaned her teeth; it was time for a bit of pampering. After applying the dye to her hair she covered it with the bag provided, cleaned her teeth and played around with the make-up she had purchased. Looking at herself in the dressing table mirror, she thought she could have passed for eighteen. Hair dye, she thought, how long has it been on? She had forgotten to check the time when she applied it. Quickly, she went into the bathroom. There were two sachets of complimentary shampoo, the one thing she had forgotten to buy. She washed out the dye and, patting her hair with a towel, went back to the mirror. It was like looking at another person. It said mousy brown on the box. She must have left it on too long, as her hair was now bordering on dark brown and, with her fair eyebrows, it didn't look quite right. But it was done, and it had certainly changed her appearance. Switching on the small kettle she made a cup of tea. Wrapped in a large bath towel, she lay on the bed. It was so very comfortable. She looked up at the ceiling feeling pleased with herself; the day had gone very well up to now. Closing her eyes she drifted off too sleep.

At Cherry Tree Crescent, Alex had arrived home smelling strongly of alcohol.

'I've phoned the police,' said Carol. Alex turned and glared. 'I just told them she'd run away. They came round and took an old photo of her and some details. They want to talk to you, give them a call, the number's on the pad.' Carol went into the kitchen and put the kettle on. Alex made the call, trying to look concerned, but Carol knew better. Within the hour there was a knock at the door. As Alex went to open it he could see the officers through the glass.

'Hello sir, PC Truman and WPC Evitts, Cromwell Lane Station. Mr Dean?'

'Yes, come in,' said Alex. They walked into the living room.

'I'd like to take a statement from you. Hopefully we may be able to shed some light on why your daughter has run away, which may help us to find her. Can you think of anything that may have been upsetting her? Was she being bullied at school or anything like that?' asked Truman. Alex's face was reddening and Truman picked up on it straight away.

'If there's anything at all, what about money? Has she got much on her?' Alex's eyes widened. He jumped up and ran into the bedroom. Feeling under the bed he pulled out the box and hurriedly removed the lid.

'Bitch,' he said under his breath. Walking back into the living room he said, 'over fifty pounds'. The officers looked startled.

'Fifty pounds,' said Truman, 'she could be anywhere in the country by now. Why didn't you tell us earlier?'

'I've only just realised the money was gone,' said Alex.

'Right, we have to get back to the station and forward her picture and details further afield. Before we go, is there anything else you have to tell us?' The officers looked directly at Alex. 'Nothing at all?' reiterated the officer; there was an uncomfortable silence in the flat. 'OK, we'll get back and widen the search.' The officers stood up and left. As they walked to the car Truman said, 'She's left because of him, could you feel it?'

'Yes,' replied Evitts, 'he's already been drinking. Did you smell it on him?'

'Noted,' said Truman. They got into the car and headed back to the station.

Lisa woke with a startled intake of breath. Slowly she realised her surroundings. Then, moving her neck from side to side with her arms raised above her head, she stretched and yawned simultaneously. Turning to the clock on the bedside cabinet she noticed it was just after seven o'clock. Remembering that the evening meal was now being served, she combed her hair, reapplied her make-up and pulled on a clean t-shirt and jeans. Studying her reflection in the wardrobe mirror she knew she could easily pass for eighteen, probably older.

She went down the stairs; the door opposite reception had a sign marked 'dining room.' Entering the room she noticed an elderly couple sitting at the window table eating what looked like a huge portion of steak and kidney pie, and a middle-aged businessman, tucking into a large piece of black forest gateau. Just then the man she had met earlier at the reception desk came in.

'Ah, Miss Grove. Good evening. I almost didn't recognise you – your hair colour...'

'Yes, just thought I'd have a change,' she replied.

'Looks very nice, madam.' He led her across the dining room to a table set for one. He pulled out the chair and she sat down.

'Your menu, madam. Soup of the day is asparagus, I will be with you shortly.'

'Thank you,' she replied. Within five minutes he returned.

'Are you ready to order, madam?'

'Yes, thanks. I'd like the soup followed by the lamb, please,' said Lisa.

'Excellent choice, madam.' She thought that if she had asked for a bowl of cornflakes she would have received the same reply. He took the menu from her and disappeared into the kitchen. She imagined him quickly putting on a chef's uniform and rushing around preparing the food, then quickly changing back again to bring it to the table, as she had not seen any other staff. A bit like a comedy she had seen on television recently staring David Niven, where he had played six different characters. Visualising it, she smiled. If he was alone, he was very efficient, as the food was on the table within a few minutes, and very enjoyable. After the meal she went back to her room. Feeling very full she lay down on the bed to let her food go down. She started to think about home and what they had done about her running away. When she weighed up the advantages and disadvantages of being here or there she thought stuff them, I'm OK on my own.

The two police officers had sent the relevant information to all the main constabularies. They had drawn a blank with the local hospitals and every on-duty officer in the area was on the lookout for her. They informed their superiors of the situation and it was decided to handle it as a straightforward runaway. If there was any foul play, she had run away from it. As a minor, they had to go through procedure, regardless that in a couple of months she could legally leave home and probably would. Like so many kids in the area, when the first opportunity to get out of there presented itself, they usually took it. Not always the right choice, but that was life. Usually they were back within a few weeks, tails between their legs, happy to be home. But there was always the exception. Another twenty-four hours and the press would be involved.

The next morning Lisa got up just before eight o'clock, showered and went for breakfast. She needed to earn some money, get a job of some kind, but how? Lying about her age was going to catch up with her sooner or later. She decided to head back into the city. She had noticed an open market on the bus journey out, which could be a good place to get a job without too many questions. She could afford one more night in the B&B and then, with no money coming in, she would be on the streets.

The traffic going back into the city was horrendous. She didn't like buses at the best of times but this was ridiculous; it probably would have been quicker to walk. Eventually she saw the canvas tops of the market stalls and got off the bus. The market was only just coming to life and stallholders were beginning to set up. She spotted a man in his thirties running a fruit and vegetable stall. 'This is the one,' she thought.

'Excuse me,' said Lisa, 'I'm looking for some work.'

'It's a bit early in the morning for that, ain't it darling?' came the reply, a cheeky grin on his face. 'Only joking,' he added, 'I only make enough to cover myself these days, love. Some of the stalls take people on casual-like, but I never told you that. Have a look down the other end of the market. Clothes stalls are the ones to try.' Lisa thanked him.

'You're welcome,' came the reply. As she walked on he shouted, 'What are you doing tonight anyway?' She turned, smiled, then carried on walking. Pretending to look interested in the clothes on the stalls, she was actually eyeing up the owners; none of them looked very busy. It was the sort of market that did most of its trade at weekends. She noticed a stall that sold mostly women's clothing. The woman running the stall sat on a stool reading a newspaper with a cigarette in the corner of her mouth.

'Excuse me, I can see it's not very busy at the moment, but do you need an assistant? I'm a good worker,' said Lisa.

'I thought you were winding me up for a minute then,' said the woman in a very broad midlands accent. 'I need someone this Friday and Saturday. If you want the job, be here at half seven sharp Friday morning.'

'Yes I do, I mean I will. My name's Sue,' she said, using her new alias.

'Hello Sue. See you Friday,' came the reply. The woman's head then went straight back into her newspaper. Lisa walked on through the market feeling quite proud of herself. 'Well, that's two days sorted,' she thought, 'three to go.' For the rest of the morning and most of the afternoon she tried various shops and stalls for more work but had no luck. By three o'clock she had had enough. Catching the bus back to the B&B her legs ached and she wanted nothing more than to lie down for a couple of hours then get something to eat.

After dinner she spent the evening in her room pampering herself, but still racking her brain as to how she could earn some money. She decided to try a few shops the next day. By half past nine she was in bed and it crossed her mind that tomorrow night she just might be sleeping rough.

After breakfast the following morning, Lisa packed her holdall and went down to reception. She rang the small bell on the desk and the same man appeared, in another one of his many roles.

'Ah, Miss Groves, have you enjoyed your stay with us?'

'Yes thanks,' replied Lisa.

'I'll get your bill.' He went behind a small desk and pulled out a receipt book. 'Was the room and restaurant to your satisfaction?'

'They were great, thanks,' replied Lisa.

'Right, let's have a look, that's two nights plus two evening meals, that's twenty-five pounds please.' Lisa had the right amount of money ready and handed it over the desk to him.

'Thank you very much. Hope to see you again in the future, Miss Groves. Goodbye.' Lisa returned the compliment, picked up her holdall and left through the front door.

The remainder of the day dragged by, with no luck trying to find work in the shops and market stalls. Her mind was now focused on where she was going to sleep that night. She could possibly scrape together enough to stay one more night in a B&B, but would then be completely out of money. She had to get that job on Friday morning.

The police had now become very concerned about Lisa's whereabouts. There had been no sightings of her, her friends and family had not heard from her in seventy-two hours, and the case had now been assigned to Detective Inspector Mike Robinson and his team. DI Robinson had a lot of experience in the field of missing persons, especially children. As Robinson arrived at Cromwell Lane Police Station he introduced himself at the reception desk.

'Good afternoon, sir,' came the reply from the constable manning the reception, 'I'll take you through and let the sergeant know you've arrived.' The constable pressed the button on the desk, which released the side entrance door. Robinson followed the constable down the corridor to a large briefing room.

'Make yourself at home, sir. There's some fresh coffee,' he said, pointing to a large coffee percolator, 'I'll get Sergeant Rhodes.' The constable left the room and Robinson poured a cup of coffee. Slowly he walked round the room, briefly reading articles on the walls of recent and past cases. The door opened and two of Robinson's team walked in: DC Joe Bradley and DC Paul Shaw.

'Hi guys,' said Robinson 'there's coffee over here and it's fresh. I think they're trying to spoil us.'

'Cheers, Guv,' said Shaw. They both poured a coffee.

'Have you had the full SP yet, Guv?' said Bradley,

'No, but I have a good idea what we are up against.' With that the door opened and the young constable from the desk came in. Behind him was a tower of a man: Sergeant Ian Rhodes, 6 feet 6 inches tall, weighing in at around 18 stone. As he entered the room both the detective constables lowered their coffee cups from their lips. Rhodes' presence had that effect on people who didn't know him. A broad smile appeared on Robinson's face and the sergeant returned the expression.

'Ian Rhodes,' said Robinson, 'it must be fifteen years.'

'Good to see you, Mike,' came the reply.

'So you gave up the special patrol group activities then.'

'Yes,' said Rhodes, 'getting a little to old for all that now. I've been based here now for best part of eight years … let's just say it's a little quieter. I like to let the youngsters take care of that side of the job now.'

A further eight officers entered the room, all assigned to the missing girl's case. 'OK, I think we're all here, let's get started,' said Robinson, 'Truman, would you like to take over?' said Sergeant Rhodes. Truman came forward with the paperwork he had gathered on the case, placing it on the desk.

'Right, Lisa Dean, fifteen year-old girl,' he handed out photographs as he spoke. 'Blonde hair, blue eyes, very attractive, mature for her age. Not many friends, no known boyfriends. Has fall-out with her parents, packs a bag on Sunday morning, slips out without either parent knowing she's gone. Took approximately fifty pounds in cash from a box under father's bed, hasn't been seen since. Looks like there have been some domestic problems at home but they're not talking about it. No friends or family have seen or heard from her. Father seems a bit of a drinker, but has no previous. That's basically all we have.' Truman concluded his report and Robinson stood up.

'Right then, I want media coverage. If she's still out there, someone has seen her; we just have to let them know we are looking. With fifty pounds in her pocket she could be anywhere in the country by now.' He held Lisa's photograph above high. 'I want this photograph in every newspaper and on every news broadcast in the country by morning. I assume it's already gone to other constabularies?'

'Sorted,' said Truman.

'DC Shaw, I want you to check every A&E within a fifty-mile radius.'

'OK, sir.'

'DC Bradley.'

'Sir?'

'You've got the street. Anyone knows anything, I want to know.'

'Straight on it, sir.'

'Truman, I want the father down here for an interview ASAP and bring the mother in; I don't want him to feel he is being suspected or interrogated in any way.'

'Right, sir.'

'OK, guys, let's get to work; time isn't on our side.'

3

Janie

By early evening Lisa was exhausted, she had walked on and off all day and just wanted to sit down and rest. It crossed her mind to use the rest of her money for one more night of luxury, but then what? She would not even have enough money for a drink. Walking around the subways she noticed more and more people who looked as if they were in the same position as she was; buskers who were not really that good, making passers-by pity them rather than applaud them, even people trying to beg for small change. Lisa realised that until you are one of them you do not truly see them, or choose not to see them, as the case may be. As the evening wore on Lisa looked for a quiet little corner to rest. She tried a couple of secluded alleyways, but after a closer inspection of the surrounding area she found used syringes, condoms, broken bottles and decided it was probably best not to stay there. A small gully at the side of some shops led her to six huge wheelie bins crammed with cardboard boxes. Checking that nobody had seen her go down there, she arranged a pile of the boxes in the corner, like a tunnel. One more check up the alley then she climbed in, it was not quite the B&B but she needed to rest. If she was going to get that job in the market the next morning, she had to be fresh and on time. Exhausted, both physically and mentally, it didn't take long for sleep to take hold of her.

PC Truman rang the Dean family's phone number; Carol was sitting on the sofa with the phone on her lap, watching it intently. The phone rang and she instantly picked it up, barely giving it time to ring out.

'Lisa?' said Carol in a distressed voice.

'Hello Mrs Dean, this is PC Truman from Cromwell Lane.'

'Oh, sorry, is there any news? I'm worried sick.' Carol's voice was trembling, already thinking the worst.

'Detective Inspector Robinson has taken over the search for Lisa. He'd like to have a chat with you and your husband. If I send a car round to collect you would you come straight in?' Carol hesitated. Alex had returned from the club and had had one too many; again she tried to cover for him.

'I'll come straight away but my husband isn't well, I think the stress of all this is getting to him.' Truman did not want to let her know that it was him they wanted to interview.

'Right, it's getting late now, so what I'll do is have a car outside your flat at half eight in the morning. The press are getting involved so don't be surprised if any reporters turn up at your flat. Don't listen to any stories – as of now there have been no sightings of Lisa. If we hear anything you'll be the first to know. Try to get some rest, Mrs Dean. It's going to be a long day tomorrow.'

'Thank you, Constable Truman. We'll be waiting outside in the morning.'

Lisa was sleeping soundly when the sound of a bottle breaking instantly alerted her. She tried to stay still but her body was trembling with fear. Someone was rummaging through the bins. Staying as still as she could she hoped whoever it was wouldn't move the boxes. A series of coughs, spits and verbal gobbledegook made her realise it was a drunken tramp. If he found her, as drunk as he was, she could still be in serious trouble. After ten minutes of unsuccessful rummaging, the tramp started to move boxes. Lisa could not believe what was happening; he had made a tunnel with boxes right next to her. He climbed into the tunnel completely oblivious to Lisa's presence. She stayed still and tried to breathe very quietly. About half an hour went by, but it felt like hours to Lisa. The tramp started snoring and coughing almost rhythmically, while Lisa lay still, listening. She grew more weary, but every time she started to fall asleep, a loud snore or cough would bring her back to her senses. At about half four in the morning the tramp got up; the smell of urine was overpowering. Lisa could hear him mumbling to himself as he shook himself down. She heard his footsteps as he walked off down the alley. After a few minutes, when she had convinced herself he had definitely gone, she climbed out of the box, peeping in the direction of the alley entrance. It was starting to get light. Moving the boxes away from the stench of urine, she climbed back in, hoping to get another couple of hours' rest; it didn't take her long to go back to sleep.

When Lisa woke she listened for a short time, then crawled out of the boxes, again observing the entrance to the alley. Opening her holdall she checked the time on her small travel clock. It was seven o'clock – half an hour to get over to the market. Holding up the small compact mirror she had bought with the cheap make-up, she brushed her hair, applied a small amount of make-up and headed down the alley. The main street was already teeming with people. It was about a ten-minute walk to the market so she had to hurry.

Many of the stalls were already set up. Lisa walked through the market until she came to the stall where she had been offered work. A young girl was putting clothes on hangers.

'Excuse me, is the lady that runs the stall about?' asked Lisa.

'She's just gone to get a coffee,' replied the girl. 'She won't be long.' After a few minutes the woman turned up holding two coffees and some toast in a bag.

'Hello,' said Lisa, 'I'm here for the job you offered me.'

'Sorry girl, you're too late,' said the woman.

'But it's not even half past seven yet,' replied Lisa, her voice almost frantic.

'First come in this line of work, girl,' replied the woman.

'But I need this job!' Lisa's voice was now raised, attracting the attention of onlookers.

'Don't raise your voice to me, girl, or I'll give you what for.'

'Please, I need this job,' she pleaded.

'Maybe next week.'

Lisa was gutted; tears filled her eyes as she rushed, almost running, out of the market and down the subway. Sitting on the cold stairs she started to cry. She could not remember ever feeling this low. What was she going to do now?

It was just approaching half past eight. Carol and Alex Dean left the flat, Alex pulled the door shut behind him. The police car was already waiting down below. They were met at the entrance by WPC Evitts.

'Morning Mr and Mrs Dean, I have a car waiting for you.'

'Thank you,' said Carol, Alex just nodded. Evitts opened the back door and they both got in. Aware of the attention they were attracting, Evitts quickly drove off.

'Detective Inspector Robinson is heading the investigation into Lisa's disappearance; he's waiting at the station. He'd like to ask you a few questions that might just help us put together a few pieces of the puzzle as to why Lisa has run away,' said Evitts.

'I can't understand it,' said Carol. 'This isn't like Lisa at all. We have our little ups and downs, every parent does with teenagers, but she has never done anything like this before.' Alex just sat there looking straight ahead, almost trance-like. They arrived at the station; Evitts jumped out of the car and opened the door.

'If you'd like to follow me, I'll take you to the briefing room,' said Evitts. Pushing the car door shut behind them they followed the WPC in through the rear door of the station. They went into a room that contained nothing but a table and four chairs.

'Please take a seat. Can I get you both a drink?'

'No thanks,' said Carol. Alex gestured with his hands as if in verbal shock.

'I'll tell DI Robinson you're here.' Evitts left the room, closing the door behind her.

'What are we going to do, Alex?'

'What do you mean?' he replied.

'They're going to ask questions.'

'And we're going to answer them,' said Alex.

'Yes, but...'

'Yes but nothing. Just choose your words carefully.' Carol felt the hair stand up on her neck. Since he had struck her she had felt frightened and intimidated by him and with direct statements like the one he had just made, she knew that he was capable of anything.

The door opened and DI Robinson and DC Shaw entered. 'Morning Mr and Mrs Dean, I'm Detective Inspector Robinson and this is Detective Constable Shaw – I wish we were meeting in different circumstances. There has been a lot going on in the last twelve hours. There have been no positive sightings of Lisa as yet, but we now have the press involved and her picture has been forwarded to all the major TV broadcasting companies. I think we should have something to go on in the next few hours. Have you heard anything from her?'

'No, not a word,' said Carol, 'I wish she would just let us know she's safe.'

'That's exactly the approach we're going to take. I don't think for one minute she's been abducted. First things first, we need to get her to make contact with us, just acknowledge that she's safe.'

'What would you say your relationship with your daughter is like at present', asked Robinson, 'I know they can be a bit of a handful at this age.'

'I get on really well with her. This is completely out of character,' said Carol.

'What about you, Mr Dean?'

'OK,' replied Alex, 'but like you said, she's a teenager.'

Robinson scrutinised Alex's face; he looked uncomfortable.

'You had a fall-out with her Mrs Dean, the day she left – what was it about?' Carol tried to think her way round the actual truth.

'Nothing bad, as I remember,' she replied.

'It must have been to her. Within two hours she packed a bag and left.'

At this, Alex jumped in, 'What? Are you saying it's our fault she's gone?'

'What I'm saying, Mr Dean, is that something happened at home to make her not want to be there and that sounds pretty important to me.' Alex stared down at the floor.

'Can I ask you both a personal question about Lisa?' Alex and Carol both looked up.

'If it's going to help find her, yes,' said Alex.

'Is Lisa sexually active? You see, I think there may be a boy involved here.'

'She's never brought any boys home,' said Carol.

'At this age they sometimes don't, especially if he's older, or got his own place. It's possible she may be being sheltered by someone. As I said before, I don't think for one minute anything untoward has happened to her.'

'God, I hope you're right,' said Carol, the pressure showing on her face.

'I've some calls to make. Would you bear with me? DC Shaw will get you anything you need. I'd like to get a press conference arranged for this morning, if that's OK?' they both nodded in agreement. 'Don't worry, we'll find her. I'm sure she's safe.' Robinson stood up and left the room.

'Tea or coffee?' asked Shaw.

'Coffee, please,' replied Carol.

'Tea,' said Alex.

'Just give me two minutes.' Shaw went to get the drinks.

In the incident room, Robinson was talking to Bradley.

'Alex Dean isn't telling us everything.'

'In what way, Guv?' asked Bradley.

'Whatever's been going on in that flat has driven her away, whether it's between the girl and him or his wife I'm not sure, but I get the feeling this young girl's just had enough; she's packed her bags and left, you mark my words. Still, whatever the reason, it's our job to find her and bring her back, so I want the press here for a briefing at ten-thirty sharp, OK?'

'I'll get straight on it, Guv.'

Lisa counted her money. She had decided that there was no point in feeling sorry for herself, she just had to get on with it. She had just under thirteen pounds. Her priority was to get something to eat, then decide what to do from there. There was a café on the other side of the market: a good breakfast inside her would set her up for the day.

The café was full of market people laughing and joking with each other. Lisa ordered a full breakfast and a mug of tea, then sat down by the window watching the world go by. She started to daydream about home. What had her parents done about her running away? Come to think about it, had they done anything at all? Had they just accepted the fact that she had gone? What will happen at school when I don't turn up for days?

'Hello, full breakfast.'

'Oh, I'm sorry,' said Lisa. The woman who had taken her order was standing over her, breakfast in one hand, a mug of tea in the other.

'I was miles away,' apologised Lisa.

'I could see that, love. Here, enjoy,' replied the woman. Lisa thanked her and began eating. It was a full breakfast in every meaning of the word, with two of everything. At least I'm not going to starve, thought Lisa; she hadn't realised just how hungry she was. People in the café glanced over; aware of their eyes on her she slowed down, not wanting to draw attention to herself. After finishing her breakfast she sat back in her chair and took a large breath, wondering what the world had in store for her that day. Slugging back the last mouthful of tea, she reached under the table and grabbed her holdall. Leaving the café, she glanced left and right. Choosing the subway, she headed in the direction of the city centre. If there were any opportunities to be taken, that was where she would find them.

Cromwell Lane Police Station was buzzing with reporters. The constable on the main desk was trying to contain them in the main entrance, but there were far too many to accommodate. It was almost half past ten.

'Can I have your attention please? Please, a bit of quiet.' The constable raised his voice to be heard. 'Very shortly I'll be taking you through to the briefing room. Please let the TV cameras get in position at the front. You'll all get the opportunity to ask questions at the end of the briefing, OK? Just give me two more minutes.'

It was very quickly turning into a full-scale search. Representatives from all the major television and radio stations were there, plus countless tabloid reporters. Bradley's head appeared around the edge of the door. 'We're ready for them now,' he gave a thumbs up to the constable.

'OK people, if you'd like to follow me.' They swarmed after the constable, every camera and microphone known to man about their persons. A large table stood at the front of the briefing room with two large jugs of water and four glasses. Facing the table were thirty or so chairs which filled up very quickly, TV cameras getting priority seats at the front, with radio station microphones and photographic cameras clamouring for the best viewpoints. Robinson entered the room, followed by Alex and Carol Dean, with Shaw behind them. As they took their seats, a dozen cameras flashed simultaneously, trying to capitalise on every expression.

'Morning,' said DI Robinson, 'I think everyone's aware of the situation.' A large photograph of Lisa was on the back wall. 'The young lady in the photograph, her name is Lisa Dean, she is fifteen years old and was last seen on Sunday morning at approximately ten-thirty in the morning. We are very concerned about the whereabouts of Lisa. We think she has run away from home. At this time we do not suspect foul play but are keeping every option open. If anybody has seen Lisa, please contact your local police station immediately. Lisa was wearing a blue-green, short-sleeved t-shirt, jeans and trainers, and she has a blue Slazenger sports holdall. Lisa's parents would like to say a few words to the cameras before any questions. Thank you.'

Robinson gestured to Carol. Nervously, Carol asked which camera she had to look at and a cameraman raised his hand.

'Lisa,' Carol was already trembling, 'if you're watching this, please get in contact with us. Whatever's happened we can work it out. If you're in trouble in any way, we can sort it out, just come home.' A tear rolled down her cheek, she was struggling to hold herself together. Alex said nothing. His eyes remained fixed on the table in front of him.

'OK,' said Robinson, 'questions one at a time please.'

A thin man wearing small round spectacles stood up.

'Is there a boyfriend involved?'

'We're not sure on that one,' replied Robinson, 'but we don't think so.'

'Has she ever done anything like this in the past?' a voice at the back asked.

'No, it's totally out of character,' said Robinson.

Another man shouted out, 'What about money, has she got any?'

'Yes,' replied the DI, 'about fifty pounds in cash.'

'That's a lot of money for a fifteen year-old – she could be anywhere with that amount of money,' came the reply.

'Precisely, that's why we need your help. The more media coverage the better. Right gentlemen, we have a photograph of Lisa for all of you, plus a description of what she was wearing when she was last seen. Thank you very much.'

With that, they all stood. Carol was now weeping uncontrollably. Her obvious distress and personal loss was sending the photographers into a photographic frenzy. By lunchtime, Lisa's photograph and description were being broadcast on all television stations. The following morning her face would be in every newspaper.

Within hours, sightings were coming in from all over, as far afield as Scotland, Wales, the West Country and London. The problem now was deciding which ones were genuine. Then one call in particular stood out from the rest. A Mr Maguire living in the Birmingham area claimed that just two nights ago she had stayed at his house. Bradley and Shaw were sent to chase up the lead, arriving in Birmingham just after two o'clock.

'Right,' said Shaw, 'we're looking for the Hagley Road – that's the A456.'

'Got it,' replied Bradley as he scanned a local *A to Z*. 'Looks like we have to go through the centre, so just keep following the signs for the A456. Once we are on the main Hagley Road it should only take twenty minutes or so.' The city centre was as hectic as ever. Forty-five minutes later they managed to twist and turn a path out onto the main Hagley Road. Another fifteen minutes found them getting close to their destination, Lordswood Road.

'Hamilton Avenue, should be next left,' said Bradley. Shaw turned in and pulled up outside the Maguire's. Shaw locked the car as Bradley went up to the house and rang the bell. The door opened and Margaret Maguire stood in front of them.

'Mrs Maguire?' asked Shaw.

'Yes,' she replied.

'Detectives Shaw and Bradley. We had a call from your husband concerning a missing girl.'

'Oh yes, come in. Phil said you were coming. He'll be back in five minutes. He's just popped out to put some petrol in the car – he won't be long.' They went through into the living room. 'Please have a seat. Can I get you both a drink?'

After such a long drive they both accepted Margaret's offer, 'Coffees for both of us please, no sugar.'

They heard the front door open and close.

'I'm back, love.' Phil Maguire's voice sounded down the hallway. As he came in to the living room both the detectives stood up.

'Hello,' said Phil, guessing who they were.

'Mr Maguire, pleased to meet you. Detectives Shaw and Bradley. We came as soon as we got your message concerning the missing girl.' They all sat down.

'It was definitely her,' said Phil, 'absolutely positive, one hundred per cent. As soon as I saw her picture on the midday news I knew it was her.' Shaw reached into his inside pocket and pulled out Lisa's photograph.

'Take one more look,' he said.

'Yep,' said Phil without any doubt, 'she looks older than in this photo but it's definitely her. My daughter went out for a drink with her at our local on Monday night. They came back here and she stayed the night.'

'How did she meet her?' asked Shaw.

'She told me they worked together at the pizzeria. I had no reason to doubt her word.'

'What about the next morning?' asked Shaw.

'Well, they relaxed here till about half ten, had some breakfast then I took her into Birmingham. She got a train to London, said she was going to stay with her sister.'

'I see,' said Shaw. 'How did she come across to you? Was she upset in any way?'

'Quite the opposite, she appeared to be very happy-go-lucky.'

'Will your daughter be home soon, Mr Maguire?' asked Bradley.

'Yeah, Sam should be back in an hour or so, traffic willing,' Phil replied as Margaret came in with the coffee.

'Are you waiting to see Sam, officers?' she asked.

'If you don't mind, Mrs Maguire, she might just be able to answer a couple of questions for us.'

'In that case, you must be hungry – I'll make some sandwiches.'

'Honestly, Mrs Maguire, we're OK. Don't put yourself out for us.' They were famished but didn't like to say so.

'It's no problem, we were going to eat anyway,' said Margaret, disappearing into the kitchen, feeling useful and enjoying every minute of it.

Lisa had spent most of the day looking for any opportunity to earn some money but vacancies were few and far between. How nice it would be to have the use of a bathroom, she thought, just to have a wash and clean her teeth. She was beginning to appreciate some of the basic things she had previously taken for granted. Walking through the main shopping area she approached a huge electrical wholesaler, where what seemed like a hundred television sets of all shapes and sizes were in the display windows. Suddenly, her face appeared on every screen in the window. Frozen to the spot, she could not believe her eyes. In a split-second, the reality of what she was seeing kicked in; just about every policeman in the country was looking for her. Lowering her head she quickly scurried off. Well clear of the main shops, Lisa started to think about her image on the television screen, remembering the day the photograph was taken.

Originally, Jinder was in the photograph with her. That was over twelve months ago, hanging around in the shopping centre at home. It brought a smile to her face; they were happy times. A sudden glance at her reflection in a shop window made her stop and look at how she had changed. Now with brown hair and make-up, she felt as if she was an older sister to the image on the screen. Her parents could not have given the police a worse photograph; it was almost as if they did not want her to be found. The worry of discovery was gone as quickly as it had come. She decided to find a store with a public toilet and get cleaned up; if she was to find work of any kind she had to be presentable.

Sam Maguire arrived home from work, closing the front door behind her she shouted, 'Mum, I'm home.' Her voice boomed down the hall. Her father got up, looked at the two detectives, smiled and said, 'She's home.' They smiled back, pleased that their wait was over. Her father stepped into the hall; instant eye contact told her that there was a problem.

'What's wrong?' asked Sam.

'It's OK, love. The police are here – they want to ask you a few questions about Lisa.'

'Lisa?' said Sam, 'What's happened to her?' Sam followed her father into the living room and the two detectives stood up.

'Hello Sam, Detective Constables Shaw and Bradley. We are investigating the disappearance of a young girl, Lisa Dean.'

'God, when did this happen?' asked Sam, with genuine amazement.

'Last Sunday,' replied Shaw.

'It can't have – she stayed with me on Monday evening.' The room fell silent as the penny dropped, then Sam's bottom jaw nearly hit the floor.

'I suppose I should tell you how I met her,' said Sam.

'That would be very helpful,' replied Bradley.

Sam told them everything, from meeting in the pizzeria to the night out in the local and her so-called sister in London.

'I hope she's OK,' said Sam.

'Well, this is why we need as much information about her movements over the last few days as we can get. Hopefully, we can then find her as quickly as possible. Are you sure there's nothing else you can tell us, even the slightest detail?'

Sam had an intense look on her face, racking her brains for the slightest bit of information that might help.

'She seemed very intent on going to London. Dad dropped her at New Street station.'

'Yes, it looks like that's where we're going to find her. If she tries to get in touch with you in any way you must contact us straight away. This is my number, I can be contacted twenty-four hours a day,' said Shaw. 'We've got your number. If we need to ask any more questions we'll be in touch. Thanks for all your help.' Both men stood up and shook hands with Sam and her father. As they left, they thanked Mrs Maguire for the food and drink.

'Looks like we've got another long drive,' said Bradley.

'Yep, I'll call the Guv and let him know the situation.' They both climbed into the car and sped off down the road.

By six o'clock that evening, Lisa had come to terms with the fact that she was going to spend another night on the streets. With the weekend now fast approaching, it was going to be very busy on the streets. Crowds of people out for a good time meant that there would be a large police presence; she had to be very careful. As the evening went on, Lisa watched people moving from bar to bar, some choosing the busy restaurants. Gradually, their voices grew louder as the alcohol flowed and their spirits rose. Every now and then a scuffle would break out between groups of lads who had had too much to drink, but the police were quick to calm them down and send them on their way, rarely having to arrest anyone. By midnight, Lisa was exhausted, taking every opportunity to sit down and rest, but not wanting to draw attention to herself. Each time she saw a police officer or heard the sound of a siren she would start to walk again, always at a quickened pace, as if to give the impression she had a destination. Her stomach was tense with hunger. People walked past her with burgers and hot dogs; there must be a late night burger bar nearby she thought. Turning a corner at the end of the High Street she saw a mobile fast food bar, surrounded by a large group of people falling around laughing and joking about their exploits that evening. Contemplating whether or not to get some food, hunger got the better of her. Pushing her way through the crowd she finally got to the front.

'Burger and chips please, oh, and a can of Coke,' said Lisa.

'Onions?' came the reply from a large fat man behind the counter.

'Yes, please.'

'One pound fifty, please, love.' Lisa gave the man a five-pound note. Close by, unnoticed by Lisa, she was being observed by a partially drunk, scruffy looking middle-aged man. Pushing her holdall high onto her shoulder, she picked her food up off the counter and started walking down the road. Without taking his eyes off Lisa, the man screwed up the remains of his burger into a serviette and dropped it in the bin. Slowly he walked behind her, keeping just enough distance not attract her attention. Lisa crossed the road and walked into a long row of bus shelters, looking for somewhere to sit and eat. The man saw his opportunity; increasing his pace he crossed the road. He approached without looking directly at her, giving her no reason to expect what was about to happen. He grabbed her by the throat and slammed the back of her head into the shelter. Taken completely by surprise, her food went flying across the pavement, a searing pain in the back of her head sent her dizzy.

'Don't make a fucking noise.' His face was threateningly close to Lisa's.

Lisa's eyes were wide with fear, the grip on her throat was so tight she thought she would soon pass out. Her words barely audible she croaked, 'What do you want?'

'That depends on what you've got,' he replied, the stench of cigarettes and alcohol were all too familiar to her.

'What's in the bag, bitch?'

'Clothes.'

With one hand still around her throat, he started to feel around her pockets. He quickly found her money and pocketed it.

'Is that all you've got?'

'Yes' she replied, tears now running down her face. He tightened his grip on her throat.

'You better not be fuckin' lying to me.'

'I'm not, that's everything I've got.'

Across the road, three girls heading in the direction of a taxi rank were laughing and joking as they walked. One of them noticed what she thought was a courting couple in the bus shelter.

'What do you think's going on over there then?'

'Go on, girl,' one of them shouted and they all laughed. Lisa struggled; this could be her only chance of help. The man raised his other hand and slapped her hard across the face, knocking her almost senseless. Her vision clouded as she struggled to maintain consciousness.

'Did you see that?' one of the girls said. Lisa slid down the shelter to the floor.

'HEY YOU BASTARD!' the girl shouted, running across the road, her temper raging with what she had just witnessed.

'Janie, come back, don't get involved.' Her friends called.

As she entered the shelter, the man was pulling the holdall off Lisa's shoulder. Lisa heard the girl's voice, giving her a last small hope; who was she?

'Leave her alone, you bastard!' As the man looked up, Janie's stiletto heel hit him in the face. He reeled back in pain, blood pouring from just below his left eye. With both hands raised towards his face, Janie lashed out with a kick square in the groin. The man was beaten, he crawled away, one hand raised in a gesture of defeat. Within seconds he was gone, disappearing into the night. Janie immediately lifted Lisa's head off the ground.

'Can you hear me? You're OK now, he's gone.' Lisa tried to focus on her saviour's face. Janie's two friends came running over.

'Is she all right? Shall we call an ambulance?' Lisa tried to stand up.

'Woh, sit there for a minute, girl. You took a good one on the side of your face. That's going to hurt in the morning.'

'It hurts now,' said Lisa, her head still swimming, 'thanks for helping me.'

'You're welcome, just wish I could have got another shot on him. Did he take anything?'

'I'm not sure,' replied Lisa. Getting to her feet with the aid of the three girls, she pushed her clothes back into her holdall and checked her pockets. 'He's taken my money,' she said.

'Good job that's all he got. Come on, there's an all-night café at the station. We're going that way – you can get a drink and get tided up.'

'It's OK, honest, I'll be all right.'

'Well, you don't look all right. Come on, that waster might still be around.' One of the girls carried her bag, Janie held on to her arm and they set off for the station. As they passed the taxi rank Janie said, 'You two jump in a cab, I'll see she's OK.' Janie knew her friends had had too much to drink and needed their beds.

'Are you sure, Janie?' came an almost thankful voice.

'Yeah, go on.'

'Call you tomorrow, take care love,' said one of the girls with a look of sympathy.

'Bye,' said Lisa, 'and thanks.'

Janie and Lisa walked the short distance to the café. It was virtually empty except for a couple of station workers taking time out for a coffee, and an old man who didn't seem to know where he was.

'Sit yourself down; I'll get some drinks. Coffee OK?'

'Yes, thanks.' Janie went to the counter; with everything that had happened to her in the last hour or so it was the first time Lisa had really looked at Janie. Observing her very closely she had not realised just how tall she was; at least 5 foot 11 in her heels, short brown hair and a striking figure. She obviously looked after herself. Her dress sense was a bit revealing, her short skirt and very tight top attracted a lot of male interest. But Lisa didn't care about that; she had been there when she needed her and for that she was very grateful. Janie came over with two mugs of coffee, placed them on the table and sat down facing her.

'Looks like you've had a bad night out all round. You haven't told me your name,' said Janie.

'It's Lisa.'

'Pleased to meet you, Lisa. I'm Janie.' With everything that had been going on, Lisa had forgotten to use her alias from the bed and breakfast.

'Do you live local, Lisa?' Lisa's head dropped, she found it very hard to lie to someone who had been so good to her. 'Or should I say, how long have you been on the streets?' Lisa's head popped up. 'Don't worry, I know the score, I was on the streets myself for nearly three months, I know how hard it is. How old are you?'

'Eighteen,' lied Lisa.

'It's me you're talking to,' said Janie in a patronising voice.

'Nearly sixteen,' replied Lisa.

'God, I bet your parents are worried sick.'

'I don't think so,' said Lisa.

'Like that is it?' asked Janie.

'I can't go back there and I don't think they'd want me back to be honest.' Janie looked at her quietly for a few moments.

'Look, you can stay at my place tonight if you like, it's not very big but it's safer and warmer than the street. You look like you could do with a good night's sleep anyway,' said Janie.

'Thank you, I'd appreciate that,' said Lisa, gratefully. They drank their coffees.

'Sorry, Janie, I haven't got any money, that man took what I had.'

'That's OK, I've got it covered. Come on, let's get a cab, there's a taxi rank just outside.'

They walked down to the taxi rank. The city was very quiet by now, so there was no problem getting a cab. Climbing into the rear of the cab, Janie gave the driver the address and they sped off. Slowly, a nice warm feeling of being safe crept over Lisa; she hadn't felt like that for a long time. There was something about this girl Janie, a confidence that made being with her feel very secure.

4

The game

As they drove on, Lisa was noting in her head the names of the roads and the area they were in. As far as she could see, it was a residential area called Moseley.

'Next right,' said Janie to the cab driver 'Wellington Road, number 12A.'

'OK,' replied the driver. They pulled up outside the house, Janie paid the driver and they stepped out of the cab.

'Home sweet home,' said Janie with a smile on her face. 'Come on, we're upstairs.' Lisa followed Janie into the house, which was divided upstairs and downstairs into two two-bedroom flats.

'Come on in, Lisa, make yourself at home.' Janie switched on the lights and Lisa was gob-smacked. From her impression of the outside area, she had expected a dingy little flat; how wrong she had been. The decoration was immaculate, with a beautiful red leather suite, thick shag pile carpet and state-of-the-art hi-fi and television. Separating the suite from the television was a beautifully carved coffee table that Lisa thought must have cost a fortune.

'Jesus Christ, Janie, this is beautiful. How did you afford all this? You must have a very good job.' Janie just smiled.

'Come on, I'll show you where you can sleep.' Lisa followed her along a narrow hall. 'Bathroom on the right, my room on the left, spare room,' Janie pushed open the door, 'If you want a shower before you go to bed just help yourself. I'm going to turn in. See you in the morning.'

Lisa looked straight at Janie, 'I really do appreciate this, Janie.'

'That's the second time you've said that tonight,' Janie replied with a hint of laughter in her voice.

'No, I really do.' Lisa felt herself filling up with emotion.

'Get some sleep; we'll talk tomorrow. Good night.' Janie went down the hall into her room and closed the door behind her.

Lisa emptied the contents of her holdall onto the bed; she had never seen such a large bed and the sheets were like silk. Quietly, Lisa tiptoed down the hall into the bathroom, showered and wrapped herself in a huge bath towel she found hanging on the back of the door. Back in her room she climbed into the bed; the sheets felt wonderful against her skin and she felt so relaxed that she fell asleep in an instant.

Lisa woke, having completely lost track of time. After a good stretch and a last appreciation of the silky sheets, she got out of bed. The flat was silent; no sign of life in the living room or the kitchen. Lisa wondered if Janie had gone to work; the display on the hi-fi said ten o'clock. Sitting down on the sofa Lisa looked around the flat. The décor was so tasteful, she started to dream a little – if this was my place, she thought... The click of a door opening snapped her out of her daydream; Janie walked across the hall into the bathroom. Lisa tucked her feet under her body, feeling very relaxed. A few minutes later Janie came out of the bathroom.

'Morning, Lisa.'

'Morning,' she replied.

'Did you sleep well?'

'Can't remember sleeping that well, I was out like a light.'

'Good, I think you needed it. Right, what would you like for breakfast?' asked Janie.

'Just a coffee will be fine,' Lisa replied.

'Is that with or without a bacon roll?' Lisa smiled in reply. 'I'll put the grill on.' Janie went into the kitchen and began preparing the breakfast.

At Cromwell Lane Police Station, Robinson and Rhodes were in the briefing room scrutinising the white board. All the information they had on Lisa was written down in front of them and there was not a lot to go on. Shaw and Bradley were in London chasing the lead from the Birmingham sighting.

'I want to interview the mother without the father present,' said Robinson, 'If I can find out why she left I think we'll have a better chance of finding her. At the moment with what we have, we're just banging our heads against the wall.'

'I'll call and say there's some paperwork that needs dealing with, see if we can get her down here without him suspecting anything,' replied Rhodes. The phone rang.

'Cromwell Lane Police Station, Sergeant Rhodes speaking, can I help you?' He handed over the phone to Robinson, 'It's Shaw, Mike.'

'Hi Paul, anything happening your end?'

'No Guv, drawn a complete blank up to now. Nobody at the station saw her arrive, the street is quiet, the Met have got all their guys on the lookout for her. It's like she just disappeared.'

'OK, I want you to stay down there for another couple of days, keep your ear firmly to the ground.'

'Will do Guv. Anything turns up I'll contact you,' replied Shaw.

'OK Paul, bye for now.' Robinson hung up. 'Right Ian, get Carol Dean down here, I want to find out what's been going on in that flat of theirs.'

Janie came back into the living room with two huge bacon rolls and two mugs of coffee.

'I bet you're ready for this aren't you?' said Janie. Janie handed Lisa one of the huge rolls, Lisa tucked in as if she had not eaten for a week. After they had eaten they sat back with the mugs of coffee.

'This is a beautiful flat, Janie, how do you afford it all?'

'Let's just say my job pays well,' said Janie.

'I wish I had a place like this.'

'I'm sure you will one day. Right, are you in the shower first or me?' asked Janie.

'I'll go if you like.' Lisa jumped to her feet.

'Help yourself to shampoo and anything else you fancy.'

'Thanks,' said Lisa as she walked towards the bathroom door. Janie reached for the television remote control and sat back, flicking through the channels. Fifteen minutes or so later Lisa came out of the bathroom.

'Bathroom's free, Janie.' Janie jumped off the sofa and went to the bathroom, leaving Lisa standing, drying her hair with a towel. A news bulletin started on the television and Lisa glanced towards the screen. A newsreader announced 'There is still no sign of the missing fifteen year-old, Lisa Dean. Police are asking the public to be extra vigilant in the search for the teenager.' Her picture was on the screen. She leapt over the sofa, scrambling for the remote and turning the television off as fast as she could to keep the image from Janie.

'Lisa, get me a couple of towels – they're in the airing cupboard,' Janie called.

'OK, two ticks.' Lisa passed her the towels and Janie came out of the bathroom.

'What are we doing today then Lisa? I don't have to work till tonight. I don't think you have anything planned, do you?'

Lisa smiled, shaking her head. 'No,' she replied, her heart still pounding from the close call.

Rhodes had contacted Carol Dean; he had told her they wanted to run over a few details concerning family and friends. Alex was still drinking himself stupid in the confines of their home; she arranged to be at the station for lunchtime. By one o'clock Alex was asleep on the sofa. Carol thought it would be a good two or three hours before he woke. She gently pulled the front door behind her and set off for the station. She arrived within half an hour and was recognised by the duty officer as she approached the main counter.

'Hello Mrs Dean, I'll tell DI Robinson you've arrived.'

'Thank you,' she replied. Seconds later the counter security door opened.

'This way please, Mrs Dean.' The constable showed her through to an interview room. 'Can I get you a drink?'

'No thanks,' said Carol.

'The DI will be with you shortly.' The constable left the room, closing the door behind him. Carol sat staring at the wall, wondering if there had been any progress in finding her daughter. The loud click of the door startled her as Robinson came in.

'Hello Mrs Dean, how are you bearing up?'

'I'm coping the best I can,' replied Carol.

'Could I get you a drink?'

'No, the constable already offered, thank you.'

'Right, we've had a positive sighting of Lisa, she's been in Birmingham.'

'Birmingham?' said Carol, 'Why on earth would she go to Birmingham?'

'I can't answer that, but I do know she stayed at a young girl's parents' house – they're a hundred per cent sure it was her. The problem we have now is that the girl's father took Lisa to New Street station and we think she caught a train to London, but that's where the trail stops. I've a team of officers down there now, but I still have one dilemma that I can't work out.' Carol looked up.

'What's that?' she asked.

'Why does an apparently perfectly happy fifteen year-old gather up her clothes, steal as much cash as she can from her father, then disappear without a trace?' Carol felt backed into the corner, trapped.

'Mrs Dean,' said Robinson, putting both arms on the table and leaning forward, 'if there is something you would like to tell me,' he paused and looked straight into her eyes, 'in confidence of course, I'm here. I have a feeling there is something and it's going to be a major part of the puzzle.' Carol felt her body trembling, she wanted to tell him everything, but what about Alex? He would surely kill her.

'I know you've had words with your husband lately.' Carol touched her face. 'Yes, we had noticed,' said Robinson. As she felt the bruise on her face it enraged her to think that after all these years together and the loyalty she had showed him, he could still hit her. Looking down at the table she began to share the burden which had tormented her.

'He's been messing with her; it's been going on for months. I didn't know what to do about it. I didn't believe it at first, but it just got worse and worse. The more he drank the worse it got. Last Sunday was the final straw. She found out I knew what he'd been doing and that was it. When I was in the bathroom she packed her bag and left. I'm disgusted with myself. What kind of mother stands by and watches something like that happen to their child?' Tears ran down Carol's face; she looked up, making eye contact with Robinson.

'It's not for me to judge your actions, Mrs Dean, but you've spoken out now. Now I can do something about it.' Carol sobbed loudly, placing her head in her hands, no longer able to control her emotions.

'He'll kill me if he finds out I've talked to you,' her voice desperate and shaking.

'He's not going to find out, not just yet anyway,' said Robinson. 'First we're going to find Lisa, then we're going to throw the book at him.'

Robinson offered to drive Carol home but she did not want to draw attention to herself, it was only a short bus ride home anyway. As she walked along Cromwell Lane towards the bus shelters she did not notice the figure of her husband, Alex Dean, standing over the road in the doorway of the off-licence. When she had left the flat earlier that day, he had heard the front door close and followed her. His facial expression clearly spelled out his thoughts; still partially under the influence of the morning's drink, under his breath he hissed 'I'll shut your mouth once and for all, you fuckin' bitch.'

After dressing, Janie took Lisa on a tour of the city. Knowing that Lisa had only seen it from a negative perspective, Janie had decided to show her the city the way it was supposed to be viewed. A short walk down the road brought them to the bus stop.

'It's only about twenty minutes into town from here,' said Janie, 'we can have a look around some shops and try on some clothes; I think you need some additions to your wardrobe, Lisa. Then we can get something to eat. I have to be back about five-ish to get some rest before work this evening.'

Janie was enjoying Lisa's company; it was like having a little sister stopping over. As the day went by, a firm friendship was founded. Lisa couldn't remember having had fun like this. Janie was spoiling her rotten; all Lisa's troubles felt miles away. If only I could have a life like this, she thought. They arrived back at the flat just after a quarter past five.

'Thanks, Janie, I've had a great day. I wish I could repay you,' said Lisa. 'I'll get my stuff together and let you get some rest before you go to work.'

'Where are you going?' asked Janie.

'I'm not really sure, I have to find a way to earn some money. I can't sponge off people. Something will turn up, I know it will.'

'Why don't you stop a couple of days?' suggested Janie.

'I don't want to outstay my welcome, Janie, you've already been very good to me.'

'Tell you what, why don't you work for me?'

'Doing what?' replied Lisa, surprised and shocked.

'Housekeeper,' said Janie. 'You can do the ironing, tidy the flat, get the shopping, prepare some meals; don't worry, I'll keep you busy. What do you think?' A broad smile appeared on Lisa's face. 'Are you sure?'

'I wouldn't have asked if I wasn't sure – what do you say?'

'Janie, I'd love to,' answered Lisa, still beaming.

'Well, that's it then, you officially work for me.' They hugged each other, with what looked to be the start of a great friendship.

Carol had spent the afternoon tidying the flat and, after finishing the housework, settled down with a coffee to watch the television. Alex was nowhere to be seen. Unknown to her, he had spent the afternoon at his club, drinking. The image of Carol leaving the police station angered and tormented him; what had she told them? Was it safe to go home? So many unanswered questions fired the flames of his anger.

It was just before seven o'clock; Carol had fallen asleep on the sofa. Alex arrived home, very quietly closing the front door behind him. Entering the living room, he took a quick glance at Carol over the back of the sofa then went into the kitchen. He took a can of beer from the fridge and sat down at the table slamming the bottom of the can onto the table. The sudden noise woke Carol. Startled, she looked at the clock, her eyes squinting, not fully adjusted to the light.

'Alex, is that you?' she shouted; there was no answer. She got up from the sofa, stretching as she stood and went into the kitchen, where Alex was still sitting at the table.

'Alex, you startled me. Didn't you hear me call?'

'You've been to the police,' said Alex, accusingly.

'What are you talking about? I haven't,' replied Carol. His eyes turned and staring straight at her he said, 'If you know what's good for you, don't lie to me.' Carol instantly realised that one, he was drunk and two, he knew where she had been to that lunchtime.

'I had to, they called me in, it was just routine, I didn't want to bother you. I know how stressed you are with the whole situation, I told them you're not well.'

'You're lying,' growled Alex.

'Why would I lie to you, Alex?'

'I told you, if you know what's good for you, don't lie to me.' Terrified by the anger on his reddened face, the urge to run for the front door was almost overpowering, but she knew she would not get even halfway there. He stood up and pushed the chair away from himself, 'I want the truth, everything you've told them.' Carol backed away; any second now she was going to bolt for the front door. He picked up the can and gulped down the beer; this was her chance. She turned and ran, stumbling as she went, panic taking over all her senses. Halfway down the hall a sudden yank on her hair stopped her in her tracks, pain seared through her scalp.

'Where are you going, bitch?' said Alex as he dragged her back along the hall towards the living room. Carol screamed for help at the top of her voice. Alex opened his hand and unleashed a thundering slap across her face, then covered her mouth, gripping her broken jaw so that she felt sick with pain. He knelt down beside her.

'Nobody's listening, bitch, we're on the eighth floor, remember,' Alex hissed. Carol looked into his eyes; all she could see was pure hatred. What could turn a man who was once so kind into a monster of this proportion? He dragged her the rest of the way into the living room.

'Now, tell me everything you told them.' Carol knew that in the state he was in, if she told him the truth she would be lucky to get out of the flat alive.

'They wanted to know if she has friends in the Birmingham area, there was a definite sighting there of her, they were just following up a lead.' SMACK. He punched her square in the face. Her nose exploded and with her head back, blood poured down her throat. She felt the room spin. In a split-second the realisation of what was happening kicked in; if she did not defend herself, this would be the end of her. She lunged, both her hands grasping his face, her nails sinking into the flesh on his cheeks and forehead. The counterattack took him by surprise; he had not expected her to retaliate so aggressively. As he fell backwards,

Carol continued the attack, fighting her way on top, tightening her grip on his face. The blood from Carol's nose poured onto Alex's face, temporarily blinding him. Alex pulled up his knee, slamming it into her ribs, completely knocking the wind out of her. Carol gave a loud groan and fell to the ground, releasing her grip on his face. The pain in her chest was excruciating – she tried to take a breath but the pain overwhelmed her. Alex stood up, blood rushing from the wounds inflicted by her nails. Looking down at his wife attempting to curl up into ball on the floor, Alex raised his hand to his face touching one of the wounds.

'You fucking bitch,' he sneered. Drawing back his leg he kicked her in the stomach with all his might, spat on her, then casually walked to the bathroom.

In the flat next door, Geoff and Phyllis Stone, a middle-aged couple who kept to themselves, had their ears firmly against the wall.

'I'm sure I heard her shout for help, Geoff,' said Phyllis,

'Well, there's definitely something going on,' replied Geoff, 'I'm going to phone the police. That bloke's a nutcase, always coming home drunk.' Geoff, a teetotaller, was anxious. 'Anything could be going on in there.' He pulled on his jacket and rushed down the stairs to the public telephone across the street.

Carol, semiconscious, attempted to get to her feet. Alex was still in the bathroom. This was possibly her last chance to escape. Swaying from side to side, she staggered towards the hall. Alex heard movement and his rage suddenly hit an all-time high. He ran into the living room; Carol tried to reach the door but was not fast enough. He again grabbed her hair and Carol moaned; the pain in her ribs was unbearable. He pulled her back with all his might, throwing her backwards across the living room and over the coffee table, the back of her head slamming on to the edge of the television cabinet. The sound of the impact was sickening. Carol lay on the floor, no movement or sound of breath, a trickle of blood running out of her right ear. Alex stood over her, showing no remorse, and muttered 'That'll teach you, bitch.'

Geoff Stone dialled 999. 'Which service?' came the reply.

'Police please, I want to report a disturbance.'

Cromwell Lane Police Station was given the details of the call and as soon as the address was given, a fast response unit was sent to the flats. Robinson was informed of the call and he headed straight to the Deans' flat. Two constables from the fast response unit were first to arrive.

Geoff Stone met the two policemen at the entrance to the flats. 'I made the call, I think there's a fight going on in the flat next to mine.'

'OK sir, do you want to show us the way?' Stone took the policeman up the stairs to the eighth floor.

'Is the lift broken, sir?'

'No,' replied Geoff, 'but you don't want to be going in them lifts, not with the kids round here.' They arrived at Flat 32,

'Thank you sir, you can leave it to us now,' said the constable, knocking hard on the front door. He left it a few seconds; there was no answer, the flat was silent. He lifted the letterbox and peered through. He saw no one.

'Police. Can you open the door please?' Still no sound.

Stone was standing at his front door. 'They're still in there and she was shouting for help.'

The two constables were discussing forcing the door when Robinson arrived, out of breath, having also used the stairs.

'DI Robinson,' he said, showing them his ID. 'Break it down, there's a woman in there who could be in danger.' The larger of the two constables ran at the door. It shook but remained closed. The other constable joined him; they both hit it at the same time, smashing the lock and ripping out a huge chunk of the doorframe. They rushed down the hall to the living room. Carol was lying in the same position as she had fallen. Robinson saw Carol, flat on her back, eyes wide open.

'Careful guys, he might still be here.' Robinson approached the kitchen door; he pushed it with his foot. As the door opened he saw the figure of Alex Dean, sitting at the kitchen table, his head in his hands, sobbing and mumbling to himself.

'PLACE BOTH YOUR HANDS ON YOUR HEAD,' demanded Robinson. No response from Dean. Robinson gestured to the two constables; all three of them rushed him at the same time. With no resistance from Dean they slammed his head down onto the table, pulled his arms up behind his back and quickly applied the handcuffs. Robinson ran back into the living room, knelt down beside Carol and placed two fingers on her neck, hoping he could find the slightest sign of life, but it was not to be. Robinson went back to the kitchen.

'Read him his rights. I don't think there are any other suspects to take into consideration. I'll radio in for an ambulance and get the ball rolling.'

By nine o'clock Janie had showered, changed into some blatantly revealing clothes and was putting on her make-up. Curious, Lisa asked Janie where she worked.

'In a club,' replied Janie.

'What, like behind the bars and that?'

'Kind of, I'm a hostess, I keep the important guests happy,' said Janie.

'I see, and they pay you to have a good time. I wouldn't mind a job like that myself,' said Lisa, wistfully.

The reality was that Janie had been a prostitute for the best part of eight years. She had left home at sixteen, had a short spell on the streets and found the only way she could survive was to sell her body. It had been hard at first, but she had learnt to switch off. One positive thing that had come from it was her independence. The other girls working the streets either had pimps or were junkies, but not Janie. It may have been an undesirable occupation, but Janie went with whom she wanted when she wanted. Anything she earned was her own and that's the way it was going to stay.

'I'm off out, Lisa, don't wait up – I'll be very late. See you in the morning. Remember, if you want anything help yourself.'

'OK, thanks again, Janie. See you in the morning.'

Janie left the flat and stepped into a waiting taxi.

'Good evening, miss.' The driver greeted her as usual and they pulled away. Lisa peered from the front window, watching until the vehicle disappeared from sight.

Alex Dean was taken back to Cromwell Lane Police Station and charged with the murder of his wife. He had not spoken a word since the time of his arrest. As far as Robinson was concerned, it was an open and shut case. But as for Lisa, if this got into the papers, the chances of finding her would be even less than they were already. However, this was not the kind of thing you could keep quiet. As soon as the press got hold of it, knowing the case background, they would spread it all over the papers.

The following morning Lisa lay in bed enjoying the luxurious feel of the sheets on her body. It was just nine o'clock; she had had an early night so by this time felt wide awake and refreshed. She had not heard Janie come in; it must have been late as there was still no noise from her room. Lisa got out of bed and went into the living room, switching on the television, as was her normal routine. She made tea and toast and carried it back into the living room. A news bulletin began.

'Police are investigating the murder of Mrs Carol Dean, the mother of the missing teenager, Lisa Dean. They have arrested her husband, Alex Dean, on suspicion of murder.' Lisa stared at the television. She dropped the mug and plate she was holding. In a state of shock, she felt the walls closing in on her, then fainted, falling in a heap at the side of the settee.

'Lisa, wake up! Lisa can you hear me? What's happened?' Slowly, Lisa opened her eyes, her head still fuzzy; she did not know how long she had been out. Janie was kneeling down beside her.

'Thank God, I thought I was going to have to call 999. I don't know how long you were down there, I only got up for a drink and there you were.' Lisa's eyes were full of tears.

'Janie, something terrible's happened. I have to come straight with you.' Janie helped Lisa back to her feet and they sat on the sofa. Tears were running down Lisa's face, she was trying to be strong.

'It can't be that bad, girl,' said Janie, taking one of Lisa's hands in hers and trying to rub warmth into the cold fingers.

'I've just found out on the TV, my mum has been murdered.' Lisa burst into loud sobbing.

'Jesus fucking Christ, girl, where did that come from?' said Janie, dropping Lisa's hand, a look of absolute shock on her face.

'My dad's been arrested for murder.'

Janie reached her arms out to Lisa to hold her and, putting her head on Janie's shoulder, she cried her heart out. After a short time Lisa raised her head.

'Janie, the police are looking for me, they have been for over a week, since I ran away. I can't go back, if I do they'll put me in care.'

'Can I tell you something, Lisa?' said Janie, quietly, 'We're like two peas in a pod. I left home at fifteen and I've been on my own ever since. I wouldn't wish my youth on anyone, but I got through it, and so will you.' Janie smiled at Lisa; again she held her close. 'Have you worked out what I really do Lisa, how I really earn a living?'

'You're a hostess, that's what you said.'

'That's partly true. I'm on the game and have been for best part of eight years. I'm not proud of it, but when I was your age it was the only way I could survive and it's given me a pretty good life.' Lisa looked stunned. 'Are you shocked?'

'A little, but it doesn't change the way I feel about you, you're still the best friend I have.'

'That's nice. Well, I don't think we have any more secrets. Let's try and find out about your parents.'

Robinson had contacted Bradley and Shaw in London, explained the situation and ordered them back. They had drawn a complete blank and

Robinson was starting to think it was time to look closer to home. But then, of course, she no longer had a home. More and more he felt sure that unless this girl handed herself in, she was going to be swallowed up, never to be seen again, just another missing person.

For the next month, the police had many sightings of Lisa but none of them came to anything. Slowly, the profile of the case lowered until Robinson's team was reduced to just five officers. Lisa kept her head well down; she stayed in most of the time, just going out when she had to, mostly taking care of the flat, her relationship with Janie growing stronger as the days passed. Saturday night was Lisa's favourite time. Janie always found time to take Lisa out on the town, even if just for a few hours with her friends. Lisa's appearance had changed so much that there was little chance of her being identified. Every few weeks she would recolour the roots of her hair and diligently did nothing to arouse any suspicion, especially with Janie's neighbours, but most of them kept to themselves. Lisa constantly watched the news in the hope of some information about her parents. The last thing she had heard was that her father had been charged with murder and was remanded in custody, awaiting trial. She knew that this could take a long time and made a conscious effort to get on with her life, and it wasn't turning out too badly.

5

A new career

It was June 1986, just over twelve months after Lisa had left home. Her father had been found guilty of murder and sentenced to life imprisonment; it had been a hard time for Lisa when the trial had been taking place. All the memories had come flooding back, those fearful nights waiting for the click of the bedroom door. But she had come through it and life was good. Lisa was now sixteen years old and in a position to start earning money. Janie was still taking good care of her, providing everything she needed and for that she was truly thankful.

Janie was out working most nights, but she always saved Saturday night for the two of them. As Janie always said to Lisa, 'I don't mix business with pleasure,' which was difficult to comprehend in her line of work. Occasionally, Janie would entertain her regular clients at the flat and Lisa would just keep out of the way. They were never there more than an hour and the money was always left in the same place on the coffee table in the living room, sometimes as much as sixty pounds. Most people wouldn't get that much for a week's work. Lisa had enquired in some local shops for work, but the money they were paying was atrocious, not enough to survive on. Lisa wondered what Janie would say if she decided to go on the game, probably go mad? She decided to ask her thoughts on it.

That night while Janie was getting ready to go out, Lisa tapped on the bedroom door.

'Come in, Lisa, what's up?'

'I've been thinking, Janie; you make a lot of money doing what you do. Do you think I could?' Janie stopped what she was doing and just sat there, an uneasy silence surrounding them.

'Did I hear you right – you're thinking of going on the game? Just like that, you're thinking of going on the game? Do you think I enjoy what I do, being pawed every night by old men stinking of beer and god knows what else?' Lisa suddenly wished she hadn't made the suggestion. 'When

I asked you to stay here do you think I was looking to start up some kind of escort agency? I took you in to try and stop that happening, so don't you dare even let that cross your mind again. Have you got that?'

'Yes, I'm sorry; I just wanted to try and earn some money myself. I always feel like I'm just sponging off you.'

'Don't worry. If I feel you're sponging off me I'll let you know.' Lisa smiled. 'Now, I don't want to hear any more talk about going on the game, you got that?'

'OK,' replied Lisa.

'Now go and make us both a coffee before I have to go out.'

Lisa went into the kitchen and put the kettle on. When she had made the coffee they both sat down on the sofa.

'I may be a little later tonight, got a client at the Victoria Hotel, should be a good little earner.'

Half an hour later Janie was off out as normal. The taxi pulled up and Lisa watched from the window until the cab was out of sight.

'Different drop off place tonight driver,' said Janie.

'Right you are, miss,' replied the driver, 'you just direct me.'

'Victoria Hotel,' said Janie.

'No problem.' The driver had worked out the nature of Janie's work, but it was a good regular booking so, what the hell? If he didn't take it, another cab would. They arrived at the hotel and Janie had the fare ready; she was a regular booking so was charged the same price anywhere within the city centre. The driver asked if she wanted to be collected.

'I'll give you a call when I'm ready,' Janie replied.

'OK miss, bye for now.'

Janie had been told to go to reception and ask for Mr Talbot. The receptionist gave Janie the room number, looking down her nose at her with contempt. Janie had become accustomed to this. All these hotel jobs were the same, the hoteliers knew what went on when these businessmen were in town, but chose to ignore it, good for business and all that. Janie got into the lift; fifth floor, suite number 115. 'Suite,' she said to herself, 'this bloke must have some money.' It was usually just a double room. She knocked at the door and within a few seconds a man opened the door. He was casually dressed but still smart, designer stubble, not the typical businessman type.

'Mr Talbot?' asked Janie.

'Yes,' he replied.

'Hi, I'm Janie. I'm here to keep you company for the evening,' she said with a broad smile on her face; he returned the expression.

'Come in and make yourself comfortable.'

As she walked down the hall into the main lounge she felt his eyes on her body; the short skirt she was wearing didn't make it hard for her to walk the walk. He followed her and offered her a drink.

'Whatever you're having will be fine,' replied Janie. Talbot poured two large scotches and gave one to Janie; she raised her glass to his: the glasses chinked together.

'What would you like to do, Mr Talbot? You've got my complete attention.' He held her hand, then led her into the bedroom, placed his drink on the bedside cabinet and lay on the bed. Janie kicked off her shoes and climbed on top of him straddling his hips.

'Just lie back and let me relax you.' Janie started to undo his shirt, rubbing his chest with the palms of her hands. Suddenly, he grabbed both her wrists and rolled over so that he was on top.

'So, you like to be on top.'

He released her wrists; as she lay back she could feel his body hardening against her. He unbuckled his belt and pulled it from his trousers. He then unzipped his trousers revealing his aroused body. He pulled up her skirt and aggressively grasped at her underwear.

'Slow down, you'll enjoy it more if you relax,' said Janie.

'Just shut the fuck up.' His aggression made Janie freeze. She would get punters like this from time to time; you just had to tell them the right thing.

'OK, OK you're in charge,' she lay still. Her knicker elastic snapped and he threw the garment aside, plunging himself into her. This was not like the normal aggressive sex she had had to deal with in the past; this was frightening, he was immensely powerful. He grabbed her throat and instinct made her grab at his hand.

'That's it, fight back, I like it like that.' Still thrusting himself into her body, his left hand came across and crashed into her face. She instantly saw stars, her head was swimming and again he hit her, still squeezing her throat with his other hand.

Janie tried a last desperate attempt to get him off, thrusting her hips up, she rolled to the side; they both rolled over and off the side of the bed, crashing down to the floor. It took him by surprise, but seemed to excite him. Janie threw out a fist, which he caught.

'That's more like it.' It was as if it was a game to him. He grabbed her hair, banging the back of her head on the floor. With his trousers round his knees it was difficult for him to stand. He got to one knee; again he grabbed her throat and the waist of her skirt. He threw her onto the edge of the bed, she tried to keep her legs together but he thrust his hand between, squeezing her inner thigh. The pain was so intense that her legs opened. Again he thrust himself into her body, the more Janie struggled the more excited he became. She reached out, her nails sinking into his face; his left hand came round in a hooking motion. The punch hit Janie squarely on the jaw – CRACK; the noise was sickening, she was out cold. This did not stop him, he continued his attack slapping and punching any part of her exposed body that he could hit. His aggression became frenzied until the point when he climaxed. Then, just as if it had been a normal sexual experience, he dressed, took a crisp twenty-pound note from his wallet and threw it on her broken body.

As he left the suite, he looked both ways down the hall to make sure that no one saw him leave. He went down the stairs and left the building via the rear emergency exit, casually disappearing into the night.

Slowly, Janie regained consciousness, her mind clouded from the beating she had sustained. Her eyes were so badly swollen she could hardly see. As she took a breath, a great pain engulfed her chest; at best her ribs were cracked but more likely broken. She tried to move, but her whole body felt smashed, the pain in her jaw was excruciating; she had to get help. Slowly she crawled along the edge of the bed, trying to reach the phone on the bedside cabinet, every movement was a colossal effort. Finally, her hand reached the receiver. She lifted it and the light on the front of the phone flashed. A few seconds later, a voice came onto the line.

'Can I help you?' Janie could not answer, dropping the receiver she hoped it would alert their attention.

'That was strange,' said the girl on the reception desk, 'I just had a call from suite 151. The phone's off the hook but there's no reply.'

'Maybe it's just been knocked off accidentally,' said her colleague.

'I'll send up room service, just to be on the safe side,' she replied. Five minutes later a young girl from room service was outside suite 151. She knocked the door and waited; no reply. She knocked louder. Janie heard the knock but could do nothing about it; it had taken all her strength just to pick up the receiver. The girl at the door had been told that she must get a reply, so decided to enter with her staff key. She opened the door shouting 'Room service.' There was no sign of anyone. 'Hello?' she called, glancing around from room to room. As she opened the bedroom door the sight stopped her in her tracks: bed clothes covered in blood, a girl half on half off the bed, clothes torn from her body, her face grotesquely beaten.

'Oh my God!' She ran back to the main sitting room, fumbling to pick up the telephone receiver. 'Hello! Hello! Come on!'

'Reception, can I help you?'

'This is room service. I'm at suite 151, call an ambulance, there's a girl up here – I think she's dead!'

The next fifteen minutes in the hotel were chaotic, with managerial staff running everywhere. The first-aiders had been called and had established that she wasn't dead, but there was nothing but reassuring comfort they could give her, the nature of her injuries were so severe. The police and ambulance arrived virtually together. Janie's injuries were stabilised and she was taken to hospital. The entire floor of the hotel was taped off for forensic investigation, just in case it became a murder scene.

Steel House Yard CID took charge of the case. Two young detectives, waited for the go-ahead from the forensic team. First, they had to establish who the girl was and who had been in the suite with her. The hotel had no record of a girl staying at the suite, only a Mr J Talbot. A message was received from the hospital saying that the victim was out of danger and her injuries were not life-threatening. The detectives moved into the crime scene. Detective Constables Gillman and Elms gathered up Janie's personal possessions.

'Bingo!' said Gillman, flicking through her diary, 'Home address. We need to let these forensic guys do their job here. I'll head over to her house; you get down to the hospital. See if she's in any kind of position to give a statement, or just get a description of her attacker.'

'OK,' said Elms 'I'm on it.'

'When I've informed next of kin and found out what she was doing there, I'll meet you at the station,' replied Gillman. The detectives went their separate ways.

Gillman had no problem locating Wellington Road, Moseley, a well-known part of the city's red light area. Already, Gillman had put two and two together regarding the occupation of the young girl preparing for a stay in the main city hospital. All he had from the diary was the name Janie. He found flat 12A and knocked on the door. It was just after half past ten and he could see lights on in the flat; he knocked again. Lisa had heard him the first time and was peeping out of the corner of the bay window, contemplating whether to open the door or not. 'What the hell, I can't hide forever,' she thought. Already changed for bed, she pulled on her dressing gown and went downstairs. Opening the door but leaving the chain on, Lisa asked, 'Can I help you?'

'Yes, I'm sorry to disturb you at such a late hour.' Taking his identity card and badge from his inside jacket pocket, Gillman introduced himself. 'Detective Gillman, Steel House Yard Police Station. Can I come in? It's about Janie.'

'What's happened?' replied Lisa, immediately concerned.

'Shall we go inside?' said Gillman. Lisa closed the door and took off the chain to let Gillman enter.

'Is she OK?'

'Let's sit down,' replied Gillman, seeing that Lisa was starting to panic. They went into the flat and sat down on the sofa.

'Janie was assaulted tonight. She's in a bad way, but her injuries are not life-threatening,' said Gillman. He paused for a moment, then added 'And you are?'

'Lisa Dean.' As soon as she said it she thought 'Shit, and to a policeman as well.'

'Are you related to her?'

'No, we're flatmates. Can I go and see her?'

'Yes, of course, but can I ask you a few questions first?'

'Of course you can, I'll get dressed.' Lisa jumped to her feet and ran to her bedroom, 'Just keep talking,' she shouted to him. Gillman stood up and walked down the hall towards her bedroom.

'What was Janie doing in the Victoria Hotel this evening?' Lisa thought for a second or two then replied that Janie had been meeting a friend.

'Do you know who he was?'

'No, might have been a girl friend, she never said.' As he stood in the hall, the door was ajar and in the reflection of the mirror in her room he caught a glimpse of her as she pulled a t-shirt over her head, and found himself staring at her partly clothed body. As Lisa turned, he instantly diverted his eyes away. She came out of the bedroom,

'Shall we go?'

'Sure, we can talk on the way. Do I know you?'

'I don't think so,' replied Lisa. As they left the flat and headed towards the car Gillman racked his brains to remember how he knew this girl.

Janie had been taken to the Birmingham General Hospital A&E. After an examination she was found to have a broken jaw, three broken ribs, concussion and severe bruising around her inner thighs, throat and eyes. She had regained a good level of consciousness, but had been in so much pain the medical staff thought it best to sedate her. Surgery was required for her jaw, but the ribs and bruising were just going to take time to heal.

Elms was waiting patiently at the hospital when Gillman and Lisa arrived. Gillman introduced Lisa to Elms then they all went through to see Janie. She was still in a cubicle waiting to be taken to a ward. As soon as Lisa saw her she realised the severity of the beating she had received. Tears rolled down Lisa's face as she reached out and held Janie's hand.

'What has he done to you?'

Janie did not respond. Gillman put his hand on Lisa's shoulder.

'Don't worry; she'll heal. I think we should let her rest this evening. Come on, I'll get you a drink, you look like you need one.' As they left the cubicle a nurse approached Lisa.

'We haven't got a full name or next of kin contact details for Janie, could you fill them out for us?'

'I guess I'm her next of kin,' said Lisa, 'but I don't know her surname. I bet that sounds stupid, but it's true.'

'Just give us as much information as you can,' replied the nurse. 'She's going up to Ward 23 in the next few minutes so you won't be able to see her till tomorrow.' Straightaway the police officers' minds were doing overtime. 'Doesn't know her flatmate's name? Very strange,' thought Gillman. The officers gave each other a puzzled look.

'Let's get that drink – there's not a lot we can do here tonight.' They went to the hospital's reception area and had a coffee.

'I'll come over and get you in the morning from your flat if you like, see if she's able to talk,' said Gillman. Lisa thanked him. Gillman had taken a fancy to Lisa; there was something about her. In the last twelve months she had grown into a beautiful young woman. He had no idea she was only sixteen years old. He dropped her back at the flat and told her he would pick her up at nine o'clock. Her name and face were so familiar, but from where? He decided to go back to the station and check the computer for some answers.

Twenty minutes later Gillman arrived back at the station. It was starting to fill up with usual drunk and disorderly types. He steered past a couple of officers trying to restrain a large and very drunk man. The desk sergeant spotted him,

'You're late back this evening.'

'Yeah,' replied Gillman, 'some paperwork I have to complete for the morning.' The sergeant was then distracted by the large man the officers were trying to restrain. 'Just take him to the cells lads, I'll bring the paperwork to you.'

'OK Sarge,' replied one of the constables, 'Come on mate, just take it easy and you can have a nice bed for the night.' The tussling went on all the way to the cells. Gillman slipped by into his office and logged into the computer.

'Right,' he said out loud to himself, 'Lisa Dean,' he typed the name into the search screen and pressed enter. Virtually straight away the name came up on the screen. Lisa Dean, sixteen years old, missing person since

June 1985. The file had been updated with details of the murder of her mother and her father's imprisonment for the crime.

'I knew it,' he said out loud. The Greater Manchester police were dealing with the case, headed by a DI Robinson based at Cromwell Lane station. He flicked through a list of numbers, and then dialled the number for the Central Headquarters of the Greater Manchester Police.

Next morning at nine o'clock, Gillman pulled up in Wellington Road with DI Robinson from the Greater Manchester Police Force alongside him.

'This is one case I never thought we would crack,' said Robinson. 'Right from the start I knew it was going to be a chance meeting that would find this girl. Personally, I think she was better off out of there.'

They walked up to the front door; as Gillman was about to knock the door opened.

'I'm ready,' said Lisa.

Robinson looked at her. Lisa sensed that there was something wrong.

'Hello Lisa, I'm Detective Inspector Mike Robinson, I've been looking for you.' Lisa realised what he meant straight away. They went back inside the flat and over the next hour Robinson explained her situation. She hadn't actually done anything wrong, he just wished she had come forward and saved a lot of man hours and police resources trying to locate her. Now she was sixteen with no real next of kin, she was free to do as she chose. If that meant staying in Birmingham at her friend's flat, then that was fine. At least now she had her identity back, no more false names and dying her hair. She could be herself again. Lisa felt a sense of relief after the conversation, but was still glad she had not come forward earlier and risked ending up in some dingy care home until she was of age.

Janie had turned out to be a great guardian; as far as Lisa was concerned, Janie was her only family now, and Janie needed her. Robinson said he would sort out all the relevant paperwork and be in touch if there was a problem.

Lisa and Gillman arrived at the hospital; it didn't take long to locate Ward 23 and they introduced themselves to a nurse.

'We're looking for a girl called Janie, not sure of her surname.

'Right,' said the nurse, 'that would be Janie Coleman. You haven't got long, she's going down to theatre soon.' Gillman made a note of her surname.

'Theatre?' said Lisa in a startled voice.

'Yes, she has a broken jaw – it needs setting,' replied the nurse. Lisa's face contorted as if she could feel Janie's pain. 'I'll show you where she is.'

They walked down the ward a little way. On the left was a bed with curtains drawn around it.

'In there,' gestured the nurse. 'Don't encourage her to speak.' Lisa pulled the curtains aside and stepped in, trying to conceal the horror she felt at Janie's injuries. Lisa tried to smile as the small slits where Janie's eyes used to be attempted to focus on her. Lisa reached out and held Janie's hand; Janie's hand squeezed hers. Tears rolled down Lisa's face.

'Don't try and talk,' Lisa said softly. 'This is Detective Gillman.'

'Hello Janie,' said Gillman. 'As soon as I get a statement from you I'll be in a better position to catch the animal that did this to you. Can you write, Janie?' He took out his notepad, placed it on the bed and gave her a pen. Janie picked it up and roughly wrote down a brief description of the man that had attacked her.

'That's great, Janie; all you have to concentrate on now is getting yourself well. I'll come back and see you after your operation when you're able to talk. Take care of her, Lisa, I'll be in touch shortly.'

'Thank you,' said Lisa 'what's your first name?'

'Jack,' he replied.

'Thanks again, Jack, we appreciate it.' Gillman smiled as he turned and left. Lisa turned back to Janie.

'Don't worry, Janie, I'll take care of you.'

Later that day Janie had her operation. Her jaw was wired into place which meant at least a month of minimal movement, and with the condition of her ribs and other damage she had sustained, probably a lot longer. Lisa went home. She had been informed that Janie had been sedated after the operation and would remain that way for the next twenty-four hours. The best thing Lisa could do now was try to keep the flat running as normal, so that when Janie came home it would be less stressful for her.

Lisa prepared herself some food; there wasn't much in the fridge, just a slice of ham and some salad. She sat down in front of the television with a sandwich and was about to take a bite when the doorbell rang. She got up and, looking out the front window, saw a smartly dressed, grey-haired man in his mid to late forties. At first she thought it was another policeman but some kind of sixth sense told her he wasn't. She went down and opened the door.

'Hello,' he said, 'I haven't seen you before.'

'Can I help you?' asked Lisa, wondering who he was.

'Yes, I'm here to see Janie, but you'll do fine.' Lisa realised it was one of Janie's 'clients,' as she liked to call them. She could feel her face reddening.

'Sorry, she's not here today and I, I...' she stammered, 'don't do that.'

'Oh, I am sorry, I didn't mean to offend, I normally see her after the club on Thursday, but she arranged a home visit for me this week.'

He talked about it as if he was seeing a therapist; in some ways he was.

'Could you ask her to call me?' He handed Lisa a business card.

'She's not been very well, but as soon as she's better she'll be in touch.'

'I'm sorry to hear that. She's never mentioned you.'

'I'm Lisa, her flatmate.'

'Very nice to meet you, Lisa,' he took her hand and shook it, 'bye for now.'

As he left, Lisa thought how nice he had seemed. She had always imagined perverts and drunks seeking out girls on the game but how wrong she had been.

The next day Lisa arrived at the hospital just before lunchtime. As she walked down the ward she could see Janie sitting up in bed. She smiled as she got closer. The bruising on Janie's face was starting to change colour, a sign that the healing process had started.

'Sitting up, that's a start,' said Lisa. Janie had a notepad on her lap and wrote on it that she had been told not to try to talk for a few days.

'OK,' said Lisa, 'I'll have to get you some notebooks then, that one's not going to last you long.'

Janie put her thumb up then wrote, 'My ribs are killing me. They said I have to stay in for about seven days. Can you cope on your own?'

'What do you think?' Lisa smiled.

Again, Janie raised a thumb, a half smile on her face. Suddenly the colour drained from Janie's face and she raised a hand to her chest, the pain from her ribs momentarily overwhelming her. Within a few seconds the pain subsided and Janie wrote, 'It comes on like that, one minute nothing then all of a sudden, God it's painful.'

Lisa tried to make conversation but it was hard, especially when the other person couldn't talk.

'You know, Janie, I never knew your surname was Coleman.'

'I don't use it if I can help it,' wrote Janie, 'but the police were asking; they needed information on my medical records.'

'I see,' replied Lisa 'if there's anything you want, just let me know and I'll bring it in for you.'

A nurse came over to Janie's bed.

'Hello Janie,' she said, 'the consultant wants to take another look at your jaw, just to make sure it's aligned correctly. If the pain in your ribs gets too bad just let me know and I'll give you something to ease it.' Again, Janie gave the thumbs up. The nurse checked her chart then went on to the next patient.

'What happened, Janie? Lisa asked, 'Do you want to tell me about it?' Janie picked up her pad.

'Later, not just yet, when I can talk.' The nurse came back to the bed.

'Right Janie, you're off to X-ray.'

'I'll get off,' said Lisa, 'I'll come and see you tomorrow,' she took her hand and simultaneously they squeezed. 'Take care.' Lisa walked down the ward turning once and raising her hand to say good-bye.

When Lisa arrived home she checked her money – £1.50. That wasn't going to last her a week. She didn't want to ask Janie for money; she had enough to think about. In her purse she found the business card of the man who had been at the flat the evening before, Graham Brent Architectural Services. 'Sounds very professional,' thought Lisa. Over the next couple of hours, she paced up and down the living room, 'should I, shouldn't I,' racking her brain.

'What the hell,' she said out loud. Picking up the phone she dialled the number on the card. It rang for about thirty seconds.

'Graham Brent, can I help you?'

'Hello, this is Lisa, Janie's friend, you gave me your card yesterday,'

'Hello Lisa, how are you?'

'Fine thanks. Janie has asked me to take care of business until she's back on her feet, would you like to make an appointment?'

'Certainly Lisa, but I thought you said you didn't?'

'Let's just say you're a special case.' Lisa couldn't believe what she was saying, and how calm she was with it. They arranged to meet at nine o'clock that evening, at the flat.

'I'll see you later,' said Lisa and then hung up.

For the rest of the evening Lisa was on edge. She took a shower and went into Janie's room. She didn't like going through her things without permission but this was a special case. She put on some silk lingerie that must have cost a fortune. She thought about Janie's look when she went out to work; sexy but not too revealing. She decided on a chocolate brown silk camisole top, with a cream skirt fitted above the knee that complemented her curvaceous figure. Her hair was almost back to its natural blonde. She applied some of Janie's make-up; it was almost like getting ready for a date. Looking at herself in the mirror she felt pleased with her selection; the question was, would he be pleased? Two hours before he was due to arrive and Lisa was pacing up and down again, having second thoughts about what she was about to do. What would Janie say? Would she understand? What if she didn't and she threw her out? She wouldn't do that, or would she?

At exactly nine o'clock there was a knock at the door and Lisa's heart started to race. She looked out the window and saw it was him, holding a bottle of wine, just as if he was on a date. Lisa went down and opened the door.

'Good evening, Lisa,' he extended his hands with the bottle of wine, 'for you.'

'Thank you,' replied Lisa, 'come on up.' They went upstairs to the living room, 'Would you like a drink, Graham?'

'A glass of that wine would be very nice, Lisa, would you like me to open it for you?'

'Yes please,' replied Lisa. Graham uncorked the bottle and handed it to Lisa, who poured two glasses of wine and handed one to him.

'Cheers,' he said raising his glass. 'I must say Lisa, you are looking very beautiful this evening.' Lisa thanked him and he held out his hand. 'Shall we?'

Lisa knew this was it, she had bluffed up to now, but she couldn't bluff any longer. Her sexual experience was virtually zero; her only real sexual encounter was being raped by her father, not a good starting point. She felt herself trembling. He took her hand and led her towards the bedroom.

'The end room,' she said. It was one thing using Janie's clothes and make-up, but she drew a line when it came to using her bed. As they entered the bedroom he said,

'You're trembling; you don't usually do this sort of thing do you? Don't worry – I'm not a monster, I'll be gentle.'

As she lay on the bed he slowly removed his clothes. She didn't feel threatened at all. If anything she was actually enjoying the experience. For a middle-aged man he was in very good shape. Slowly he kissed her around the neck and shoulders. She was still trembling but slowly began to relax. He was very gentle and respectful of her obvious innocence. Over the next forty-five minutes Lisa's first real sexual experience excited her beyond her wildest dreams, he was so gentle and sensual. Why this man was using call girls for sex she did not know. They lay on the bed, their bodies soaked in sweat.

'Can I ask you something, Graham?' said Lisa.

'Of course,' he replied.

'Why do you use call girls? You're such a nice man, most girls would jump at the chance to date you.'

'Janie asked me the same question when I first met her. I don't have the time for relationships, I was married once but it didn't last. You see, I'm married to my work. I'm passionate about what I do, nothing comes between me and my work, but I still have needs like any man.' With that he rolled off the bed onto his feet. 'I could ask you the same question, but I won't. Do you mind if I take a shower?'

'No, of course not,' replied Lisa.

Lisa put on her dressing gown, went into the living room and curled up her legs under her on the sofa. Ten minutes later he appeared looking his original smart self. He took out his wallet and gave Lisa sixty pounds, thanked her, held her hand and kissed it.

'Shall we say the same time next week?' Lisa was stunned; she had not expected this.

'Yes. OK.' Again he kissed her hand.

'I'll let myself out.' As the door closed behind him Lisa looked down at the money in her hand. In one hour she had made more money than most people made in a week. Suddenly, from being quite pleased with herself, the reality of what she had just done hit home. What will Janie say, not just about the fact she had gone against her requests, but with one of her regular clients? To top it off, she had used no protection or any form of contraception. She decided to see Janie first thing in the morning to tell her what she had done, and just hope she had not crossed the line too far. If she gave Janie the money she had earned, maybe she would understand.

The following morning, Lisa went to the hospital. Visiting times were quite flexible, as long as people did not overcrowd the ward. As Lisa entered the ward Janie spotted her she raised her hand and waved.

'Hi Janie, you look a lot better today.' Lisa was in a chirpy mood. The colour and swelling around Janie's eyes had improved immensely.

'I can talk too,' said Janie, but her mouth was barely moving.

'That's great. Have they told you when you can go home?'

'No, few more days yet, I'm still on a lot of medication. Every hour or so they come and prod me here and there – I keep telling them it still hurts but they keep doing it,' said Janie with difficulty. Lisa laughed. 'I think the nurse on this ward gets a kick out of puffing up my pillows – I tell her they're fine but she carries on. Anyway what have you been up to? I meant to give you some money – I bet you've run out haven't you?' Lisa diverted her eyes from Janie's. 'What's wrong?' Janie picked up on Lisa's body language straight away. Lisa took the money she had earned from her pocket and placed it on the bed next to Janie. 'What's that?' asked Janie.

'Please don't hate me,' said Lisa.

'What have you done, Lisa?'

'One of your clients came round, a man called Graham, I told him you're not well.'

'So you stood in for me.'

'Yeah, I'm sorry,' said Lisa, sheepishly.

'The last thing I wanted, Lisa, was for you to go down the same path as me.' Lisa could hear the disappointment in Janie's voice; she couldn't look her in the face. She felt ashamed, not for what she had done, but for disrespecting the wishes of her friend.

'How did you feel afterwards?' asked Janie

'OK,' said Lisa shrugging her shoulders, 'I was more concerned about you than what I was doing myself.'

'Are you going to do it again?' asked Janie.

'He asked if I was available same time next week.'

'And are you?'

'Janie, if you say don't, I won't, I don't know if I should feel like this but I actually enjoyed it.'

'With someone like Graham Brent, you will, he's a very nice man, but they're not all like that; look at me.' Again Lisa lowered her head. 'Did you take precautions?'

'No.'

'Jesus Christ, Lisa, you always have to protect yourself.'

'I never thought at the time.'

'First things first, we have to get you on the pill. If you're going to do this you have to take care of yourself.' Janie picked up her notepad and wrote a doctor's name and address on it.

'Here take this money, I don't know why you gave it to me, you earned it. Go to this address, register with the doctor and then get some contraception sorted. Just hope to God you're lucky this time.'

'Thanks, Janie.'

'I don't know what I'm going to do with you,' said Janie, Lisa looked up and smiled. 'I'll have to keep my eye on you; with your looks I'll be out of work by the time I get myself straight.'

For the next half an hour or so they chatted and Janie told her one or two things to watch out for with various types of punters. Janie said she would take Lisa to the club and introduce her to a few people, once she was back on her feet. It was how Janie got virtually all of her business and it was safer that way. The managers of the club knew what was going on, but chose to turn a blind eye. It suited everyone.

Just then a voice from behind Lisa said 'Hello girls.' Lisa turned round to see Gillman and his colleague Elms.

'Hello Jack,' replied Lisa. He nodded then looked at Janie.

'How's the patient today?' he asked. Janie, still using very small mouth movements, replied that she was slowly getting better.

'Good, do you mind if I pull up a chair?' said Gillman.

'Please help yourself,' Janie was always a little apprehensive when policemen were being friendly; just force of habit.

'From yours and the hotelier's description, we have a good lead on a guy down south. It turns out you aren't the first girl to end up seriously injured in a hotel room in the last few months. There have been two other incidents in the London area alone; it's just a matter of time before we catch him.'

'Good,' said Lisa, 'people like that shouldn't be walking the streets.'

'Can I ask you how you met him, Janie?'

'Through a friend.'

'I know you probably think it's not my business, but soliciting is not just illegal it's a very dangerous game, especially in those circumstances.'

'Who said I was soliciting?'

'Come on, Janie, I wasn't born yesterday, just hear me out and be careful.' For a few seconds there was an uncomfortable silence. 'If you need anything or remember something significant, give me a call.' He took out a business card from his jacket and gave it to Janie. She glanced at it then placed it on the cabinet at the side of the bed.

'Right, we'll leave you for now.' Both policemen said their goodbyes and left.

That afternoon Lisa made an appointment to see the doctor at the address Janie had given her. She registered herself as a patient at the practice. It was easy to obtain the contraceptive pills. After a brief check of her general health and a pep talk on the do's and don'ts of contraception, she was given a prescription, which she collected straight away.

Over the next few days Lisa visited Janie each morning. After her visit she would go home and keep the flat nice and tidy, ready for Janie's return from hospital. There were now only two days to go before her appointment with Graham and she was looking forward to it, hoping to use him as a means of gaining experience in her new career.

6

James Noakes

James Noakes, Jimmy to anyone who knew him, was twenty-three years old, average build, rather non-descript. He was very young-looking for his age and could easily pass for seventeen. For the last five years he had roamed from place to place, never really settling down or forging any relationships. Most of his life had been spent in care, through no fault of his own. He had never known his father; his mother had gone rapidly downhill, turning to drink, drugs and, inevitably, prostitution to pay for her habits. Jimmy had inherited a large property from his mother's family, which made him financially secure. The property had been sold while he was in care and the proceeds placed into a trust fund, which he inherited on his eighteenth birthday.

Sitting on the park bench staring at the ground, Jimmy Noakes was in one of his daydream states of mind. These could go on for hours; they were actually a kind of seizure. He would find himself transported back to a period in his life, usually not a very pleasant one, where he would relive the whole experience again and again. On this particular occasion he was in his bedroom, seven years old. He remembered the details as if it was yesterday. His mother had one of her boyfriends (as she called them) over. It was a large, spacious house with very high ceilings and wooden floors; the sound really travelled. Sometimes her boyfriends would stay all night, other times they would just stay for half an hour or so. His mother always had bruises around her face; he wondered if that was normal – the mothers of the children at his school never looked like that. He crept along the landing to his mother's room; the door was slightly ajar and he could hear his mother; it sounded as if she was moaning. He peered through the crack of the door, she was face down on the bed naked, the man was also naked on top of her. He had what looked like a belt; he was hitting her with it and, by the noises she was making, he thought she was enjoying it. This went on for fifteen minutes or so, then he threaded the belt buckle and put the loop over her head.

Still thrashing around on her he pulled it tight. Still moaning, she started to make a gurgling sound, and after a while, the man collapsed on her back and lay there breathing heavily. His mother made no sound. He heard the man say, 'Oh fuck what have I done?' Quickly, Jimmy ran back to his room and hid under the bed. He could hear the man swearing as he dressed. Peering out from under the bed, he saw the man walk along the landing and down the stairs. The front door opened then slammed shut. Slowly, Jimmy came out from under the bed, tiptoed onto the landing and peeped over the balustrade; he had gone. Again, he went to his mother's room and peeped through the crack. She was still face down on the bed, the belt removed from her neck; slowly he walked into the room. As he got closer he called out, 'Mummy?' She did not reply. He walked along the side of the bed, noticing that her back was scratched and bleeding. As he looked into her face he saw that her eyes where bulging slightly and her tongue was protruding from her mouth. He stood back in shock, again calling 'mummy'; still no reply. He shook her shoulder, calling her again. He knew it was not right but couldn't grasp the fact that she was dead. He put the bed sheets over her in an attempt to keep her warm.

'Excuse me, hello,' a park warden was standing in front of him, 'are you all right? You've been sitting there like that for the last two hours.'

Jimmy looked up, suddenly snapping out of his trance-like state.

'I'm fine, thank you,' he replied. Wondering what all the fuss was about, Jimmy got up and walked off down the path. The warden stood looking at him, shaking his head.

Most of Jimmy's days were spent like this. Until recently, the opposite sex never really appealed to him, but now he found himself watching girls all the time. His social skills were very poor and he really didn't know how to approach girls. He just couldn't find the right words; not going through the normal state school system had made him very introverted. His manly urges were getting stronger all the time. Constantly frustrated, he decided to do something about it. He was renting a small flat, just outside the city, in the Bordesley Green area of Birmingham. He had lived in better areas, but the flat was comfortable for now, until he decided it was time to move on again. He bought a local evening newspaper and was looking through the personal ads, girls advertising their services, massages and so forth. He decided to give one a call and randomly chose one from a list of about thirty or more. The ad said, 'Sensual massage – home visits, call Susie 7 till late.' He dialled the number. It rang out; after a few seconds a girl's voice came on.

'Hi, this is Susie. Can I help you?'

'Yes,' replied Jimmy, 'I'd like to make an appointment please.' He arranged for the girl to be at his flat at half past nine the following evening.

Lisa was excited; the previous evening Graham Brent had been round for his appointment and she had enjoyed the experience even more than the previous week. Right from the start she had been so relaxed with him that the sex had been wonderful. As before, he had kissed her hand and paid her sixty pounds, again arranging to be there the same time the following week.

To add to her excitement, Janie was coming out of hospital that morning.

Lisa couldn't wait; she had visited Janie every day for the last two weeks. The bruises on her face were clearing up nicely. The jaw and internal bruising would take considerably longer. Lisa arrived at the hospital just after half past ten. As she walked along the ward Janie was standing by her bed with her back to her, gathering the last of her personal belongings together. Lisa walked up behind her.

'Boo!' As Janie jumped, her face contorted in pain, 'Sorry, sorry, sorry,' said Lisa realising what a stupid thing she had just done.

'Jesus Christ, Lisa, have you ever broken a rib before?'

'Sorry, I never thought.' A sheepish look came across Lisa's face. Janie's face slowly changed from contorted pain to an attempted smile.

'Come on, let's get out of here.' Lisa picked up Janie's bag and very slowly they walked down the ward, stopping every now and then to say goodbye to other patients Janie had got to know while she was staying at the hospital. She had been given an outpatient appointment to have the wire removed from her jaw in two weeks' time; the consultant said she would have to be admitted as a day case. Until then, she had to have total rest, limit her solid foods and try not to talk too much. Most of the food she had in hospital consisted of high-protein drinks and what could only be described as baby food. She needed to start having at least one solid meal a day, but it would take a week or so to readjust.

The taxi arrived promptly. Lisa asked the driver to take it easy due to Janie's injuries. Within twenty minutes they were home and it was obvious to see Janie was pleased to be there. The boredom of the hospital had been driving her stir crazy. Lisa opened the front door; there was a note sticking through the back of the letterbox. She pulled it out and carried on up the stairs into the living room. Lisa put the bag down.

'Right, you sit yourself down and I'll get the kettle on. I bet you could do with a coffee,' said Lisa.

'You know, of all the things I've missed that's probably number one on the list,' replied Janie.

'Put your feet up.' Lisa walked into the kitchen glancing at the note in her hand. On the back of the folded note was written 'Miss Lisa Dean'. She opened out the note; it read:

'Hi Lisa, I have been trying to contact you concerning your mother's personal belongings. The local council has repossessed the flat at Cherry Tree Towers; virtually all the contents have been put in storage. If you would contact me on the number enclosed I will arrange for you to obtain access to the items and close any outstanding paperwork we have between us. Detective Inspector Mike Robinson.'

Lisa made two coffees and went back into the living room. Janie took the coffee, thanked Lisa and sipped it, 'Ooh, I needed that,' she said with a look of contentment on her face.

'What do you make of this Janie?' asked Lisa, handing Janie the note. Janie read it.

'I wondered when this was going to arrive,' replied Janie, 'it has to be sorted, Lisa. Don't worry, I'll come with you.'

Lisa phoned the number on the card, it was Robinson's direct number. After a brief chat, he arranged for a car to drive down to Birmingham the following Monday and collect her at nine o'clock. From there she would be taken to Cromwell Lane Police Station to conclude any outstanding paperwork on her missing person file, then on to the storage facility and her mother's personal belongings. She knew that it was going to be a very distressing event.

It was just after nine o'clock. Jimmy had been pacing up and down his flat for the best part of an hour, glancing at the clock every few seconds. 'She'll be here soon,' he thought, 'do I pay her when she walks in or after?' Pacing at a slightly faster speed, he was nervously rubbing the palms of his hands together. His anxiety was reaching new levels when the doorbell rang. For a few seconds he stood still, thinking about what he was going to say when he opened the door. His heart was pounding in his chest as he approach the door. He clicked the latch from the locked position and opened the door. A small oriental-looking girl stood before him, no more than eighteen years old, very slight build, but at the same time very attractive.

She smiled at him, 'Hi, I'm Suzie. I have an appointment with a guy called Jimmy.'

For a split second he froze, then stuttered, 'Ye-yes, that's me.'

'Hi Jimmy, can I come in?' He stood back and she walked straight past him into the living room. Closing the door behind him, he followed her in.

'OK Jimmy, straight sex is forty pounds, anything kinky is more. But we can talk about that as we go, if you like.'

'Straight sex will be fine thank you,' he replied. He could not get over how relaxed about it she was, straight to the point.

'OK, shall we go into the bedroom or stay in here?'

'Bedroom.' One word answers were all he could muster at the moment; he was still a bit numb with her approach. As soon as they entered the bedroom she kicked off her shoes, stepped out of her small denim skirt and turned to Jimmy. She put both her hands around his neck and directed him towards the bed pushing him back onto it.

'Would you like me on top?'

He was dumbstruck. She undid his belt and pulled down his trousers, exposing his aroused body. As she climbed on top of him he felt an aggression building in his body that he had not experienced for a long time, flashing back to when he was a small boy in care. A boy had taken a ball from him; he had attacked, raining blows on his head. Even when the boy was unconscious he had continued; if it hadn't been for the care worker he would surely have killed him. Suddenly he was back in the room with the young prostitute, she was still on top of him, her top now removed. Sweat was running down her naked body, it excited him even more. He rolled to one side, releasing himself from her body and turned her over.

'Remember, anything kinky is extra,' she said. Again he entered her body, he reached forward on all fours, placing his forearm around her neck, and instinctively she grasped his arm. His aggression increasing, he was now in a frenzied state. She tried to talk but no sound came out; he was choking her. Reaching over her shoulder, she attempted to scratch his face but he just squeezed tighter and tighter. Then, as he climaxed, he realised what he was doing to her, and that in another few seconds he would have killed her. She was lying face down on the bed grasping at her throat, trying desperately to draw in as much breath as she could.

'You fucking maniac!' she screamed at him, still coughing. 'What the fuck do you think you were doing?! You nearly fucking killed me!'

'I'm sorry, I got carried away,' he replied.

'Carried away? You fucking moron.' She got to her feet still clutching her throat and coughing. 'Give me my money.'

'I'm really sorry.'

'Just give me my money,' she demanded, pulling on her clothes. He took his wallet from his trousers, counted out forty pounds and held it out to her.

'You're having a fucking laugh mate, sixty quid at least. I told you, anything funny was extra.' He pulled another twenty pounds from his wallet and gave it to her. Stuffing the money into the pocket of her skirt; she hastily walked towards the front door. 'I'll see myself out.'

As she left she slammed the door behind her. Jimmy sat on the bed, a little taken aback by her reaction, but then he smiled to himself under his breath and gave a small chuckle. The Jimmy Noakes that had been under control for so many years had finally surfaced.

Lisa woke just after half past seven. All weekend she had been dreading the arrival of the car that would take her to Cromwell Lane Police Station and then on to the storage facility where her mother's personal possessions were being kept. She knew that as soon as she saw certain items, memories would come flooding back. Both Janie and Lisa were ready with fifteen minutes to spare.

'Just take it as it comes,' said Janie, 'you know it's going to be hard, but it has to be done, and once that paperwork is completed you'll be part of the system again. I bet you're really looking forward to that.'

'Yeah, really,' replied Lisa, sarcastically.

By a quarter past nine there was still no sign of the car.

'I did get the right day, didn't I?' asked Lisa.

'You took the message,' replied Janie, 'give them another fifteen minutes; if it's not here by then we'll call them.' Just before half past nine, a white Ford Granada pulled up outside, a man in a suit got out of the car, locked it and came to the front door. Before he could knock or ring Lisa opened the door,

'Miss Dean? Sorry I'm late, the traffic was horrendous. DC Shaw, I'm your ride to Cromwell Lane.'

'I'll just get my friend, two ticks.' Lisa went back up to the flat. 'It's him, Janie.'

'OK,' Janie shouted from the bathroom, 'give me a sec.' Five minutes later they both walked out to the car.

'I didn't know there were two of you.'

Lisa introduced Janie.

'I'm here for moral support,' interrupted Janie.

'Sounds good to me,' said Shaw, opening the rear door of the car. 'Shall we go? It's a long drive.' They climbed in. 'I'll have you there in no time,' he said. The car roared off a little too quickly for their liking; they exchanged worried looks.

Over two hours later they arrived at Cromwell Lane Police Station.

'There you go ladies, on time, safe and sound,' Janie nearly commented but bit her lip instead. 'I'll take you in, get you a drink and let the governor know you're here.' After the journey they had just had, something stronger than coffee would have been more suitable. He had got into the outside lane on the motorway and stayed there all the way to Manchester. As a policeman, he should have known better, but he gave them the feeling that he thought he was above the law. They went into the station via a rear security door; Shaw led them to a room off a long corridor and they sat down.

'Right, I'll get you those drinks – tea or coffee?'

'Coffee please, no sugar,' they replied.

'Make yourselves comfortable, I'll let the DI know you're here.' Shaw left the room. They hadn't been waiting long when the door opened and a face familiar to Lisa entered the room: Mike Robinson.

'Hello Lisa, how are you?' he asked.

'Fine thanks, err?'

'Mike will do,' he anticipated she would not remember his name or not know how to address him. 'Shaw said there were two of you.' Janie stood up and Lisa introduced her to Robinson.

'I've arranged for some food for you a bit later on. But first shall we clear up the missing person paperwork? It's been on my desk longer than I can remember. Let's go to my office – it's a bit more comfortable there.' Shaw came in with the drinks. 'We can take them with us,' said Robinson, gesturing towards the door. It only took about an hour to complete the paperwork; most of it was just signatures, confirming that it actually was her. What it meant in reality was that Lisa was now officially a listed person again: she could sign on and receive benefits, get herself a bank account, national insurance number, credit cards and all the things that girls of her age would normally take for granted.

'Right,' said Robinson, 'now that's all out the way we'll go and get some lunch then get down to the matter of your mother's personal belongings.' It was plain to see from Lisa's face that she was dreading this part of the day. Janie reached out, putting her hand on Lisa's shoulder; a friendly smile eased Lisa's mind for now. After lunch, Robinson explained that some of the items from the flat had been used as evidence in the case against her father so they would still be in a police storage facility, but the majority had been put in council storage. As they left the station dining area, Robinson asked to speak to Lisa alone.

'I have nothing that Janie can't hear about,' replied Lisa.

'I just wanted to tell you some things that your mother said to me. I think I was possibly the last person that spoke to her, next to your father.'

'It's OK,' said Janie 'I need the little girl's room anyway.' Janie disappeared down the corridor.

'You know, Lisa, your mother loved you very much; it was because she came to the police that your father killed her. She spoke out about what he was doing to you. She wished to God that she had come forward earlier. Don't hate her for it, we all make mistakes and your mother paid the ultimate penalty for it.'

'That may be so,' replied Lisa, flatly, 'but I'd never let something like that happen to a child of mine.'

Lisa had hardened over the past twelve months, mostly for the better. But now she came across as a lot older than her years. A small part of her childhood had been stolen from her and for that she could thank her father. Janie returned.

'How we doing?' she asked, a smile forming on her face.

'I think we're just about done,' said Robinson returning the smile. 'Let's get DC Shaw to take you to the storage facility, it's only about fifteen minutes from here. Any other paperwork that needs signing can be sent to you in the post.' Robinson located Shaw, said goodbye to the girls and assured them that after they had been to the storage facility, the young detective would take them home. Less than half an hour later they arrived at the council storage warehouse. After a short explanation and another form signing session, a man led them to a large room.

'Top left corner,' he handed them a list, 'it's all labelled, but if it's not on the list it's not yours,' said the little man abruptly, as if the warehouse contents were his own personal possessions. As he turned and walked away Janie sneered at him.

'He's a charmer, isn't he?' said Shaw, and they all laughed. 'Right, I'll leave you girls to have a good look through your stuff. If you don't mind, I'm going to put my head down in the car for half an hour or so – we still have a long drive a head of us.'

They set about going through some of the boxes. Lisa noticed the three-piece suite; she had fallen asleep on that once or twice. She found a couple of small boxes with her own things inside, but there wasn't much stuff she actually wanted – most of it was old and just brought back bad memories. As far as the beds were concerned she would have liked to see them burn. In the corner she noticed a small metal box, one of her last memories of home; the box had contained all her father's personal information. She moved a few items to get at it. Janie could see Lisa was making a beeline for the small box and asked if it was important.

'I'm not sure yet,' she replied. She pulled the box out. The clasp was very tight; it hadn't been opened for a long time. Picking up a knife from a box of kitchen utensils, she prized the clasp open. It was just as she remembered it on that day she had left home: the medical card, passport and the wallet she had taken the fifty pounds out of were all still in there, but no cash, unfortunately. Then something stopped her in her tracks: photographs of her and her father on holiday. Lisa was sitting on his shoulders holding an ice cream; she looked so happy. There were others of them playing in the sea. She couldn't remember when or where the photographs were taken; they were not even a distant memory to her. There were some excellent pictures of her mother and father walking hand in hand. A tear ran down her face.

'Why, Janie?' she whispered, tears rolling down both cheeks. Janie put her arm around Lisa's shoulders.

'Let it out girl,' she said. Lisa cried, all the pent-up emotion pouring from her body.

Lisa placed to one side the things she wanted to keep. The furniture was of no value to her. The little man with the attitude came over.

'You have one week from today to move it all or it will be sold at auction to cover the cost of the storage,' he said, almost pleased with himself.

'I only want what I will take with me today – I don't care what happens to the rest of it,' Lisa told him.

'Right, I'll get the forms for you to sign.'

Lisa and Janie finished separating the boxes. 'I hope the policeman doesn't mind me bringing this stuff back in the car,' said Lisa. The little man came over, clipboard in hand.

'Just sign on the dotted line and I'll take care of the rest of it. Make sure you have everything you want. It'll all be gone by dinner time tomorrow.' Lisa took the board, briefly read the form and signed it. Twenty minutes later they were ready to go. Most of the things she was taking were hers anyway, a few of her mother's things had a little sentimental value, but most of it was junk as far as she was concerned.

'Hello girls,' said Shaw, refreshed from his sleep. 'How are we doing?'

'Fine,' replied Lisa, 'just about ready to go. You don't mind if we put some of these things in the car do you?'

'No problem,' replied Shaw, and started to load the car. Lisa thanked him; it didn't take long for the three of them to load the car. Lisa checked with the little man that everything was signed.

'Of course it is,' he said in his arrogant manner. So they set off back to Birmingham. Lisa was happy to have dealt with the situation; she could finally leave her previous life behind her.

Since his encounter with the young prostitute, Jimmy continually scanned the personal ads. Every evening he had purchased the local paper, contemplating whom he was going to call next. He didn't like the idea of them coming to his flat; the next time, he decided, he would go to them. If they couldn't accommodate him he would simply move on to the next ad. He read the column over and over and randomly he selected one: 'Michelle. Your place or mine. Relaxing massage.' He dialled the number; it rang out for at least a minute. He was just about to put the receiver down and choose another when a voice said, 'Hi, Michelle here, can I help you?' Her voice was sultry. He got the feeling the girl on the other end of the line was more mature, more experienced than the previous one.

'I'd like to make an appointment please.' He arranged to meet her at nine o'clock the following evening; the address he was given was a house in Edgbaston, an affluent suburb of Birmingham. He bought a Birmingham street guide and looked up the road, thinking out loud he said 'Belfort Road'. Scanning the index, he found the road easily.

The next evening he set off just after eight o'clock, giving himself plenty of time to get there. He caught a bus into the city centre then walked; it was less than half an hour on foot. Still ten minutes early, he walked up and down the road; number 22 was the house he was looking for. He stood on the other side of the road looking at the house. The houses were all typical – similar-looking three-bedroomed, semi-detached properties. He waited until exactly nine o'clock then checked up and down the road; he didn't like the idea of people seeing him going in a house like this. He crossed over and walked up the path, closing the gate behind him. He glanced over his shoulder as he knocked on the door. A woman opened the door, fortyish, peroxide blonde hair, he could see she was fighting to maintain her figure; her clothes were very tight, which did her no favours. With a large smile on her face she welcomed him. 'Jimmy I take it?'

'Yes,' he replied. She invited him in. As he stepped over the threshold, again he glanced over his shoulder. She could see that he felt edgy.

'Can I get you a drink, Jimmy, something to relax you a little?'

'No, I'm fine thanks,' he replied.

'Take off your coat and sit yourself down.' He put his jacket on the back of a chair and sat down. There was a strong smell of cigarettes; he got the feeling this woman didn't take very good care of herself, he was beginning to wonder if he had done the right thing. She wasn't as appealing to him as the last one. Kneeling down in front of him she asked, 'What would you like Jimmy? I can start with a massage to relax you before we...'

'Straight sex' Jimmy interrupted, abruptly.

'Ooh you know exactly what you want then, that'll be forty pounds, I like the money up front.' Her tone had changed to a business-like approach, just like flicking a switch. Jimmy pulled out his wallet and gave her the forty pounds. As soon as she had the cash her tone changed straight back to soft, friendly and pleasing.

'Let's go up to the bedroom and get a little more comfortable.' She took his hand and led him up the stairs, glancing over her shoulder with a gentle smile. The room was very sparsely furnished; he got the feeling this room was used for one thing only. Jimmy sat on the bed; she climbed on behind him kicking off her she shoes as she went. With both hands firmly on his shoulders she started to massage his upper back. He was very tense; she had been in the game a long time and could sense it.

'Try to relax, Jimmy.' Softly, she kissed the back of his neck. She unfastened the buttons on his shirt, 'How would you like me, Jimmy?' It was like a trigger to him, he turned and pushed her down onto the bed.

'Steady tiger,' she said, his eagerness surprising her. Piece by piece he pulled at her clothing until she was naked in front of him.

'You don't hang around do you?' she murmured, again startled by his impatience. She started to undo his belt. He looked down at her naked body; it wasn't excitement he felt, it was more like rage. He hated the way these women sold their bodies, but at the same time he wanted them. As soon as she undid his trousers he pushed her arms down and forced himself between her legs.

'Don't rush, Jimmy, take it easy,' she said. He didn't hear her. He plunged himself into her body, the rage building with every thrust. Pulling himself from her body he turned her so she was face down.

'Take it easy!' she shouted, frightened by the aggression in his movements. Again he plunged himself into her body. She cried out with pain but it only excited him; the flashbacks again starting to happen. In his mind he was surrounded by children, taunting him, laughing and ridiculing him. He grabbed the back of her hair forcing her face into the pillow. The children were still laughing, pointing, calling out names, 'Freak!' He lashed out hitting anything he could. His body was tense, enraged with anger. Still he forced her face hard down into the pillow; she was frantically trying to breathe. Her hands reached behind her, trying to find some leverage to release herself, but he was too strong. Jimmy was still in a trance-like state, pounding her body harder and harder, infuriated within his dream state. She was weakening rapidly, not an ounce of breath left in her body. With a cloudy haze forming in her eyes, she no longer had the strength to escape. As she slipped into unconsciousness, Jimmy continued, faster and faster. How much time passed he didn't know before he slumped on top of the woman, her body collapsed face down in a heap. He rolled off her expecting a verbal attack, like the one from the last prostitute, but she lay completely still. He reached over and lightly touched her shoulder. Gently he shook her, instantly remembering the day he found his mother dead; the similarities were frightening. Her face was turned away from him so he walked round the bed to look at her; a cold shiver went down his spine. Her eyes were wide open, her mouth agape, as if trying to snatch a last gulp of air. Panic ran through his body. 'Fuck,' he whispered, then, shouting aloud, 'I've fucking killed her!' He paced to and fro across the room, frantically rubbing the palms of his hands together and speaking aloud to try and calm himself. 'Don't panic Jimmy. Come on. What do I do? Have to get away. Can't be seen.'

A steadiness came over him. He pulled on his clothes then meticulously wiped the door handles and furniture, cleaning anything he thought he had touched. Finally, he went back to the bedroom to take a last look around, checking that there was nothing left to incriminate him. He went down the stairs and peered out of the front room window checking the street; it was dark and there was no sign of any neighbours or passers-by. Grabbing his jacket from the chair he left the house, pulling the front door quietly closed behind him. Keeping his face down, he hurried the opposite way down the road to which he had arrived, disappearing around the corner.

7

A business arrangement

It was dark when Shaw's car arrived back at Wellington Road. Lisa and Janie had both fallen asleep in the back of the car.

'Wakey, wakey ladies,' said Shaw 'you're home.' Slowly, both girls sat up, stretching and yawning almost simultaneously. Shaw got out of the car and stretched his legs. Opening the rear door he said, 'If you open up I'll bring the boxes up.' Lisa thanked him. The journey had taken its toll on Janie; Lisa could see she was in pain, occasionally she would hold her side, a grimace on her face.

'Come on Janie, let's get you upstairs, you look like you need a rest. I'll help with the boxes.' Janie didn't need telling twice. Lisa and Shaw moved the boxes up to the flat, stacking them in Lisa's room. When they had finished Lisa put the kettle on.

'Tea or coffee?' she asked. 'Sorry, I never got your first name.'

'Paul,' replied Shaw, 'coffee would be great, thanks.'

'I bet you're shattered,' said Lisa.

'It's certainly been a long day, but you get used to it though in my line of work. Still, I'm not looking forward to the drive back.'

'Can I get you a sandwich or something?' asked Lisa.

'Sure you don't mind?'

'No, course not. Couple of sandwiches be OK?'

'That would be great, thank you,' said Shaw. He didn't fancy jumping back into the car and heading straight back, after all, he had been up and down the motorway three times already that day. Lisa gave Janie a coffee, which she took gratefully. Two ham sandwiches and a mug of coffee later, Shaw thanked the girls for their hospitality and started his journey back.

Lisa and Janie changed into their dressing gowns and sat in front of the television, both feeling exhausted after a very long day. By half past ten they were both fast asleep on the sofa. Sometime in the early hours of the morning, Lisa sleepily found her way to her bed.

Some hours later she woke and lay in bed feeling refreshed after what had been a taxing previous day. Since Janie had been attacked, Lisa had been trying to think of ways to reduce the chances of it happening again. Janie had always been her own boss when it came to clients, but she still relied on the club for her introductions and hotel work. Inevitably, they had taken a cut of the money. Now that Lisa was becoming involved, she thought of a proposition. They could advertise themselves, working only from the flat, reducing the chances of walking into a trap as Janie had. It had the potential to be a good business arrangement, also a lot safer. After breakfast she decided to put it to Janie and see what she thought. At least while Janie was recovering Lisa could give it a go and see if it worked; they had nothing to lose.

Lisa got up, showered and went into the kitchen. There was no sign of Janie stirring. Lisa glanced at the clock and saw that it was just before ten o'clock; no wonder she felt refreshed, she had slept for nearly twelve hours. Janie's bedroom door opened and a very tired-looking Janie came out of her bedroom, her face attempting to control a very painful yawn. Lisa stuck her head out of the kitchen, 'Coffee?'

'Oh yes, please,' replied Janie, her mouth moving barely more than that of a ventriloquist. Slowly she sat down on the sofa, still feeling extremely fragile. 'Have you been up long?'

'No, only about ten minutes.'

'God, what time did we go to bed?'

'Must have been about three o'clock,' said Lisa, coming into the living room with two mugs of coffee in one hand and a plate full of toast in the other.

'Oh great, I need that,' said Janie.

'Janie, I've been thinking,' said Lisa.

'You don't want to do that too often,' replied Janie, grinning as she attempted to slide a small piece of toast into the restricted space in her mouth.

'No, seriously, while you're recovering, I thought I might place an advert in the personal column of the paper.'

Janie paused, putting her toast back onto the plate.

'Are you serious?' asked Janie, 'Do you know how dangerous that can be, going to someone's house you've never meet before?'

'No,' interrupted Lisa, 'I don't mean like that. I thought maybe I could work from here – it would be safer.' Lisa dropped her head sheepishly.

'You see, the thing is, I only use the flat for clients I know well.'

'It was just a thought,' replied Lisa, 'after what happened to you at the hotel, I thought all your clients from the club were checked out.'

'So did I,' replied Janie, 'and nobody's been down to see what's happened to me.'

'I just thought we should look after each other a bit more, and what could be safer than working from home. If we don't like the look of them, just turn them away.'

'God, you sound like you've been doing this for years,' said Janie, finding herself impressed by the maturity Lisa was showing, 'I'll have a think about it,' she said, 'you just concentrate on keeping Graham Brent happy for now.'

At half past ten Michelle Summers had not arrived at her mother's house; she always visited her mother on Mondays, Wednesdays and Fridays. This had been her routine since her mother had been confined to a wheelchair; she had arrived as regularly as clockwork. Michelle only lived two streets away and on the rare occasion that there had been a problem she would ring. Her mother waited until eleven o'clock. There was still no sign of her. She called her but the phone just kept ringing out. Her motherly instinct was telling her that there was a problem. She was physically unable to just pop out and check on her daughter, so she decided to give the local police station a call and explain the situation. Hopefully, with the latest drive in community policing, they would assist her. After a five-minute phone conversation with the desk sergeant he said he would send a car to the address. He took her details and said he would get back to her. Two hours later a car arrived at Belfort Road; two young police constables had been given their first assignment. Both had recently completed their training and after a couple of months working with experienced officers, it was time to let them find their own feet.

'Number 22,' said PC Alder, a tall, gangly young man; if it wasn't for his height, he wouldn't have looked old enough to be a police officer.

'That's it there, look,' said his companion, PC Goode, exactly the opposite in stature, his build and square features making him look considerably older than his age. They got out of the car and glanced around.

'Nice, quiet little street,' noted Alder.

'I bet they aren't half a price,' replied Goode. They went up to the front door and rang the bell; there was no answer. Goode looked through the letterbox while Alder peered through the front bay window.

'It doesn't look like there's anyone in,' said Alder, 'I'll take a look round the back.' He went to the side gate and found it locked. With one foot on the fence he reached over the gate, his long frame easily reaching the bolts. He went down the side alley and into the garden. Goode followed close behind him. Before them was a beautifully manicured garden.

'Someone's got green fingers,' said Alder.

'Yeah, it's nice isn't it?' agreed Goode. Alder peered through the kitchen window,

'Don't look like anything's out of place,' he said.

Goode tried the patio door; it opened, 'Not very clever, gone out and left the back door unlocked. Come on, better check it out.' They stepped into the room. Everything looked in place, a bit lived in, but OK.

'Hello, Police. Anyone home?' called Alder. There was no reply.

'I think this lady's just gone out, or maybe she got lucky last night and just never came home?'

'Maybe,' replied Goode, 'we're here now though, so we should just check the rest of the house.' They went up the stairs. Again Alder called out, just in case the owner was in bed, but there was still no reply. Goode checked the bathroom. Alder pushed open the front bedroom door and stepped in; he felt the hair on the back of his neck stand up. Michelle Summers was in the same position that Jimmy Noakes had left her; face down, naked, with her head turned slightly to one side. Alder froze; he had seen dead bodies before, but to discover one in these circumstances was a first.

'Alright mate?' shouted Goode from the bathroom; he could see his colleague standing in the bedroom doorway, motionless. Goode approached him, 'What's up mate?' he pushed past Alder into the room.

'Oh fuck,' said Goode, instantly reaching for his radio. 'Bravo 30 to control, over.'

'Yeah Bravo 30, what's up lads?' crackled the response.

'We've got a dead body.' It was a short, sharp, shock for both young police constables. The controller told them to back off out of the house the way they had entered, being careful not to touch or disturb any potential evidence. Within ten minutes a car arrived and Sergeant Ernie Hewitt, a highly experienced officer, took charge. CID were informed and the scene of crime officers started their investigation.

It was after noon when Jimmy woke. He had spent most of the night pacing up and down the living room and it was nearly five in the morning before he finally went to sleep. He had been racking his brains; had he left any incriminating evidence? Before he left the house he had wiped everything he thought he had touched and was certain that nobody saw him enter or leave the house. There was nothing he could do about body fluids; he just had to make sure they couldn't identify him; he did not have a criminal record so, theoretically, if he went to ground, they could never connect him to the murder. Thinking about what he had done, he felt no remorse; as far as he was concerned it was just another slag off the street.

Sitting down with a mug of coffee, Jimmy silently contemplated what he was going to do next. The rent on his flat was paid a month in advance, so if he moved out for a few weeks he wouldn't be missed. Nobody ever called on him, except the landlord and that was usually about a week before the rent was due. He decided to get a lunchtime paper and see what rental accommodation was available. The more he kept on the move, the harder it would be to track him down. He set off for the local newsagent where he purchased a newspaper then went into a nearby café to get some lunch and scrutinise the property pages. In a short time he had highlighted a couple of one-bedroom flats that stood out; one was in the Moseley area of the city, the other in Kings Heath. Both were relatively close to each other, the price was right and most importantly to Jimmy, both were furnished. He decided to call after he had eaten to see if they were still available. Again he turned to the personal ads; it was becoming an obsession. He noticed that the dead woman's advert was still in the paper; how long would it be before they found her? The longer the better, as far as he was concerned. He carried on reading the ads. 'Petite oriental beauty. My place or yours.' He liked the sound of that. Quickly, he closed the paper, 'Have to wait, have to stay in control,' he said to himself. But he was not in control; the urges were getting stronger, he actually enjoyed the violence he had inflicted upon the woman. It was just a matter of time before he struck again.

Lisa and Janie were relaxing on the sofa watching an old black and white movie on the television; Janie had a soft spot for old romantic movies.

'I've been thinking about what you said, Lisa, about the ad in the paper.'

'What do you reckon?' replied Lisa.

'Well, the way that club has treated me, I don't think I owe them anything; still not a word. It would be safer, at least we can control who comes through the door.'

'So, are we going to give it a go?' asked Lisa.

'I'm not exactly in any sort of shape at the moment,' replied Janie, 'but you can give it a trial run for a couple of weeks if you like, and see what sort of business you get.'

Lisa jumped up, 'I'll get a pen and paper.' She dashed to her room and was back in a flash. 'Right' she said, curling her legs up on the sofa, 'what about … let's think blonde bombshell.'

'Yeah, really,' said Janie, 'bit corny.'

'No, I know,' said Lisa. 'How about blue-eyed blonde offers relaxing massage, 7 till late.'

'Sounds like you just read that straight out of the paper,' said Janie. Lisa wrote it down.

'Sounds catchy to me… Have you got an old newspaper, Janie?'

'Yeah, should be one under the coffee table.'

Lisa got the paper and looked at the start of the ads section, 'To advertise in this section call… here it is,' she wrote down the number.

Lisa phoned the number and arranged for the ad to go into the paper on Thursday, Friday and Saturday evening. It worked on the basis that if you advertise for three nights you got one free. She paid with her new credit card; it was the first time she had used it. Once the ad was set up and paid for she felt pretty pleased with herself.

'Right then,' said Lisa, again sitting back down on the sofa, a big smile on her face, 'all we have to do now is see what happens.'

At Belfort Road the scene of crime officers were carrying out forensic tests. The fact that all of the door handles and surfaces had been wiped of fingerprints had confirmed to the officers that it was a murder scene and not just a terrible accident. Two CID officers arrived at the scene: DI Tony Hammond and DC Jack Gillman, both from Steel House Yard, Birmingham Central Police Station. They showed their identity cards to the young constable stationed at the front gate.

'Thank you sir, SOCO are in there now,' he told them. As they passed through the gateway they could see a forensic officer, dressed in white paper overalls, dusting the front door for prints.

'Ah,' said the forensic officer, 'first decent prints I've had in the whole house.' He stood aside to let them pass by into the house, where the rest of the forensic team, also dressed in white, were searching for prints and placing anything of the slightest interest into plastic bags. They went up the stairs and met Sergeant Hewitt who was standing on the landing looking into the bedroom.

'Hello sergeant, DI Hammond and DC Gillman, Steel House Yard CID. What you got for me?' The sergeant stepped aside. Michelle Summers' body lay in the same position that Jimmy had left it. A young woman in white overalls was carefully gathering forensic evidence from the body and its surrounding area. Hammond nodded to her and introduced himself.

'Hi, nice to see you could make it,' she murmured. Hammond got the feeling she wasn't exactly friendly with CID.

'Well,' she said, 'Fortyish female, approx time of death 10pm, suspect asphyxiation, bruising around the back of the neck and head, I'd say she was held face down by a very powerful person or persons. Also bruising around the inner thighs. She died during whatever sexual act was being forced upon her, and believe me it *was* forced upon her; I'll be able to tell you more after the autopsy.'

Sergeant Hewitt spoke, 'Her name's Michelle Summers. She was a known prostitute. The neighbours said she had a lot of men coming and going from the house of an evening.'

'Have you got statements confirming these allegations?' Hammond asked.

'Yes, but no descriptions of the men that visited her,' Hewitt replied.

'Ain't that just typical,' replied Hammond.

The forensic officers completed their crime scene investigation and extensive photographs of the crime scene and body were taken before the body was moved.

'I want uniform to do a door-to-door of every house in the street and approaching streets. Somebody's seen this person – we just have to jog their memories,' said Hammond.

'I'll get straight on it,' said Gillman.

A team of officers went about the task in hand. It appeared that nobody had seen anything. The officers had the feeling that there was a kind of resentment against the woman; as much as she had tried to keep it to herself, her occupation was widely known and was not acceptable to the local community.

Jimmy Noakes was travelling down the Alcester Road on the number 50 bus. He had used his street guide to locate the flat on Sandhurst Road in Moseley; it was a lot closer to the Kings Heath flat than he had thought. He had spoken to a woman on the phone who told him to be there for three o'clock to view the flat; if he liked it, she said he could move in any time he wanted. He watched for the names on the side streets: Dowels Close, Hillcrest Road, it was the next one. He jumped to his feet and quickly moved to the front of the bus. As he looked through the glass door he saw Sandhurst Road go by. The bus came to a halt, Jimmy stepped off and started walking back up the road; it was only about 100 metres or so. Walking down Sandhurst Road checking the numbers, he noticed a woman standing about half way down the road. He looked at his watch; it was just three o'clock. As he got closer he made eye contact.

'Mr Noakes?' she asked.

'Yes,' Jimmy replied. She offered him her hand and as he shook it she smiled.

'You found it without too much trouble then?'

'Yes, no problem,' Jimmy replied, returning the smile.

'Well, this is it. There are four flats in each block, eight in all. Number eight is vacant at the moment but I've had a lot of enquires about it, so if you like it I'd move fast. Right then, shall we go in?' They walked up to the front door and the woman sifted through a bunch of keys in an attempt to select the correct one.

'You'll have to excuse me, I haven't been back to the office all day, I have that many keys on me,' she fumbled with them until she found the right key. Finally, she opened the door.

'Sorry about that. OK, there's a pay phone in the reception hall, but you can have your own, you just need to contact the phone company and get it connected.' They went up a flight of stairs, first on the left was number 8, she opened the door. It was a one-bedroomed flat in excellent decorative order, fully furnished. Jimmy liked it straight away; it had everything he needed.

'I'll take it,' he said.

'Gosh, that was quick,' she replied.

'It's just what I want, perfect location.'

'Do you work nearby, Mr Noakes?'

'Sort of,' said Jimmy. But what was going through Jimmy's mind had nothing to do with work, already the urge to call another girl was overwhelming him. After a short discussion about the rent, Jimmy was given a key. He paid two months' rent in advance, said goodbye and headed back to his old flat. He decided to spend that night in his old flat and move out the next morning. All he really needed was a few personal belongings.

At Steel House Yard Police Station an incident room had been set up. Hammond and Gillman were facing a board containing various photographs of the victim and a list of phone numbers, all of which had made calls to the victim's house in the last month. Some had already been checked out, but one in particular interested Hammond.

'All these numbers and only one is a pay phone, Bordesley Green, over at East Birmingham. I've got a feeling,' said Hammond, 'that when we find the person that made that call, we'll find our murderer.'

'It's a bit of a long shot, sir,' replied Gillman.

'It's just a hunch, but I want that box checked for prints. If we can match up with that one they found on the front door of the victim's house we're onto him.' The forensic officers moved quickly; the box was cordoned off and checked from top to bottom with a fine-toothed comb. It was a bit rough but, as Hammond had suspected, the thumbprint was found to be a match for the one at the victim's house.

The following morning Hammond and Gillman drove over to Bordesley Green. They found the phone box and Hammond was looking around the immediate area, deep in thought. It was a labyrinth of alleys and flats, any one of which could have been the residence of the person they were looking for.

'Where do you start?' said Hammond, 'I feel sure the suspect's in this neighbourhood. I think we'll get uniform to do a door-to-door and try to narrow down the sheer scale of the problem. We might just get lucky. I want to know if we have any sex offenders in the local area, mentally ill, anyone with form.'

As the two officers stood discussing the task in hand, Jimmy Noakes closed the front door of his old flat, his personal belongings packed into two bulky holdalls. He walked down the alley onto the main road and past the phone box where the two men were talking, unaware that they were police officers. As Jimmy continued in the direction of the bus stop, the officers would never know how close to their assailant they had just been.

After a struggle on two buses with his oversized holdalls, Jimmy arrived at his new flat. He was glad to be out of the old one; it was a dark and dingy place, not a touch on this place. It didn't take him long to put his belongings away and already it was starting to feel like home. On his way through the city he had bought a paper – Thursdays were always a good day for adverts, especially personal ones. Scanning through the paper he quickly found his way to the personal adverts. As he read them the wording alone excited him. There were so many girls and, by their names and descriptions, they were of all cultures and races. One in particular caught his eye, 'Blue-eyed blonde offers relaxing massage, 7 till late.' He checked his watch, it was just before three o'clock. Feeling through his coat pocket he found some change, picked up the paper and went down to the pay phone in the entrance hall to the flats. Again, he checked the ads then dialled the number. It rang out for a few seconds then:

'Hi, this is Lisa, can I help you?'

'Yes, I'd like to make an appointment please.' Over the next few minutes Lisa arranged for Jimmy to be at the flat that same day at seven o'clock. Their flats were no more than half a mile apart. When Jimmy hung up he went straight back upstairs, a look of excitement on his face.

At Wellington Road, Lisa was feeling all sorts of emotions: fear, excitement, apprehension. She kept asking herself if she was doing the right thing. At nine o'clock she had her usual client, Graham Brent. He was such a lovely man and never made her feel as if she was a prostitute. But with the new client it would be different. She could not imagine how she would cope.

Janie arrived back from a hospital appointment. Lisa had offered to go with her but Janie knew that the advert was going in that day and said it was best she stayed at home, just in case anyone called.

'Hi Janie how did it go?' asked Lisa.

'OK,' said Janie, 'I just wish they would see you at the time they give you the appointment for. Hanging around in that place is soul destroying.'

'Guess what,' said Lisa. Janie sat on the sofa looking exhausted and stressed.

'What?' replied Janie, wearily.

'I got a phone call from the advert, seven o'clock tonight.' Lisa's excitement and nervousness was obvious.

'That didn't take long, it's only been in the paper about four hours,' replied Janie. 'It's that blonde hair and blue eyes, they're suckers for it. You'd better start getting yourself ready.'

'I think I'll do just that,' said Lisa smiling. She went into the bathroom, poured herself a bath and contemplated the evening ahead.

By six o'clock Lisa was as ready as she was ever going to be. Janie had advised her to go light on the make-up to show off her youth, as this was always popular, especially with older clients.

'Make sure you let him know how much it is before he even comes near you, and don't let him bully you. I'll be in my room, any problems just shout,' said Janie.

'You sound like my mother,' replied Lisa, grinning like a Cheshire cat.

'Joking apart Lisa, just remember what you're getting yourself into. Look what happened to me and I thought I could handle them.'

'Point taken, I'll be careful,' said Lisa.

Jimmy used his street guide again and looked up Wellington Road. It was only a fifteen-minute walk from his flat, but he set off with an extra ten minutes to spare. As he approached Wellington Road his heart was pounding; he was not really sure whether it was excitement or fear of who would answer the door. He walked along the road noting the numbers on the doors, '12, 12A, that's the one,' he thought to himself, 'it must be the upstairs flat.' He rang the bell. Upstairs Lisa heard the bell ring out and jumped to her feet.

'Calm down, take a deep breath, relax, go down there, smile and ask him in. I'll be in my bedroom if there's a problem. Good luck,' said Janie, then she got up and went to her bedroom. Lisa took a deep breath and went down to open the front door. Jimmy was on the top step looking towards the road.

As he turned Lisa smiled, 'Hello, you must be Jimmy.'

He was dumbstruck. Her eyes were the deepest blue he had ever seen, her hair long and blonde, just as the ad had said. But there was something else about her; he felt an innocence that he had not expected. She was possibly the most beautiful girl he had ever laid eyes on. The open smile on her face made him feel welcome, something he had not experienced in a long time.

'Are you all right?' Lisa asked. Jimmy suddenly snapped out of his trance.

'Sorry, yes, Jimmy, that's me, you must be Lisa.' She invited him in and they went upstairs to the flat.

'OK Jimmy, what can I do for you?' he looked at her, hating the idea of her innocence being spoiled.

'How long have you been doing this, Lisa?' She had not expected to be questioned.

'Not long,' she replied, concerned and uncertain.

'You should stop now,' said Jimmy,

'Sorry?' replied Lisa.

'You're far too young and beautiful to be throwing your life away doing this,' he told her.

'Thank you for the compliment but time's money,' said Lisa, regaining her composure. Her statement enraged Jimmy. He went into his pocket and pulled out his wallet.

'How much?' he took forty pounds and thrust it towards her, Lisa looked at the floor, at once ashamed, afraid and confused. In an instant he calmed down.

'I'm sorry I frightened you, please take the money, how I choose to spend it is my business.' He gestured the notes towards her and Lisa reached out and took them.

'The truth is, I've been with other girls on the game but you don't look like them,' said Jimmy.

'That's very flattering Jimmy, but I am and that's all there is to it. I have to survive.' They continued to talk for almost an hour, Lisa found herself telling him about her time on the streets. Jimmy reciprocated by telling her about his time in care, something he had never spoken to anyone else about. Jimmy noticed Lisa glance at the clock.

'Have I had my time?' he asked.

'Nearly,' she replied.

'I've enjoyed talking to you, Lisa, can I see you again?'

'If you want to,' replied Lisa.

'Same time next week, is that OK?' asked Jimmy.

'Next week then,' she said. Jimmy got up and walked towards the door. It was the first time anybody had been able to tame Jimmy Noakes; unknowingly Lisa's beauty and innocence had done what no other had been able to do. As he left the flat he turned, smiled and said goodbye. Lisa went back upstairs where Janie was settling herself on the sofa.

'Well, how did it go?' she asked.

'He didn't touch me, he just talked for a whole hour, then gave me forty quid and, to top that, booked to see me next week.'

'You're a jammy cow you are,' said Janie.

'He was a bit of a weirdo,' replied Lisa, 'had me worried at first, but in the end seemed like a nice bloke.'

Janie smiled, 'Well, congratulations, looks like we're in business.'

The rest of the evening went to plan. Graham Brent, Lisa's regular client, kept his appointment as normal. By half past ten Lisa had taken a shower, made herself a coffee and was relaxing on the sofa. Janie had gone to bed. Lisa smiled to herself; this was turning out to be a very lucrative business arrangement.

8

The net tightens

Over the next week, the police stepped up their investigations. Every house and flat within a five-hundred-metre radius of the phone box in Bordesley Green where they had found the prints received a call. DI Hammond, playing on his hunch, had insisted they get an answer from every property; any they could not get an answer from had to be noted and followed up. After many hours of knocking on doors, uniform had reduced the number down to fifteen, mostly flats. One or two of them were obviously unoccupied and the owners were identified and located. A local Asian businessman called Hasan Khan owned six of the remaining flats; Hammond decided to pay him a visit. Khan owned a large carpet store on Coventry Road, which seemed like a good place to try and find him. As Hammond and Gillman walked quickly into the shop a young man came over.

'Can I help you?' he asked with a welcoming smile.

Hammond pulled out his warrant card. 'I'm looking for Mr Khan, is he in?'

'I'm not sure,' came the reply. On seeing the warrant card the smile disappeared and the young man instantly clammed.

'It's OK, Haggie,' came a voice from behind a huge pile of carpets. 'Good day officers, can I help you?'

'Are you Mr Khan?' asked Hammond.

'Yes, is there a problem?'

'No problem. We believe you own and rent six properties in the Bordesley Green area.'

'Yes, that is correct, but I didn't know that was against the law?'

'No sir, it's not,' replied Hammond, a smile appearing on his face, 'what we're trying to do is identify the people who live in them. We believe that one of them may be able to help us with our enquiries.'

'Well, I have a list of all the people that rent properties from me, I will help you any way I can,' said Khan.

'Thank you, sir,' replied Hammond, 'that's much appreciated.'

Khan took them to the back of the store to a small office. Khan's administrative abilities left a lot to be desired; the desk was piled high with invoices. Either he was doing a lot of business or it hadn't been touched for months. He started sifting through a pile of paperwork, 'It won't take long – please make yourself at home.' Hammond looked at Gillman with an expression that said this was going to be a long day.

Jimmy sat at the table in his new flat, sipping a cup of coffee; the newspaper he had bought the previous day was laid out on the table in front of him. He still had the image of the young girl called Lisa he had met the night before in his mind. He could not understand how such a beautiful young girl could fall into such a sordid lifestyle. But that did nothing for his hunger. He liked talking to her, he had an urge to protect her, a strange sensation he had not experienced before. Again Jimmy scanned the personal ads. As he read them he tried to imagine what they would look like. 'Young oriental beauty offers sensual massage. Can travel.' He decided to give this one a call. Pulling the front door behind him he went down to the pay phone and dialled the number. A girl answered in broken English. The address she gave him was a high-rise block of flats on Bristol Road, just outside the city centre; he arranged to be there at nine o'clock that night. After what had happened the night before he was a little apprehensive, but his hunger for these women was now consuming him.

After nearly an hour and two cups of coffee, Mr Khan could still not put his hands on the relevant paperwork; he swore blind it was there but Hammond and Gillman doubted it had ever existed.

'Mr Khan, I think we are getting nowhere fast. Best thing we can do is take a drive over there. You do keep spare keys for these properties I take it?'

'Yes, all of them,' replied Khan.

'Right, you get the keys and we can clear this up as quickly as possible.' Twenty minutes later they were driving along Bordesley Green Road. Gillman had ticked all the properties on the list that Khan owned, six in all. They parked by the phone box in which they had found the fingerprint.

'OK, Mr Khan,' said Hammond, 'we are in your hands. Would you please take us to the nearest property you own.' They got out of the car. It was only a short walk to the first property, a two-bedroomed flat. Khan rang the doorbell.

'A young couple rent this flat,' said Khan, 'always on time with the rent, very nice people.' The door opened.

'Hello Mr Khan.' A young man in his early twenties stood at the door.

'Who is it, Jamie?' asked a voice from inside.

'It's only Mr Khan.' the young man replied. 'The rent's not due till the end of the month.' Hammond intervened by showing his warrant card.

'Sorry sir, we've been making some inquires in the area concerning the murder of a young woman.'

'We only got back off our holidays yesterday, we had a couple of weeks at the mother-in-law's down south.'

'That's fine, sir,' said Hammond. 'We're just trying to identify the tenants of these flats; we won't take up any more of your time. Good day to you.' As the officers turned away, the young man closed the door. Gillman ticked off the flat on his list.

'Right, Mr Khan, and the next one.'

'It's just round the corner,' said Khan. They followed him for twenty yards. 'Here we are,' again Khan knocked on the door, 'this is rented by a nice quiet young man, always pays his rent well in advance,' he raised his hand and grasped his forehead, 'What was his name?' Khan racked his brain, 'Jimmy, that was it, Jimmy Stokes. Yes, I remember now, very nice young man, very polite and respectful.' There was still no reply. Hammond and Gillman both looked at each other, both thinking the same thing. Gillman looked through the window; there was no sign that anybody was in.

'Open it up, Mr Khan,' said Hammond.

'But this is somebody's home, I cannot just walk in.'

'Look at it this way, Mr Khan, either you open the door or I get a search warrant and open the door. Now that takes time and if I get held up you get held up.'

'When you put it like that, time is money, officer.' Khan got the feeling that if he didn't open up then more questions would be asked, maybe one or two that he really didn't want to answer. He fumbled with a large bunch of keys, finally finding the right one. As he pushed the door open he shouted, 'Hello Mr Stokes, are you there?' There was no reply. The officers sidestepped Khan and walked into the living room. Cautiously, they moved around the flat, scanning each room for any sign of evidence without disturbing anything. Hammond opened the wardrobe door; there was nothing in there. He tried the chest of drawers; again, empty. 'When was the last time he paid you, Mr Khan?' asked Hammond.

'Well, to be honest he only ever paid me once, and that was for four months. He has just under two months left.'

'Didn't you find that a bit strange, Mr Khan?'

'I'm just a humble man, Mr Hammond, trying to earn a living. When somebody offers me rent in advance, I just take them at face value and we are all happy.'

Hammond turned to Gillman, 'I want SOCO down here – let's find out if we've hit the jackpot.' He then turned to Khan, 'You, Mr Khan, are going to tell me everything you can about our Mr Stokes, every last detail.'

Forensic officers examined the flat. Sure enough, the prints matched those found at the murder scene. Khan's description was vague – dark hair, average build, young looking – it could have been any young man on the streets. At least they had a name, however: Jimmy Stokes. That in itself was a breakthrough. They decided to clear out of the flat and put twenty-four hour surveillance on it; if he came back they would be waiting for him. Hammond arranged for Khan to go to the station and help with a photo-fit of the suspect, hopefully they would then have a bit more than just a name to go on.

Back at the station, Hammond and Gillman were in the incident room clutching cups of coffee and considering the evidence and information they had gathered. 'We've got a murdered woman in Edgbaston, a flat where the suspect lives and fingerprints tying the suspect to the murder. What I'd like to know is, did the suspect know the victim or was it just a random meeting?' Hammond paused for thought. 'Jack, I want you to check the personal ads in the local papers, see if Michelle Summers had an advert to attract more business. As far as our suspect is concerned, we have to keep this from the press. If he knows we are on to him he'll disappear. We have to at least get an ID on him before the press get hold of it.'

They kept up the surveillance on the flat in Bordesley Green but to no avail; he was long gone. Mr Khan, however, had, with the help of a photo-fit expert, produced an ID picture. Had they realised just how good a likeness of their suspect it was, they would have made it public, but for now they kept it under wraps.

Jimmy arrived at the flats, it was approaching a quarter to nine. Compton Towers was on Bristol Road, just five minutes walk from the city centre. He got into the lift and pressed the button for the sixth floor. The smell of urine was overpowering. As he stepped out of the lift he looked left and right in an attempt to get his bearings; '40, 41, must be this way,' he thought. He walked past a couple of flat doors and turned right through a set of swing doors. There were three more doors to his left; '42, 43, 44, this is it.'

Standing in front of the door Jimmy took a deep breath then rang the bell. It seemed as if he had waited minutes, but it was probably about thirty seconds. He had the feeling that the occupant was watching him through the spy hole on the door, then the door opened.

'Hello,' said Jimmy, 'I have an appointment.' Standing before him was a young oriental girl; Japanese, Chinese, they were all the same to Jimmy. She was very thin to the point of being frail. Her hair was tied back in a ponytail and she wore a long t-shirt dress with a thin belt loosely tied around the waist.

'Jimmy, com-in.' Her accent was very strange. He closed the door behind him and followed her into the living room, looking at her body as she walked down the hallway. She obviously knew he was watching her by the way she moved.

'My name Sunli. I charge forty pounds for up to one hour, OK?' Jimmy nodded. 'OK Jimmy, what you like me to do for you?' Jimmy was already aroused. She untied the small belt from her waist and let it fall to the floor. As she stepped forward towards Jimmy she gestured for him to sit down on the sofa; he followed her lead and sat down.

'How you like me?' she climbed onto his lap, pulling the t-shirt dress up. Raising her arms, she pulled the dress over her head, exposing her naked body. Holding the lapels of Jimmy's jacket she lay back, pulling Jimmy forward. He controlled her weight down to the floor. She rolled over, so that she was on top of him and started undoing his shirt. Placing her hands on his chest she drew her nails down his body towards his groin. Jimmy grabbed her wrists and sat up pushing her backwards off his body, she lay on her back in a submissive gesture. Jimmy undid his belt and trousers exposing his aroused body; she licked her lips. With that Jimmy raised his hand and slapped her hard across the face.

'Dirty bitch,' he said. The slap shocked her but she didn't panic. She just lay there submitting to his abuse. In an attempt to calm him she reached out with her hand to caress his body. He hit her again, even harder across the other side of the face. Her expression changed this time, fear was starting to set in. He pushed her legs wide apart and thrust himself in her, still she submitted to his aggression. As he thrust into her body his anger grew.

'Fuckin nip.' His face was enraged and looking into his eyes she knew she was in trouble. She started ranting at him in her native tongue; he hadn't got a clue what she was saying, he really didn't care, it was just another excuse for him to hit her. How many times he slapped her face he did not know. Enraged by her ranting he punched her square in the face and blood exploded from her nose; it looked as if she was about to pass out. Jimmy grabbed her hair and shook her head. 'Wake up bitch!' he shouted. Her eyes opened in a semi-conscious state, he pulled himself from her body and turned her over face down, raising her body he plunged himself into her. Again he grabbed her hair pulling her up almost straight. Blood poured from her nose down the front of her body.

'Stop, please stop,' she begged, almost choking on her own blood.

'Shut the fuck up,' he forced her down on all fours and pounded her exhausted and broken body. Her hand reached out towards an ashtray perched on the side of the fireplace. She grabbed it and with all her remaining strength turned sideways and smashed him in the side of the head. Jimmy reeled back and Sunli fell flat on her face. Jimmy put his hand to the side of his head and a small trickle of blood ran down his face. 'Fuckin bitch.' Her belt was on the floor by his side. He picked it up still in a loop, lunged forward and threw it over her head. She tried to grab it but the blood on her hands made it slip through her fingers. Again Jimmy pulled her onto all fours, choking her with the belt he entered her body. As he squeezed the band of leather around her throat she was totally helpless, no match for an enraged maniac. Slowly, she fell into unconsciousness, her body went limp but still Jimmy squeezed, as if trying to drive every last sign of life from her body. It was at least another five minutes before he climaxed, his body tense and a look of wild excitement on his face.

The whole scene was a grotesque mixture of blood and sweat. He stood up with his hands covered in blood. Picking up her dress, he wiped his hands then threw it onto her naked body. 'Teach you, fuckin bitch.' His body still fired with adrenalin, he went into the bathroom and rinsed his hands and face with cold water. He checked the cut on the side of his head in the mirror – it wasn't deep but it was very swollen. As he looked into his eyes there was a fleeting moment of remorse, but there was no going back now, he was in too deep. He walked back through the living room, briefly glancing at the lifeless body in front of the fireplace. Slowly he opened the front door; there was no sign of anyone in the hall. Pulling the front door closed behind him, he walked briskly towards the lifts. He pressed the button to call the lift and the door opened immediately; it probably hadn't moved since he arrived. Being careful not to be seen, Jimmy left the flats, jogged across the main road, and walked off in the direction of the city centre.

Lisa and Janie had phoned in a pizza; they had decided to have a quiet night in. The advert in the paper had attracted at least six new clients.

Janie had stayed in her room, constantly alert for any sound that might mean Lisa was in trouble. Since the incident at the Victoria Hotel, Janie had become almost paranoid of every man she came into contact with and there was no way she was going to let anything like that happen to Lisa. Janie had acquired an almost motherly instinct towards Lisa. As they sat on the sofa working their way through a fourteen-inch ham and pineapple pizza, Lisa said, 'Janie, you know that Jimmy?'

'The one who likes talking a lot?', said Janie

'Yeah, that's him,' replied Lisa. 'He wants to see me twice a week.'

'You got a problem with that?' asked Janie. 'I guarantee another month and he'll lose interest and move on. As long as you can handle him and he keeps paying, it's easy money girl, don't knock it.' Lisa picked up another slice of pizza, 'I wish I could get work like that. God, you're like a bloody counsellor,' said Janie. Lisa laughed and they both tucked into the pizza.

The following week, Jimmy saw Lisa twice; how he could afford it she did not know. But as Janie said, 'Just keep taking the money,' so she did. He told her he wanted to get her out of her present life, into something safe and respectable. Not once did he attempt to touch her; the thought of violating something so beautiful was unimaginable to him. He had tried to blank out of his mind the fact that she was a prostitute. On the second visit that week Jimmy asked, 'Hypothetically, what would you do if someone offered you a huge sum of money?'

'Well,' Lisa replied, 'that would depend on how much money it was.'

'Say, about a quarter of a million.'

'Now that's a lot of money,' said Lisa, 'You're not offering are you?' They smiled at each other. 'Well,' said Lisa, 'I think I'd buy a nice house, probably travel a bit and go and see one of those financial advisers to make sure it would last me all my life.' Good answer, thought Jimmy. He paid Lisa forty pounds and arranged to see her twice the following week.

Samantha Yates, Sam to her friends, was a first-year psychology student. Since arriving at college she had built up a good friendship with Sunli, helping her to improve her English. For no apparent reason, Sunli hadn't been at college all week. Sunli never missed school as her education was paramount to her. She had arrived in this country with her parents just two years previously and her parents had instilled in her the importance of getting a good education. At just eighteen years of age she had left her parents and moved to Birmingham to pursue an education in psychology. Sam tried ringing her but had no luck. After college that Friday she decided to go round to Sunli's flat. Sunli had never invited her to the flat, which seemed a little strange considering how long they had known each other, but Sam was worried about her. She arrived at the flat just after half past five. It was easy to find and only a short bus ride from her parents' house. She knew the number of the flat but not the floor it was on. In the foyer there was a plan of the flats. She identified flat 44 on the sixth floor. The lift took ages to arrive and she almost gave up and used the stairs. When it finally arrived and the doors opened a red-faced young couple stepped out, trying hard not to grin or laugh. She stepped into the lift and as the doors closed, had a little chuckle to herself. A few seconds later, she was on the sixth floor. Following the numbers on the doors she quickly found number 44. She knocked the door and waited. No reply. She knocked again a little harder. Still nothing. She bent down and opened the letterbox, 'Sunli,' she shouted, then the smell hit her. It was so awful she reeled back. 'What the hell is that?' she said to herself. Sam knocked the door of the next flat. The door opened just a little; a chain was on the door and she could just make out the face of an elderly woman peeping through the crack.

'Can I help you?' asked the woman.

'I'm trying to find my friend – she lives in the flat next to you, have you seen her this week at all?'

'I don't buy things from the door, goodbye.' The door slammed shut.

'Great, that's all I need,' she said aloud, and opened the letterbox of Sunli's flat again.

'Sunli, are you in there?' Again the smell overpowered her; instinct told her that all was not well. She remembered seeing a pay phone down in the foyer. She got back in the lift and went back down to the ground floor. Picking up the receiver she dialled 999 and asked for the police. Twenty minutes later, two police officers arrived at the flats. As they entered the foyer Sam rushed over to them and introduced herself.

'Right, madam,' said one of the officers, 'what seems to be the problem?'

'I'm worried about my friend. She hasn't been in college all week and she's not answering the door of her flat, it's not like her at all.'

'OK, what's the number of the flat?' Sam gave the number and they all got into the lift. One of the officers took out a notepad and recorded Sam's and Sunli's details.

'Sunli, Sunli Chun.'

'She's an oriental girl then?'

'Yes, Chinese, her family live down south somewhere, but I'm not sure whereabouts.' Sam showed them the way to the flat. 'I've tried knocking. The next door neighbour isn't all there so she's no help, and there's a horrible smell in there.' The policeman opened the letterbox and looked in; the smell hit him straight away. He stood up and turned to his colleague, the colour draining from his face, and gestured to his partner to do as he had. With the same reaction, the second officer stood up and said, 'I'll radio the station.' Both officers were experienced enough to have a good idea of what was waiting for them inside the flat. It wasn't the first time they had smelt death. The larger of the two officers rammed the door with his shoulder. The frame shook but the door remained closed. Two more forceful blows and the latch broke. 'Stay there miss,' said one of the officers. The two officers entered the flat. As they walked down the hall towards the living room the smell intensified. It had been a week since Sunli had been murdered and the heating in the flat had been switched on for all that time, speeding up the decomposition process. 'I think we can safely say she's dead,' said one of the officers, 'I'll radio in. You take care of the young lady outside, don't let her in what ever you do.'

CID were informed and Sam was taken to the police station to make a statement. She tried to give any information she could in relation to her friend's untimely death. Scene of crime officers cordoned off the area around the flat, establishing almost instantly that it was a murder scene. Hammond arrived at the scene within a few minutes. Gillman walked in breathing hard, 'Sorry I'm late sir, family do, you know what it's like trying to get away,' he said.

'Same again, Jack, our forensic friends are going to tell us the same story as the Belfort Road murder, I just know it,' said Hammond.

'When the press get hold of it they'll have a field day. I can just see it now, two murders in a fortnight and the police are keeping it quiet.' The forensic officers said that the most likely cause of death was asphyxiation due to strangulation; she had been beaten and raped before and after her death. The characteristics of the murders were so similar and his fingerprints were found all over the bathroom sink and living room area. He was either getting very sloppy or just didn't care any more. Either way they had to catch him before he struck again.

Back at Steel House Yard Police Station, Hammond and Gillman found themselves in a predicament. 'Do we hold a press conference and risk losing him?' asked Hammond, 'or do we keep quiet and risk being dragged across the coals by the public for not informing them that there's a killer out there?'

'I think that decision has been made for you Tony.' They spun round, startled by the voice at the rear of the room. Detective Superintendent Harvey Catel was standing in the doorway, 'If the press get wind that we've been keeping something like this quiet, we'll all be out of a job. First things first, get that press conference organised ASAP.' He had been watching the case develop from a distance. Normally he wouldn't interfere, but he didn't like the way this one was going. If somebody's head was going to be on the block it wasn't going to be his.

Later that evening, Gillman was sitting at home reading the evening paper. As he flicked through the adverts his attention was brought to the personal ads. He noticed the phone number of the murder victim in Edgbaston. It caught his eye because he had traced every call to it for a month. Grabbing his car keys, he headed back to the station. Pulling out the file on the latest victim, Sunli Chun, he scanned it for her phone number. He laid the paper on the table open at the personal ads and started scanning down the columns. 'Bingo, "Young oriental beauty offers sensual massage. Can travel." So that's what he's doing, he's randomly choosing his victims from the evening paper personal ads.' He grabbed the phone and rang Hammond, explaining what he had found; it was a major breakthrough. The problem they had now was that there were over sixty adverts on that night alone – where would he strike next?

A press conference was called the following morning. Before the conference, Hammond gathered his team in the incident room to fill them in on the night's developments. A constant hum came from the room as if all the officers were talking at the same time.

'OK, everyone listen in,' said Hammond. 'You all know by now we are having a press conference in just over an hour. We've had some significant information overnight. The young student, Sunli Chun, was on the game, apparently trying to pay her way through college. Both murder victims had adverts in the local evening newspaper. It turns out our murderer appears to be working his way through the personal ads. The chances are he has already contacted other girls in those ads; let's just hope he hasn't had time to do the same to any of those. So every personal ad in the paper has to be chased up. From experience, it's going to be hard to get these girls to talk to us at all, but we must get across to them just how dangerous this man is.' Gillman handed out photo-fit pictures. 'This is the only picture we have to go on,' said Hammond,

'James Stokes, average build. Not a lot, but it's all we have. I just want to reiterate, make sure these girls know just how dangerous this man is. If they are so afraid that it takes them out of circulation till we catch him that will suit me fine. OK people, let's do it.'

The room became a hive of activity with people making phone calls and exchanging notes.

'OK Jack,' said Hammond, 'let's get this press conference over with.' The press were filled in with all the information Hammond wanted them to know. They all received a photo-fit picture and the name of the suspect. It was reinforced that on no account was this man to be approached. As soon as the conference was over and after some questions that Hammond really didn't want to answer, the room quickly cleared.

'Let's hope this flushes him out,' said Hammond.

'Either way, sir, he's going to know we're on to him and it will be interesting to see what he does next.'

9

The deal

Jimmy was sitting at his living room table; he had just warmed up a can of ravioli and was watching the television. He was feeling happy because tonight he was going to see Lisa. He couldn't get her out of his mind; to him she was the perfect girl; when they chatted he hadn't a care in the world. The news came on the television. 'Tonight in Birmingham the police are on the lookout for a man called James Stokes, wanted in connection with the murder of two local prostitutes.' A photo-fit of him came on the screen, 'Shit!' said Jimmy. The newsreader continued, 'He is believed to be living in the Bordesley Green area of the city. If you have any information concerning the whereabouts of this man, please contact Steel House Yard Police Station. The number appeared on the screen. 'This man is believed to be very dangerous. On no account should he be approached.'

Jimmy put down his knife and fork. 'James Stokes... tossers!' But as he said it he knew it was just a matter of time before they closed in on him; the photo-fit was pretty good. He decided that night he would make Lisa an offer that would get her out of her sordid life, and would also ensure that his money was safe until, one day, he could get his life back, get his money and get the girl of his dreams.

Hammond's team had been slowly contacting all the people in the personal ads; he had split up the list and given six members of the team ten ads each. It was a long, tedious job. As soon as the girls found out that it was the police making enquires they all clammed up. Gillman decided that the best way to contact them was to try and make an appointment. He managed to arrange three appointments that afternoon. As he read through his list he thought, 'Just one more, that should keep me busy for the rest of the afternoon. Let's see...' he scanned the list. 'Blue-eyed blonde offers relaxing massage, 7 till late.' 'Right, I'll try that one.' He dialled the number and Janie answered, 'Hello can I help you?'

'Hi,' replied Gillman, 'is there any chance of an appointment this afternoon? I know it says 7 till late but...' Janie thought about it. Lisa was out for the afternoon; it was about time she got back to work.

'OK, just this once, I'll make an exception. Shall we say three o'clock?'

'That would be great, thanks,' Gillman replied. Janie gave him the address. 'See you at three then,' said Gillman. He put the phone down and looked at the address he had jotted down. '12A Wellington Road,' he remembered, 'the girl that was attacked at the Victoria Hotel,' he said to himself. His first appointment was at one o'clock; he grabbed his jacket and left the station.

Over the next couple of hours Gillman had differing responses to his enquiries. After informing the first girl that he was a police officer, she spat at him then slammed the door in his face. The next had offered him a free session; he had thanked her for the thought, but declined. She appreciated what he had to say concerning her well-being and with that he left. At three o'clock he arrived at Wellington Road. The last time he had been there they had been glad to see him, he wondered what the feeling would be this time. As he knocked the door he turned and glanced around the street. The door opened and he turned sharply. The last time he had seen this girl she had looked considerably less attractive. It was amazing how well her face had recovered after the beating she had received. There was no sign of scaring and no deformity to her nose or cheeks. He remembered just how bad the injuries had been; for a time he thought it was going to be a murder investigation.

'Hello, Janie isn't it?' asked Gillman.

'You're a police officer,' replied Janie.

'Right first time. I'm sorry, making an appointment with you was the only way I could be sure to get your undivided attention.'

'To think I thought I was going to make some money this afternoon. Oh well, you'd better come in,' said Janie.

Gillman followed her up the stairs into the flat. 'I must say Janie, you look a lot better than the last time I saw you.'

'Thanks,' replied Janie, 'it's taken a long time but I think I'm finally over it.'

'That's good,' replied Gillman, 'the reason I've come to see you is, you've heard about the two girls that were murdered locally?'

'I saw a little on the news about it,' answered Janie.

'There's a real chance he's going to strike again.'

'Believe me,' said Janie, 'after what happened to me we're so careful who we let through that door.'

'With the greatest respect Janie, I think those two girls were probably thinking exactly the same as you. Both the attacks took place in their own homes. Have you got any punters that are anything near this photo-fit?' Gillman took out the photo and handed it to Janie.

'Well, I haven't been working lately, but I can't say I recognise him.' Every time Jimmy had been to the flat, Janie had made it her business to be in her room. Although she always listened out for Lisa, she had never actually seen Jimmy. Other than Graham Brent who had originally been her client, she hadn't seen any of Lisa's clients. Janie offered Gillman a coffee, which he accepted gratefully. Like the previous appointment, Janie thanked him for trying to make them more aware of just how dangerous the situation was. After some general chitchat, Gillman finished his coffee, gave Janie his number and told her to ring if she had any problems, especially with punters. He had a soft spot for both the girls; it was obvious the profession they were in was purely a survival tactic. He said goodbye and asked her to say hello to Lisa for him.

Jimmy was sitting in an armchair staring out of the window. All day long he had been contemplating how he was going to strike up the deal with Lisa. He decided the best way he could conceal the movement of a large amount of money was by paying it into various bank accounts. He took out his chequebook and wrote out ten cheques for twenty-five thousand pounds. Over a period of two weeks he would ask Lisa to open various bank and building society accounts. He had thought about just transferring the whole amount, like a gift to Lisa's account, but was unsure about the law on convicted murderers or psychiatric patients being allowed to do this; would the state use his assets to keep him? He didn't know and he wasn't going to find out the hard way.

That night Jimmy arrived at Wellington Road at seven o'clock, his usual time. Lisa looked as gorgeous as ever.

'Hi Jimmy, have you had a good week?' she asked.

'Yes thanks,' he replied and they went up to the flat. 'Lisa, you know I asked you if you had a lot of money, would you get out of this game?'

'Yes,' she replied.

'Well, I want to strike a deal with you. If I tell you something, will you promise to stay calm?' The hairs on Lisa's neck started to stand up as if she had just caught a draft on her back.

'What have you done Jimmy? Are you in trouble with the police?'

'Kind of ... I've done some bad things. I've hurt people...' Lisa was already planning her exit from the flat. He was acting very calmly; it couldn't be that serious she thought. 'They're going to put me away for a long time when they catch me.'

'Jimmy, you're frightening me,' said Lisa.

'Please don't be frightened – I'd never hurt you, never.'

Janie was sitting in her bedroom and noticed that it was quieter than usual. Maybe he had finally decided to get his money's worth she thought, a slight grin appearing on her face.

'I want you to have my money, as a kind of safekeeping,' said Jimmy.

'What have you done Jimmy? You have to tell me.'

Jimmy stared at the floor. 'I didn't mean to kill them,' he said quietly. Lisa went rigid, her eyes were fixed on Jimmy; he just sat looking at the floor. Lisa's mind was starting to race. 'What do I do? What do I do?' she thought over and over, adrenalin pumping round her body. Continually telling herself to stay calm, she clasped her hands together to stop them shaking. 'Did you kill those girls on the news?' she asked.

'I didn't mean to at first, but then, slags,' Lisa saw a massive change in his temperament, 'dirty fuckin' bitches,' he spat out.

'OK, OK, Jimmy.'

'I'm sorry,' said Jimmy, 'but they weren't like you Lisa. You shouldn't be doing this sort of thing. That's why I want you to take my money. Don't worry, it's not stolen – I inherited it.' He looked at her eagerly and Lisa knew she had to play along; Janie was in her room. If Jimmy knew that he might become violent. 'I want you to listen to exactly what I have to say,' he continued, 'it will change your life.'

Still reeling from what was happening Lisa said, 'OK, I'm listening.'

'I have my chequebook here,' said Jimmy, taking it from his jacket pocket, 'in here there are ten cheques all filled out for twenty-five grand each; that's a quarter of a million pounds. Apart from five hundred pounds, it's everything I have. When my mum died, her assets were sold and I inherited the money on my eighteenth birthday. Anyway, enough of that, this is the deal. You open ten different accounts in various banks and building societies, that way you won't draw too much attention to yourself. The police have got my description and any day now they're going to find me. I want you to invest my money and at the same time have a good life, but when I get out you have to fulfil the deal. That means you and the money are mine.' Lisa's throat was as dry as a bone; she swallowed hard. Jimmy sat directly in front of her staring straight into her eyes, as if he was checking her reaction to what he had said. She thought, 'If I refuse I'm dead.' His eyes were those of a calculated killer; the only way out of this was to accept the deal, whether she intended to go through with it or not. 'So I spend the money as I choose?' asked Lisa, quietly.

'Yes, but you must also invest it,' replied Jimmy, 'for the future.' Again she swallowed hard. 'One more thing,' said Jimmy; Lisa looked straight at him, 'you must not tell another soul about the deal. It's our secret.' His eyes told her what the outcome would be if she did. 'Do you understand me?'

'Yes,' replied Lisa. Jimmy put his hand out, in a handshaking gesture. Lisa again looked straight at him and slowly she pushed her hand forward. Jimmy clasped his hand around hers tightly. 'Remember Lisa, a deal is a deal.' Not taking her eyes off him, she nodded her head. His face changed from stone cold to a cheeky grin, almost like that of a child. He opened his chequebook; just as he had said, it was filled out cheque after cheque for twenty-five thousand pounds. 'What's your surname Lisa?'

'Dean,' she replied, flatly. He filled out her name at the top of the cheque and signed it, cheque after cheque he repeated himself, tearing out each cheque as he went. Finally he put the cheques together and handed them to her. With trembling hands, she took them from him.

'It would be a good idea to pay one in today,' he said, 'I'll come and see you in three or four days, to see how you're getting on.'

Lisa nodded, still numb with what was going on. Jimmy got up and, closely followed by Lisa, he headed for the door.

'Bye Lisa,' he said, 'Four days.' Lisa whispered goodbye and closed the door behind him. Turning around she leaned against the door and slid down until she was sitting on the floor. In her hands she was holding cheques to the value of a quarter of a million pounds. She stared at them, her heart racing. 'What the hell do I do now?' she thought. She heard Janie's bedroom door open.

'Lisa!' came a shout from the living room. Quickly, Lisa stuffed the cheques inside her top and got to her feet. 'Fancy a coffee?' asked Janie.

'Yeah, two ticks, just going to get changed.' Lisa went into her room and put the cheques into the bedside cabinet. She hated herself for not telling Janie what had happened, but at the same time didn't want to get her involved; Janie had had enough trauma over the last few months.

Hammond had compiled a list of all the phone calls made to the Chinese student's flat; just like the previous murder, most of the calls turned out to be home addresses. After sending officers to check them out, it was pretty obvious they were typical, everyday punters, but again, one of the calls was made from a call box in Moseley. The forensic team again went to work. They cordoned off the phone box and it didn't take them long to identify the same prints as found in the Bordesley Green phone box.

Hammond and Gillman arrived at the phone box. Moseley Road was a very busy main road leading into the city and the large police presence there was causing a lot of traffic congestion. It was just after eleven o'clock in the morning.

'Getting a bit repetitive this is, Jack.'

'I know what you mean,' replied Gillman.

'The first thing I want you to do is check out all the local estate agents, local shop ads, stuff like that, anybody that's letting out rooms or flats in the local area, I want to know about it. He knows we're on to him. We have to step up the operation before he strikes again.'

Hammond headed back to the station. The phone in the incident room seemed to ring constantly; the public were very helpful but, unfortunately, the leads they were being given were going nowhere and it was taking up all his resources to chase them up. Jack Gillman decided to take a walk down the High Street; there were two or three estate agents down there he could check out. The first two he tried without any joy but the last one, Slater & Co., was more helpful. The young woman got out all the rental agreements they had for the local area.

'All these flats are local,' she said. Gillman scanned the paperwork; nothing jumped out at him. 'Oh, hang on; we recently took on some flats a local businessman bought as a block. I think there were eight in all. Give me two ticks and I'll get the paperwork.' She disappeared out to the back of the office, returning a few minutes later holding some papers. 'Sandhurst Road, it's only about half a mile up the road.' She said, laying the paperwork on the desk for Gillman to see. He studied the names in the index. 'Sullivan, Bancroft, Noakes, Silk,' he stopped short, 'Noakes J, James Stokes, James Noakes do you remember this man?'

'Let me see, number eight, yes, very quiet chap, jumped at the property.'

Gillman went into his inside jacket pocket and pulled out the photo-fit picture. 'Did he look anything like this?'

She studied the photo. 'Yes, that's a pretty good likeness, bit too chubby in the face, but yes, I'd say that was him. He's not in trouble is he?'

'Can you show me exactly where these flats are?' asked Gillman, 'it's very important.'

'Yeah sure, but I'll have to shut the shop. Can you just give me a few minutes?'

'Certainly,' said Gillman, hoping that she would not take too long; he was eager to get there.

The previous evening, Lisa had sat in and watched the television. Unable to focus, she had annoyed Janie by constantly flicking through the channels. What had happened between her and Jimmy had been constantly on her mind. Janie had twice asked if she was OK; she just said she was tired. She decided to take one of the cheques and try to open an account. Taking some ID, she headed into Kings Heath, just a short bus ride away. Lisa decided to use the first bank or building society she saw when she got off the bus. Fifteen minutes later Lisa got up and stood by the bus doors waiting for the stop. The doors opened and almost straight in front of her was the Yorkshire Building Society.

'Oh well,' she said to herself, 'in for a penny, in for a pound.' Standing in the queue she started having second thoughts. 'What if they say it's not a real cheque, and he's just winding me up? No, he wouldn't do that.' Her mind was doing overtime.

'Next please,' called the cashier. Lisa suddenly snapped out of it. 'Hello madam, can I help you?'

'Yes, I'd like to open an account please.' Lisa presented the cheque to the cashier. After a short discussion to determine what kind of account she wanted, all the necessary forms were completed. Lisa was told to wait ten working days to let the cheque clear before she could draw on it. The cashier gave Lisa an account book. Lisa thanked her and left. Standing outside the building society, she couldn't believe what was happening to her. She opened the book and looked at the balance: £25,000. She pushed the book deep into her pocket and set off back to the flat.

Gillman waited patiently as the young woman pulled on her jacket.

'Sorry that took so long, shall we go?' As they left the shop she double-locked the front door, 'Can't be too careful nowadays can you?' she said, a broad smile across her face.

'You certainly can't,' replied Gillman. They walked along Moseley Road. After about ten minutes Gillman noticed they were approaching the phone box where the prints had been taken from.

'It's not too far now,' she said, 'next on the right.' They turned into Sandhurst Road. 'The flats are about fifty yards down on the left.'

'That's great, thank you. I think I can take it from here.' Said Gillman. The woman looked surprised.

'Don't you want me to take you in? I can show you which flat he's staying in.'

'Thanks, but I'm sure I'll be able to work that one out. Again, thanks for your help.' He replied, firmly. She looked disappointed, turned and set off back in the direction they had come from. Gillman didn't want to draw any unnecessary attention to himself. It would have been foolish to try and bring his suspect in on his own, so he decided to check out the surrounding area of the flats and call for backup. Twenty minutes later, Hammond arrived in an unmarked vehicle, along with another four members of his team. Gillman walked straight over to them, 'Flat number 8, first floor on the left. It looks all quiet at the moment. There's no way out at the back.'

'OK, let's give him a knock.' Swiftly, they moved into the building, quickly but quietly climbing the stairs. They reached the flat and the officers stood on both sides of the door. Hammond faced it and knocked: there was no reply.

'Shall I do the honours, sir?' asked Gillman. Hammond nodded. Gillman took out a thin strip of plastic and forced it in the edge of the door by the latch. A sharp shove and the door opened; they all streamed in.

'Don't touch anything,' said Hammond. On the table was a newspaper lying open at the personal ads page. 'This is him all right,' said Hammond, 'I want officers all round the flats. When he comes back he's nicked.'

Jimmy was sitting in the local park, as normal, watching the world go by. He had a feeling he was not going to be able to do this for much longer. He watched a young couple clowning around with each other. How he wished his life had been different. He had never experienced that kind of human contact, the type that is given willingly. Any contact with the opposite sex had been at a cost. He started daydreaming, he imagined himself and Lisa fooling around like the couple in front of him, just enjoying each other's company.

'Got a fag mate?' Suddenly he was brought back to reality. He sat up straight and saw a man standing in front of him, a dirty looking, unshaven man, holding a can of beer.

'Sorry, I don't smoke' said Jimmy.

'Some loose change then?' Jimmy got to his feet and looked the man up and down; suddenly he didn't feel as hard done by. Without saying a word, Jimmy walked on down the path. 'Thanks for nothing,' the man shouted; Jimmy just kept walking.

By early evening, Hammond had got twelve members of his team positioned around the flats at Sandhurst Road and every possible escape route had been closed. His plan was to let Noakes get back to the flat, then spring the trap on him. At each end of the street, one of Hammond's team was under the bonnet of a car, looking busy. When Jimmy entered the street from either end it was their job to radio ahead and let Hammond know he was approaching.

'I hate this part of the job,' said Gillman, as he stretched his arms above his head.

'I know what you mean. I can think of a lot of better ways to spend an evening,' replied Hammond. They were in a car directly opposite the flats.

'Tango 3, target sighted,' the radio burst into life. Hammond and Gillman were both instantly alert. 'Approaching from Moseley Road.' Jimmy was casually walking along Sandhurst Road. He had spent the afternoon just walking in the park, generally watching the world go by. He noticed two men sitting in a car, two more a bit further down on the other side. Then he thought about the man under the bonnet of the car – he was too smartly dressed to be messing with an engine. Jimmy was putting two and two together; there was no point in running. He half expected a policeman to be standing at the entrance to the flats.

'Nobody moves till I give the word,' said Hammond into the radio. Jimmy noticed two more men in the drive of a house opposite. This confirmed it to him; the street was swarming with police officers. As Jimmy reached the front door he had already decided he wasn't going to try and escape, just accept the inevitable. He went into the flat and closed the door.

'All units go,' came Hammond's voice on the radio. Jimmy turned his armchair round to face the front door and sat down. Hammond and five other officers swarmed up the stairs as other officers positioned themselves around the flats. With officers on both sides of the door, Hammond knocked hard on the door and waited; no reply.

'Jack.' Gillman stepped forward, plastic strip in hand. Again he forced the latch and pushed the door open. The officers rushed in expecting to have a fight on their hands. They stopped dead in their tracks. Jimmy was sitting facing them, his eyes staring into thin air, apparently oblivious to what was going on around him. Hammond walked over to him, 'James Noakes, I am arresting you for the murder of Michelle Summers and Sunli Chun. Anything you say will be taken down and used in evidence in a court of law.' Jimmy still stared into space. 'Take him away.' Two officers pulled him to his feet, handcuffed him and marched him out of the flat. Hammond looked at Gillman, 'Looks like we've got ourselves a right nutcase there, Jack.'

'Should have been institutionalised years ago if you ask me, sir,' said Gillman.

'Come on, let's get out of here,' replied Hammond, 'We can tie up this bit of paperwork then get a drink.'

'Sounds good to me, sir.'

They went back to the station, but it was all done and dusted. The evidence was so overwhelming that the conviction was just dependent upon Noakes' state of mind. Either way he was going down for a long time.

'OK, Jack, lets get that drink.'

'Now, that is a good idea, sir.' The door opened suddenly.

'Hello, sir,' said Hammond. Detective Superintendent Catel stood in the doorway.

'First-class job men, I thought he was getting the better of you at one stage, but credit where it's due,' he smiled.

'We're just going over the road for a celebratory drink if you fancy one, sir,' said Hammond.

'Thanks for the offer but I'll have to decline on this occasion – have to be elsewhere. But have a good evening – you've deserved it.'

'Thank you, sir,' they said in unison.

The following day Lisa caught a bus into the city. After opening the account the day before so easily, she had gained the courage to open more. She decided to use the same principle as the day before – using the first place she came across. It was a particularly busy morning and as she got off the bus she was jostled from side to side. It jogged her memory back to when she first arrived in Birmingham one Sunday lunchtime; she had never seen so many people in one place, the whole big city thing was very new to her.

At a street corner, a man at a newspaper booth was shouting out the headlines: 'DOUBLE MURDERER ARRESTED IN CITY.' The headline board on the front of the box carried a photo-fit picture that caught Lisa's eye; it looked very familiar. She took a pound from her purse, bought a paper and scanned the front page. Then she saw it: 'James Noakes, a 23 year-old unemployed man, was arrested last night in connection with the murders of Michelle Summers and Sunli Chun, both women were prostitutes in the Birmingham area. He has been charged with their murders and police are waiting for a psychiatric evaluation of the suspect.'

Lisa stopped reading and looked up from the paper. 'Jesus Christ, it's true, he did it!' she said to herself in amazement. Without wasting any time she rushed into the nearest bank and opened an account. By the end of the week she had opened all ten accounts. At first she had not intended to be so hasty, but now Jimmy had been arrested she thought she should cash the cheques as quickly as possible.

Two weeks after Jimmy's arrest the case had gone quiet in the newspapers. The police were tying up loose ends, making sure their prosecution was secure, but the evaluation of his mental state was still in the balance. It was this that would determine the period and place to which he would be incarcerated. After interviewing Noakes, Hammond said to Gillman 'If he's trying to fool us, he's doing a very good job of it.'

10

Going solo

Lisa had been considering what she was going to do next. The first thing she wanted to do was to stop selling her body; she had never been comfortable with the idea. As soon as the cheques had cleared she would draw on them and would tell Janie this type of life wasn't for her. Janie was a dear friend but Lisa had decided this opportunity was not to be missed at any cost. Although Jimmy was probably going to prison for the rest of his life, Lisa felt she still shouldn't tell anyone about the money; the less people that knew about it, the less chance she had of losing it. The day finally arrived; if all had gone to plan, the cheque should have cleared in the first account she had opened in Kings Heath. She took the bankbook from her bedside cabinet and caught a bus into Kings Heath. As she got off the bus, panic was setting in. 'What if it hasn't cleared?' she thought, all her dreams, plans she had for the money would be quashed. Apprehensively, she went into the bank. There was a small queue but she didn't have to wait long and within five minutes she was called to the counter.

'I'd like to withdraw one hundred pounds please,' she handed over her bankbook.

'Thank you, madam,' said the cashier. The cashier filled out a slip and passed it back to be signed. Lisa hoped that the cashier would not notice her hand shaking as she signed the slip. The cashier put the book into the machine to adjust her balance. She counted out one hundred pounds and placed it in the book. Passing the book back across the counter the cashier said 'Miss Dean, there's a lot of money in this account, would you like me to arrange an appointment with one of our financial advisers? It's a free service.' Lisa hadn't expected this.

'Err ... I'll leave it for now,' said Lisa.

'That's fine, madam. Any time you would like advice just give us a call,' she pushed a business card across the counter and Lisa picked it up. Lisa thanked her, turned and casually left the bank; inside she had an urge to jump for joy, but thought better of it. This had made her mind up; she would tell Janie of her plans that evening.

Lisa and Janie had prepared an evening meal of spaghetti bolognaise. It was their favourite meal, but their clients didn't appreciate the smell of garlic, so it was a rare treat. Lisa was trying to pluck up the courage to tell Janie her plans.

'Janie,'

'Yeah?'

'I'm packing it all in,' said Lisa.

'Packing all what in?' came the reply; Janie was preoccupied with her food.

'The whole lifestyle, I hate myself for what I'm doing.'

'Good for you,' said Janie; it wasn't the answer Lisa had expected.

'You don't mind after what I said about partners and all that?'

'Not at all,' said Janie, 'I'm just glad you're seeing sense before you get in too deep. What are you going to do?'

'I'm thinking of going down south.' Janie dropped her knife and fork and raised her eyes from her food, a look of shock on her face.

'For fuck's sake Lisa, I thought you were going to say you were going to get a job.' Lisa was startled by her reaction. 'Is it me? Have I offended you or something?' asked Janie.

'No, of course not, I just want to try and make something of myself,' Lisa replied; lying to Janie about the money was the hardest thing she had ever had to do. For the first time in her life she had found a true friend and was about to walk away from her.

'When are you thinking of going?' Janie asked.

'In a couple of days,' Lisa replied. Janie pushed her dinner plate forward, her appetite now gone. 'I'm sorry Janie, I don't want to fall out with you over this.'

Janie smiled, 'I won't fall out with you, you silly cow, I'll miss you.' Lisa felt herself filling up, tears forming in her eyes, 'I'll miss you too, but I just have to do this.'

'Well,' said Janie, if that's your calling girl, go for it. If it doesn't work for you, just jump on a train; you'll always have a home with me.' That was too much for Lisa and tears started running down her face. Janie got up; 'Come here.' They put their arms around each other. 'One day I'll make it up to her,' Lisa thought.

The next morning Lisa caught a bus into the city. Two more cheques should have cleared that day and she had decided to withdraw enough cash to get her to London and stay somewhere comfortable for a couple of weeks. She walked down Colmore Row. There were a number of banks on this street and she had opened accounts at four of them. As she approached the first one, she noticed a sign on the door of the next building: 'Craddock and Co. Independent Financial Advisers'. She remembered what the cashier had said to her at the bank in Kings Heath. With nothing to lose she went in, up two flights of stairs into a large reception area. Sitting behind a desk was a frumpy looking woman, her middle-age spread straining against her tight blouse. 'Good morning, can I help you?' she asked.

'Is it possible to see an adviser?' replied Lisa.

'I'm sorry,' she was told, 'if you haven't an appointment that won't be possible, but I can make you an appointment.' Just then Simon Clark, a partner in the firm, was about to take a coffee break. As he walked through the reception Lisa caught his eye; he had overheard her attempting to make an appointment and, always a bit of a lady's man, his male instinct reacted automatically.

'Good morning Miss... err?'

'Dean, Lisa Dean,' replied Lisa.

'I've got an open slot Janet,' he said to the receptionist.

'But there's Mr Crowther in less than twenty minutes, Simon.'

'Not to worry, we can just breathe in a little. Miss Dean, would you like to come this way?' He gestured Lisa towards his office and offered her coffee.

'Two coffees please Janet.' The receptionist glared after him; if looks could have killed, this was one of them. 'Right, Miss Dean, take a seat. Now how can we help you?'

'Well,' said Lisa, 'I've inherited some money and I'm interested in investing it,' said Lisa.

'Is it just advice you require or do you want us to actually assist in the investments?' asked Clark.

'I haven't really thought that far to be absolutely truthful,' replied Lisa.

'Really, it depends on what you choose to invest in and, of course, how much you are thinking of investing,' Clark told her.

'Well, I have something in the region of two hundred and fifty thousand pounds.'

Clark sat up in his chair, obviously taken aback. 'You took me by surprise there, Miss Dean. You'll have to excuse me, I underestimated the level of investment we were talking about.'

The receptionist came in, 'Two coffees,' she said, putting the cups down on the desk a little harder than was necessary. Clark thanked her and she walked towards the door, turning before she left to glare again at him. 'Mr Crowther is waiting in reception,' she said flatly. Clark knew he was in for it later. He waited for the door to close completely before he continued.

'Right then, that sort of investment would make you a privileged account holder with us. I think a wise move at the moment would be property. Shares in the transport industry are also showing excellent returns. But obviously we need to discuss this in greater depth, like say, over lunch,' Lisa blushed, 'on a strictly professional basis of course. Would that be possible today, Miss Dean?'

Lisa smiled, 'Yes, and it's Lisa.'

He returned the smile and put out his hand, 'Simon.' When they had finished their coffee, Simon pressed the intercom, 'Janet, can you cancel my appointments till two o'clock please, or see if Phil can take them?'

'Simon, Mr Crowther has....'

'Thanks Janet,' he replied, releasing the button and cutting her short, 'Shall we go?'

Over lunch, Clark explained a lot to Lisa; the fact that certain investments were safer than others, but that property, especially at that specific time, was a great investment. That afternoon Lisa opened an account with his firm. It was a simple arrangement; if they didn't make money for her, they wouldn't make any themselves. To a certain degree she had given them a free hand to move her money around as required. Contracts were to be drawn up and she would come in later that week to go over them and sign the paperwork. Before going home she checked at the other banks that the cheques had cleared; sure enough everything had gone according to plan.

Jimmy had been given the date that his case would be heard in court. He had been granted legal aid on the account that he had pleaded poverty. He still wasn't saying a lot and the solicitor assigned to him appeared to be just going through the motions. As Jimmy wasn't saying much, the solicitor was going down the path of diminished responsibility on the grounds that he was mentally unstable. At least by claiming that he was insane there was a chance that he could regain his freedom one day.

Jimmy had been remanded in Winston Green Prison. He was keeping himself to himself, but there were people in there who were giving him a hard time. It didn't take long for the details of his charges to get around the prison; violent or sexual offences against women and children were not taken lightly and the prison officers seemed to disappear just at the right time. The sooner his trial was over the better; he felt sure if he kept up his act, he would be locked away under the Mental Health Act. After that, it would be a case of biding his time and keeping out of trouble.

On the morning of Jimmy's first court appearance, he had hardly slept. Convinced that he was being constantly observed he had stayed very still, only moving occasionally as if he was asleep. Just after eight o'clock, two officers came to collect him. He was to appear at Birmingham Crown Court at ten o'clock and they arrived in plenty of time, the officers chatting to each other as if Jimmy didn't exist. Ten minutes before the proceedings were to begin, Jimmy was taken into the court and placed in the dock. The public gallery off to his left was filled with members of the press, all with notepads at the ready. There were also members of the murdered women's families; none of them had set eyes on Jimmy before. A family friend had assisted Michelle Summers' invalid mother into the court. Sunli Chun's mother, father and two brothers looked down at him; her mother was openly sobbing and being comforted by her father. Her brothers were both ranting obscenities in their native tongue.

Jimmy was dressed casually and he stood bolt upright, as if he hadn't a care in the world. Hammond and Gillman arrived; they both scanned their notes and from time to time they glanced around the court, watching the last few seats filling up. A jury consisting of six men and six women had already been sworn in and they were ushered into their seats by a court clerk. Almost immediately, the words 'all rise' echoed round the court, the judge came in and with a short nod of his head, everyone sat down.

The court clerk stood and read out the charge. 'James Noakes, you are charged that on Friday eighth September 1986, you murdered Michelle Summers of 22 Belfort Road, Edgbaston, and on Friday fifteenth September 1986, you also murdered Sunli Chun of 44 Compton Towers, Bristol Road, Birmingham. How do you plead?' Jimmy was standing in the dock with his head down, chin resting on his chest. He gave no reply. The clerk repeated his question but there was still no reply.

The judge looked down at Jimmy's legal representative. 'Mr Townsend,' he said, beckoning him to the bench, 'what is the problem?'

'I'm sorry, Your Honour, I can't even get him to talk to me. I think there are very good grounds for diminished responsibility, Your Honour.'

'I have read the psychological evaluation, Mr Townsend, and I must say it is not conclusive.'

'Yes, Your Honour, I appreciate that, but he has been under constant surveillance, and I am beginning to doubt the results, sir.'

'Thank you, Mr Townsend, we will leave that to the jury to decide. Please resume your position.' Townsend stood back from the bench.

'Due to Mr Noakes' lack of response, acting on his behalf, and in his best interests, Mr Townsend is forwarding a plea of not guilty on the grounds of diminished responsibility.' A sudden roar from the public gallery forced a response from the judge, 'Quiet please,' he shouted, 'please maintain order in the public gallery. We will take a fifteen-minute recess. Mr Townsend, I'd like to see you in my chambers.'

The clerk stood. 'All rise,' he demanded. The judge left the court and instantly the public gallery became a hive of activity, the press leaving to report on the plea of the accused and family members raising their voices, disgusted with what they had just heard.

Townsend knocked on the door of the judge's chambers.

'Come in,' boomed the reply. Townsend entered. 'Ah, Mr Townsend, I get the feeling the press are keeping a close eye on this case.'

'Yes, Your Honour, the public gallery appears to be considerably more full than normal.'

'I'll come straight to the point, Mr Townsend, we all know this man is guilty; the forensic evidence is overwhelming. I don't want this to drag on for weeks and weeks. We just need a conclusion on his mental state, so we know where he will be residing for the next twenty or thirty years.'

'I understand, Your Honour, just make sure the prosecution do.'

'I can guarantee, Mr Townsend, they will be just as keen as I am to draw a conclusion on this one. Right then, let's get on with it.' Townsend turned and left the room; the judge sat back and gave a large sigh, preparing himself for what was going to be a very testing week or two.

Over the next few days the prosecution tried to reinforce the fact that there was nothing wrong with Noakes, purely that he was an evil, violent rapist who deserved nothing more than life imprisonment. The defence, on the other hand, maintained that he was mentally unstable. Townsend had been doing some digging around in his client's past. He knew that Jimmy had spent most of his life in care, but did not know how this came about. After spending a couple of very late evenings delving into some archive information, he came up with something that he knew would convince the jury of Jimmy's mental condition. For a young boy to witness the murder of his mother, and then to be left with her rotting corpse for nearly a week, surely this was enough to make anybody unstable, let alone a young child. He decided to do as the judge asked and give the jury his findings at the next opportunity.

Lisa had been following the case very closely. She had considered going to sit in the public gallery, but in the end thought it best to stay away; if she had been recognised it could have had implications on the money. Janie had told her about the visit from the police officer who knew them from the Victoria Hotel incident; if he had recognised her in court, he might just put two and two together and come up with two hundred and fifty thousand pounds. She thought she was probably being a little paranoid, but it was not every day that someone gave her a quarter of a million pounds, and with that she continued to watch from a distance.

Lisa was sitting in the flat reading the previous day's news on the case, when the door suddenly opened and, as if up to no good, she quickly closed the newspaper. Janie came in, 'Hi Lisa, what you up to?'

'Nothing,' replied Lisa, feeling guilty, 'just reading the paper.' Janie went into the kitchen and put the kettle on.

'What you doing tonight Janie?' Lisa shouted through. Janie's head popped round the edge of the door.

'Three new clients. I tell you what, that advert in the paper was the best thing we ever did, once they get over the fact that I'm not blonde with blue eyes,' she went back into the kitchen. 'Coffee Lisa?'

'Yes please, what about Friday or Saturday?' Lisa shouted back. Janie again came and stood in the doorway.

'I thought you said you were leaving on Friday?'

'I've put it off till Monday, if that's alright,' replied Lisa.

'It's fine by me girl. Why, you taking me out?'

'I thought it would be nice before I go,' said Lisa.

'Friday it is then,' replied Janie.

Later that week Lisa completed the contract with the financial advisers. The money was transferred from her various accounts into a new account at Craddock and Co., all she kept back was the first account she had opened at the Yorkshire Building Society in Kings Heath. There was plenty in there for her to live on when she moved south. Hopefully, she would get herself a job and start a whole new, respectable life.

That Friday, Townsend, Jimmy's legal representative, decided to introduce the evidence he had dug up. As it had been all week, the public gallery was full to capacity. Various people had taken the stand; some medical professionals claiming that he was totally insane, and others arguing that his insanity claim was merely a scam to keep him out of prison. The truth of the matter was that none of them really knew. Townsend had contacted a woman who had cared for him in the children's home. She had strengthened his plea of diminished responsibility by claiming that he had always had a troubled mind and that nobody at the children's home had ever been able to get to the bottom of the problem.

This was the perfect opportunity for Townsend to introduce the facts on Jimmy's childhood and the faces of the jury said it all; it was truly a masterstroke. Two female members of the jury wept when the details of his mother's murder were presented to them. By the end of proceedings that Friday, the judge addressed the jury; all the evidence for both the defence and the prosecution had been presented. Now it was up to the jury to deliberate on the information that had been presented to them and make their decision. The judge decided to send the jury to a hotel for the weekend and the court was adjourned until ten o'clock the following Monday morning.

Janie and Lisa had decided that instead of just having a Friday night out, they would turn it into a girly weekend. Lisa had tied up all her loose ends and was ready to leave first thing Monday morning. On Friday evening they both hit the town. Lisa stayed with her usual soft drinks but, as normal, Janie had one drink too many. After four hours moving from pub to pub, they decided to finish off the evening in an Indian restaurant. The longer the evening went on, the louder Janie became. After waiting half an hour for their meal Janie became impatient and, as the waiter passed, words were exchanged and an argument broke out. Lisa tried her best to calm Janie down but by now alcohol was in the driving seat and it was not long before they were asked to leave. Janie was still hurling abuse at the restaurant staff as Lisa pushed her towards the door, and into the nearest waiting taxi.

On Saturday morning Lisa stayed in bed till about ten o'clock. She had been awake for a good hour, but just lay there thinking about what the following week had in store for her. Finally she got out of bed and headed for the kitchen in desperate need of a coffee. By midday there was still no sign of Janie. From the way she looked when they arrived home the night before, it would be a surprise if Janie got up at all that day. Just after two o'clock Janie came out of her room.

'Coffee?' asked Lisa,

'Yes please,' came the drowsy reply, 'my head's pounding,' said Janie.

'I guess tonight's not going to happen now then,' said Lisa, quietly.

'Give me a chance girl, I've just got out of bed.' Janie spent the rest of the afternoon relaxing, trying to get her head together, but by six o'clock was still looking extremely fragile.

'Lets get a pizza and stop in tonight,' said Lisa, in an attempt to take away the feeling of guilt, which she knew Janie felt.

'If you're sure,' replied Janie.

'Yeah, I think I've seen enough of Birmingham for one weekend.' The relief was clear on Janie's face; she didn't look as if she had another night out left in her. Like all their weekends, this one had passed as quickly as clicking your fingers.

Lisa woke up bright and early on Monday morning. She had packed all her belongings on Sunday evening so, after a light breakfast, she could be on her way. Janie gave her a talking to, just like a mother to a daughter leaving the nest for the first time. The sound of a car horn in the street outside informed Lisa that her taxi had arrived. After a long hug and one more goodbye, Lisa was on her way, entering another chapter of her so far unpredictable short life.

Jimmy sat in his cell; the thought of spending the best part of the next twenty years or more in a room with one door and window was very frightening. All his hopes were with the jury finding him guilty but on the grounds of diminished responsibility. The familiar sound of the prison officer turning the key in the lock alerted him. The door opened, 'Right young man, it's time,' said the officer. The officer turned and Jimmy followed him along the landing to the sound of the occasional jeer from fellow inmates. It was only a short drive to the city from Winston Green Prison, hopefully the last time he would make the trip. As the prison van arrived at the courts, through the blacked-out windows of the van, he caught the occasional flash of a camera from a hopeful member of the press, trying to get that lucky picture. For the last time, two officers accompanied him through the basement of the courtroom building, up the narrow stairs into the courtroom itself. A very nervous, apprehensive feeling was overwhelming his body. Already the courtroom was full. Within a couple of minutes the jury entered the room, followed by the judge. Without any hesitation the judge addressed the chairman of the jury. 'Mr Chairman, have you reached a verdict on the charges brought against Mr James Noakes?'

'We have, Your Honour,' replied the chairman.

'How do you find the named on the charge of the murder of Miss Michelle Summers?'

'Guilty,' said the chairman.

'How do you find the named on the charge of the murder of Miss Sunli Chun?'

'Guilty, Your Honour.' The public gallery sounded like a disturbed bees' nest; there was an audible hum in the courtroom.

'Order please, order,' said the judge in a loud, almost irate, voice. 'Thank you. Mr Chairman, members of the jury, this has been a particularly disturbing case, especially for the victims' families. From the evidence presented to you, you have found James Noakes guilty of two horrific murders. From a series of professional evaluations of Mr Noakes' mental state, my findings are that these crimes were carried out while he was not of a sound state of mind.' The public gallery erupted; family members shouted abuse at the judge's decision and the din escalated. The judge struck his gavel down on the bench three times, 'Order, order,' he shouted. 'Another outbreak like that and I will clear the public gallery.' The courtroom fell quiet.

'James Noakes, please stand,' said the court clerk. Slowly, Jimmy got to his feet. 'James Noakes,' said the judge, 'Given your present mental state, I sentence you to a minimum of twenty years in a state psychiatric hospital. Take him down.' The press in the public gallery were off even before the court had been dismissed. Members of the victims' families were left to console each other in their grief. As for Jimmy, he was whisked away to an unknown destination to start what was to be a long, lonely life in captivity.

Lisa arrived at Birmingham New Street railway station. She remembered the first day she had arrived; how things had changed since then. Lisa had transformed herself from a lost child to a confident young woman, setting out on an adventure. She really was looking forward to anything that life could throw at her. In two hours she would be in London and embracing a whole new beginning.

11

Getting settled

The train arrived at Euston station. Lisa's experience had taught her not to hang around in these places; you can attract some extremely undesirable people. Trying not to resemble a tourist, she left the station as if she had a destination; the truth was she hadn't a clue where she was going. Earlier that week she had withdrawn four hundred pounds from the building society account in Kings Heath, so there wouldn't be a problem with finding somewhere to stay for the night. If the worst came to the worst, any hotel would do, before finding somewhere permanent. She thought she would take a look at the sights; it was the first time she had been to the capital. After about an hour of walking, she noticed a board advertising quality accommodation at an affordable price, next on the left. 'Sounds good,' she thought. Turning into the street she could see a large hotel with a sign in big letters: 'BUDGET', it looked respectable so she went in. The woman on the desk greeted her with a pleasant smile. Lisa booked in for just one night and thought, if it was OK, she would stay a little longer. A young man showed her to her room. The first thing she wanted to do was take a bath and take the weight off her feet. After walking for well over an hour her feet were aching. She really liked having money; in these situations it certainly made life a lot easier.

The next day she decided to go out sightseeing. Walking through the hotel lobby she noticed the headlines on a newspaper left on a chair: 'MURDERER CONVICTED: MINIMUM 20 YEARS.' She immediately picked up the paper and started reading. 'So, they had put him away,' she thought, 'twenty years, that's a long time.' A grin spread over her face. She put the paper back on the chair and carried on out of the front door, a noticeable spring in her step. She really liked being in London; it was such a vibrant city and she thought how great it would be to live there. Each time she passed an estate agent she would take a look at the rental accommodation that was available; it was affordable to her now but her money would soon whittle away. There was only one thing for it: she

would have to look outside central London, as it was just too expensive.
The next estate agent she came across she went in and picked up a couple
of property newspapers. That afternoon, back at the hotel, Lisa sat down
to study the property newspapers. Everything appeared expensive but it
did get a little cheaper further away from central London. A one bedroom
flat above a shop in Wimbledon caught her eye. Not sure where it was,
she went down to reception and got a map of the tube stations to put her
in the right direction. After a little study time on the map she decided to
call the agent's number and arrange a viewing. The man she spoke to was
helpful; she arranged to be at the flat for eleven o'clock the following
morning: all she had to do now was find the place.

The following morning, after a hearty breakfast, Lisa set off with plenty
of time to get there. The tube system confused her and she had to ask two
or three underground staff before she found the correct train. Eventually,
after one or two frustrating moments, she found herself at Wimbledon
station. With the address written on a scrap of paper, she thought it best
to get a cab the rest of the way. As the cab pulled up at the address, Lisa
glanced at her watch: 10:30, it had taken her just about an hour to get
here. The flat had a separate doorway at the side of the shop. It was one
of those shops that sold just about everything, so that would be useful. A
little way down the street she could see a café, so rather than hang around
in the street, she went in for a coffee. At precisely eleven o'clock, a man
turned up outside the flat. From where Lisa was sitting she could see he
was very busy, glancing at his watch every few seconds, then looking up
and down the street. Lisa got up, pushed in her chair, acknowledged the
woman behind the counter. Closing the door behind her she went out into
the street. As she approached the man, he quickly made eye contact and
responded, 'Miss Dean?'

'Yes,' said Lisa.

'Hello there, my name's Damien, Damien East. I'm here on behalf of
the property owners to show you around.'

'Great, shall we go in?' said Lisa. He opened the door. The first thing
Lisa noticed was a smell of fresh paint. 'That's a good sign,' she thought
to herself. They went up some steep stairs, and straight into a sparsely
furnished large lounge area. Lisa looked around; there was a three-piece
suite, which had seen better days, a small coffee table and an old
sideboard with one or two drawer handles missing.

'As you can see, it has a very nice size lounge,' said East. 'It's
advertised as unfurnished but if you want the furniture which is here,
there would be no charge for it.' Lisa was impressed; the lounge alone was
bigger than any place she had lived in, and the decoration was first-class.

'Would you like to look around on your own or would you like me to show you around?'

'You can show me around, if that's OK,' said Lisa.

'No problem, Miss Dean, it's a pleasure. Shall we start in the bathroom?' East showed Lisa the rest of the flat. There was an old pine wardrobe and a chest of drawers in the bedroom, nothing else. There were a few bits and bobs in the kitchen, not brilliant, but the decoration was excellent throughout. It was just what she wanted, but she didn't want to sound too keen, as it was a little more than she wanted to pay.

'I do like the place Mr East but..'

'Damien, please Miss Dean,' he quickly replied with a smile.

'Do you think they would move on the rent? It's a little more than I can really afford.'

'I'll try for you, but I don't think it is negotiable,' he replied.

'I see,' said Lisa.

'I have to bring a young couple down here at four o'clock,' he began.

Lisa interrupted him, 'In that case I'll take it; I don't want to risk losing it.'

'Are you sure, Miss Dean?'

'Yes, I'm sure.' After a period of filling out forms, Lisa finally had her first home. She had never before felt the way she did when East handed her the keys. Finally, everything was going right for her. She took a taxi back to the station then collected her things from the hotel; tonight she was going to stay in her own place, even if it did mean sleeping on an old sofa.

Over the next few days, Lisa made the flat her own; just a few touches that to her made all the difference. She got to know the Asian family who owned the mini-market under the flat; they were very friendly towards her. Lisa had the feeling they used her as a kind of a night watchman for them, but she didn't really mind; if she did happen to hear anybody downstairs in the shop at night she would just call the police and that was the end of it.

Lisa contacted Craddock & Co., the financial advisers, to let them know her new address. She spoke to Simon Clark who had taken her out for lunch; he told her they were very happy with her investments. She had got in just at the right time; the property market was going through the roof.

Although Lisa was financially comfortable, she wasn't meeting anybody socially. Her evenings were very quiet and she decided the best way to meet people was get a job. Not yet eighteen years old and with nothing in the way of qualifications or experience she was limited in what she could do. A little way down the High Street she had noticed a wine bar called Korky's. Every night of the week it was full of what appeared to be very well-to-do people. They all seemed to be driving expensive cars and the girls wore designer clothes and were dripping in gold. Sometimes, as she went out for a walk in the evening, she would slow down as she passed the wine bar to take a good look in; it always looked as if the people in there were having a great time. One Friday lunchtime as she passed the wine bar, she noticed a card in the window advertising for part-time staff. Inside, all she could see was a lady cleaning the tables and another replenishing the wine bottles behind the bar. Lisa thought, 'What the hell,' and went in. 'Excuse me,' said Lisa, 'could you help me? I'm interested in the part-time work.' The lady cleaning the tables looked up, her eyes glanced towards the bar, as if to say 'She's in charge.' Lisa walked over to the bar, 'Excuse me,' the woman turned round. Without being rude, Lisa took a long look at her; she was beautiful, with long black hair, dark eyes, olive skin and a figure most women would die for. She must have been in her mid-thirties but still looked great.

'I'm sorry,' she said, 'I was miles away. The job's only part-time at the moment, you see we get very busy at weekends. Have you done any bar work before?'

'Well, I'm not quite eighteen yet,' said Lisa.

'Oh I see. Do you live local?'

'Just down the High Street, above the mini-market. I've only recently moved down from Birmingham.'

'You certainly don't have a Midlands accent.'

'No, I'm from Manchester originally.'

'So, exactly how old are you?' asked the woman.

'I'll be eighteen in a few weeks.'

'What's your name?'

'Lisa, Lisa Dean.'

'Well Lisa, it doesn't pay well.'

'I don't mind, I just want the experience.'

'Well, that's the first time I've had that answer.' Lisa smiled at her. 'You'll only be doing trivial work, seeing as you're not old enough to work the bar,' the woman warned her, but Lisa said it didn't matter.

'You're very keen, I'll give you that.' The woman stared intently at Lisa for what felt like several minutes. Lisa was feeling uncomfortable but held her gaze, not wanting to let this opportunity go. 'OK Lisa, I'll give you a trial this Saturday night, 6 till 12.'

'Great,' said Lisa, 'I won't let you down.'

'Look the part, I like my staff to be smart at all times during working hours.'

'I will.' Lisa's face was glowing with excitement, 'See you Saturday.' Lisa turned and walked towards the door.

'Hey,' Lisa stopped and turned, 'I'm Angie, and this is Sue,' the lady cleaning the tables looked up and smiled.

'Pleased to meet you Angie,' Lisa called back, then nodded with a smile at the lady cleaning the tables, 'Sue.' Lisa left the wine bar and headed back towards the flat, an obvious spring now in her step.

The following day Lisa went shopping; all that was on her mind was looking good on Saturday night. Nearly five hours later she arrived back at the flat, pleased with her purchases; the outfit she had chosen would have turned heads anywhere, let alone in Korky's wine bar. She had a hair appointment booked for Saturday morning; her plans were to make one hell of a first impression. On Saturday evening Lisa left the flat and took a slow walk down to Korky's, arriving with five minutes to spare. Looking through the front windows she could see that all the lights were on but there was no sign of activity. Pushing the door open she went in.

'Hi Lisa,' came a voice from behind the bar. Hearing the door open, Angie stood up from restocking the bottled beers, 'nice to see you're on time. We're going to be a bit short-staffed tonight and it's going to get busy.'

'Is there somewhere to put my coat?' asked Lisa.

'I'll show you around. Sue will be in about seven, the other girls, Alex and Zoë, are both sick with some stomach bug. I tell you, it's all I need on a Saturday night.' Angie showed Lisa around the wine bar. 'Right Lisa, put your coat in the staffroom and I'll get the place opened up.'

'OK,' replied Lisa. Lisa hung up her coat; there was a full-length mirror on the back of the staff room door, another of Angie's attention to detail ideas. Lisa looked herself up and down, briefly turning to the side, 'I hope this isn't too short,' she said to herself. Quickly, she walked down the narrow corridor into the bar. As she walked in Angie was racking some bottles of wine in a cooler compartment. Suddenly, Angie's eye caught Lisa, she turned, 'Very nice,' she said, approvingly; Lisa blushed, 'you're going to be good for business young lady, and very popular as well, if I may add.'

'I don't know about that,' said Lisa. The door opened and Sue came in.

'Hi Sue,' called Angie. Sue was a very quiet lady; also in her mid-thirties, light brown hair with a round but very pretty face, very self-conscious of the constant battle to keep her weight in check. The wine bar job was just a bit of pin money for her. Her husband was a long-distance lorry driver, so he was away most nights. She had two kids in their middle teens, both of them out most nights, so she had taken the job to get herself out of the house. It had started as a couple of nights a week, but Angie had slowly and cleverly pressured her to work virtually seven nights a week.

'Hi Angie,' replied Sue, looking over at Lisa, 'Lisa isn't it?'

'Yeah,' Lisa replied, 'nice to meet you again.' They smiled at each other. It wasn't long before customers started arriving. Wine, shots, bubbly and generous tips; it was clear to Lisa that Korky's attracted affluent customers. By nine o'clock there wasn't a free table in the bar. Lisa was constantly on the go; it was right what Angie had said about being short-staffed.

'You look tired Lisa,' said Sue.

'Is it like this every evening?' asked Lisa.

'Fridays and Saturdays mainly, but sometimes Sundays as well. Don't worry, you'll get used to it.' By half past eleven the last few customers were drinking up; the ones that were not were respectfully being asked to do so. Once they had all gone, Angie dropped the latch on the main door and went behind the bar; she pulled out a bottle of house white, uncorked it and, placing three glasses on the bar, filled them up. Lisa and Sue were collecting empty bottles and glasses from the tables.

'Girls,' they both looked around, 'come and take the weight off your feet and have a drink.' They pulled up high bar stools. 'You did well tonight Lisa,' said Angie. Lisa smiled and thanked her. 'Has the workload frightened you off, or are you going to take the job?'

'I'd love to take the job,' said Lisa. Angie raised her glass, 'Well, that's settled then, you're officially part of the team. Cheers!' They clinked their glasses together. It took over an hour to finish clearing up and washing all the glasses. Lisa arranged to be in work the same time the following evening.

When Lisa arrived home she was absolutely shattered. She lay on the bed thinking about the evening and what a great line of work it was to be in. 'One day,' she thought, 'I'll own a place like that.' Slowly, she drifted off into a deep sleep.

It had been nearly three months since Lisa had left Birmingham and she was so happy in her new job she hadn't contacted Janie at all in that time. Things had been going so well for her and she had been so busy that it had just slipped her mind. She decided to write to Janie to let her know her new address; maybe she would come down and pay her a visit. She hoped that Janie's life was equally as good as hers.

Lisa's eighteenth birthday came and went; the girls in the wine bar had put on a little party for her after hours. It was the first time she had ever had too much to drink and, like most people, she swore she would never drink again. Time went by and life was a ball for Lisa. She enrolled at the local college on a business studies course, something she had never imagined herself doing; the job at the wine bar had given her a whole new lease of life. Working almost every evening, Lisa learned the job inside out. Angie had increased her wages on her eighteenth birthday. Of course, it entailed more responsibility: serving behind the bar and occasionally adding up the takings. Her spare time was devoted to either coursework for her business studies qualifications or reading about wines. The more she learned about wine, the greater her desire grew to one day own her own wine bar. Occasionally, she would write to Janie and let her know how she was getting on. Janie had never been one for writing but would always scribble down a few words to keep in touch.

It was just twelve months since Jimmy had been committed. He had been sent to a high-security psychiatric hospital near Leeds and was still not giving much away, keeping very much to himself. Every day the inmates were given some form of medication, either a tablet or a drink. Each time Jimmy avoided taking it, either by pretending to swallow it and then spitting it out, or passing it on to some poor, unsuspecting inmate. Most inmates were kept locked up at all times. Some were so violent they could only be removed from their cells once the drugs had kicked in and by this time they were virtually incapacitated. Jimmy came under a different category. Although he had been convicted of rape and murder, compared to some of these people he was really quite gentle. He was allowed to leave his cell for meals and trivial jobs that inmates like him were selected for.

Three or four times a week, Jimmy would undergo psychological evaluations, the plan being to rehabilitate inmates and one day introduce them back into society. The therapist he was assigned to was an experienced doctor called Henry Phelps. He was a striking figure; six feet four inches tall, very slim and with a gaunt face. On more than one occasion, the police had asked him to make evaluations on suspected murderers. So, if Jimmy was going to pull the wool over his eyes, he was going to have to be very cunning. After treating Jimmy for nearly twelve months, Phelps was convinced he was making headway. When Jimmy had first arrived at the hospital he had been very quiet. In fact, for the first half dozen sessions with Phelps he had not spoken a single word. Undeterred, Phelps persevered, trying various approaches until, slowly but surely, he had begun to get a response from Jimmy. All that was keeping Jimmy going was the thought that one day he would get his money back and, most importantly, he would have his Lisa all to himself. Every time he felt down he would think of this and a kind of half smile would appear on his face. He would just go on about his business, keeping his head down and biding his time until the authorities were convinced that it was time to release him.

12

Money matters

It was almost four years to the day since Lisa had moved into her flat. She had completed her business studies exams and achieved very good grades. Quite often, Angie would leave her in charge at the wine bar and Lisa would thrive on it, feeling that everything she wanted was happening. Then Angie would turn up and it was back to reality. Lisa was getting a lot of attention from the male contingent in the bar; not unexpectedly, she had matured into a very beautiful woman. Lisa felt that Angie resented her getting all the attention. Although Angie was still a very desirable woman, next to Lisa she was a poor second. Angie would belittle Lisa in front of customers. For now she would put up with it, as she felt she owed Angie for giving her a start in the business, but she didn't know how much longer she could take it.

It was Saturday morning; the previous evening had been a particularly late one. She got out of bed, pulled on her dressing gown, went through to the kitchen and turned on the kettle. As she did every morning, she peered down the stairs to see if there was any post and saw that there was more than usual. She went down and gathered it up. Flicking through it, most of it was junk mail, then she noticed a letter from her investment firm, Craddock & Co. They sent her annual statements about shares and properties they were investing in on her behalf. She had made a decision not to touch the money for five years. As in previous years, she didn't really understand the statements, but there was always a letter attached reassuring her that the investments were in good shape. On this occasion the statement was different, she had never had one like this before. On closer inspection she realised it wasn't a statement; it was an invoice asking her to pay £30,000 for the handling of her investments. Her jaw nearly hit the floor, 'Oh my god,' she said out loud and hurriedly read the attached letter.

Dear Miss Dean,

Please find enclosed an invoice for charges relating to your investments for the year ending 31st March, 1990. Attached is a full statement of how the charges have been accrued.

Please do not hesitate to contact me if you have any questions.

Yours sincerely

Simon Clark

Acting on behalf of Craddock & Co. Financial advisers

Lisa briefly scanned the attached statement, but it meant nothing to her. She was flabbergasted. Dressing quickly, she went down to the pay phone just across the road. After a twenty-minute conversation, the secretary Lisa spoke to arranged for her to come up to Birmingham and see Simon Clark personally. The secretary had sensed the tension in Lisa's voice and thought a one-to-one meeting was required. It had been four years since she had seen Clark; the meeting was long overdue.

The following Tuesday, Lisa got up early, ate breakfast and prepared an overnight bag. She had sent a letter to Janie telling her she would be in Birmingham for a couple of days. In the four years Lisa had been in London, she had only visited Janie twice. Janie always said, 'There's a bed at my place for you anytime.' It would be great to see her again, and see how life had been treating her. It had been a long time since Lisa had taken any time off work, so Angie couldn't really complain, even if it did leave her short-staffed for a couple of evenings and it was midweek. Two other bars had opened right by Korky's and the takings had reduced dramatically. Angie hadn't said anything to the staff, but it wasn't looking good in the long term.

The train left Euston station at nine o'clock. Her meeting was at half past eleven, so, provided that there were no delays, she had plenty of time to get there. The train pulled into New Street station at 11:10, perfect timing for her appointment. Craddock & Co. was on Colmore Row, in the centre of the legal and commercial business district of the city, just a short walk from the station. Within ten minutes she arrived at the office. As she entered she remembered those familiar stairs. Four yours previously she had apprehensively climbed them wondering what the hell she was getting herself into. Nothing had changed at the top of the stairs, the same large reception area, the same furniture, but the receptionist had changed. This was a very attractive girl, not much older than herself. 'Hello, can I help you?' asked the receptionist.

'Yes, my name's Dean, Lisa Dean, I have an appointment at...'

The receptionist stopped her in her tracks, 'Eleven-thirty Miss Dean. Would you please take a seat? I'll inform Mr Clark you're here.'

'Thanks,' said Lisa, remarking to herself on the girl's efficiency. No sooner had she sat down than the office door adjacent opened and Simon Clark stepped into the hall. Lisa recognised him straight away. He was the man that had taken her out for lunch the first time she had enquired about investing her money at Craddock & Co.

'Ah, Miss Dean,' he said smiling, and shaking her hand warmly. 'Please come into my office. Nicky would you get some drinks for us please?'

'Certainly Mr Clark,' replied the receptionist, 'Would you like coffee Miss Dean?'

'That will be fine, thank you,' said Lisa. Clark stood to the side of his office door and gestured with his arm, inviting Lisa in.

'It's been nearly four years Miss Dean, you must be very pleased with your investments.' Lisa looked straight into his eyes; her experience in dealing with people at Korky's had made her very assertive.

'Pleased, Mr Clark?' She opened her bag, pulled out the invoice and placed it on the table. He picked it up and read it.

'This is your statement of costs incurred for the handling of your investments,' said Clark.

'I know that, Mr Clark, but thirty thousand pounds? Isn't that a little steep?' The tone of Lisa's voice was edged with sarcasm.

'As agreed, Miss Dean, it is a percentage proportional to your investment returns.' Lisa stared straight at him; the penny had not quite dropped. 'Miss Dean, I think we have some talking to do. I don't think you realise exactly what has been happening with your investments.' On his desk was a keyboard. He entered a code, followed by a file name and turned the monitor round slightly so Lisa could see the screen. 'Miss Dean, this shows the way your share portfolio has been performing and the property developments we invested your money in, plus the dividend cheques we reinvested over the last four years. Do you realise what you are worth, Miss Dean?'

'Mr Clark, if I knew that I wouldn't have made this appointment,' said Lisa. His reply was quiet and calm.

'Miss Dean, on paper, you're a millionairess.'

Lisa remembered nothing else until feeling the cool water on her brow as she woke up.

'Should I phone an ambulance, Mr Clark?' asked the receptionist.

'I think she's coming round, Nicky. Miss Dean, can you hear me? Are you OK?' Slowly, Lisa's head started to clear.

'What happened?'

'You fainted, Miss Dean. Do you want me to get you a doctor?'

'No, I'll be OK in a minute.'

Nicky returned with a glass in her hand. 'Here you go miss, drink some water.' Lisa thanked her and drank the water, still feeling a bit groggy. Once her head had cleared, Clark asked her if she would like him to continue explaining her financial position, or whether she would prefer to make another appointment when she felt a little better. Lisa wanted to know the facts there and then; it all sounded very impressive, if a little hard to take in. But they seemed to be doing a good job of managing her finances, so she left it with them. She explained to Clark that one day she wanted to open her own business, a venture like the wine bar she worked in. Suddenly, it was within her grasp. For now she would just bide her time, keep learning the trade and gain as much management experience as she could.

When Lisa left Craddock & Co. her mind was confused, but in a pleasant sort of way. After all, she had just been told she was rich! Her plan was to catch a bus over to Janie's, but after what she had just been told she thought, stuff it, and got into a cab. The question now was should she tell Janie about her money? Jimmy had told her never to tell a soul, but the circumstances had changed. How would Janie take it if she told her she had left four years earlier with a quarter of a million pounds and not so much as a thank you? She had to tell her, but when? The timing had to be just right. The cab turned into Wellington Road and came to a halt outside Janie's flat. Lisa gave the driver a ten-pound note and told him to keep the change. God, it felt great to have money!

Lisa rang the front door bell; she could hear the sound of distant footsteps getting louder, a hurried pace about them. The door opened and Janie stood there with a broad smile across her face.

'I was beginning to give up on you girl!' Lisa returned the smile. Janie reached out with both arms and they hugged each other.

'It's great to see you, Janie.'

'My god girl, you get prettier every time I see you,' said Janie, beaming at her, 'It won't be long before some rich bloke is sweeping you off your feet.'

'I should be so lucky,' said Lisa. Janie took Lisa's bag and they went up the stairs to the flat. The rest of the afternoon was spent reminiscing about the past. Lisa told Janie about her job and how well she had done with her college work. A couple of times she nearly got onto the subject of money, but each time changed her mind, waiting for a more opportune moment.

Janie was still running the advert in the paper. Nothing had really changed with her life; she was still in good shape and was financially sound. As she had said to Lisa, 'I can't complain, I go where I like with whom I like.' That was her policy on life, always had been and probably always would be. Later that evening they were deciding what to do, whether to go out or get a takeaway. Lisa preferred to stay in; she knew if Janie got out on the town, after a couple of hours the alcohol would take over and they would probably end up in trouble. Lisa still hadn't forgotten the fiasco in the Indian restaurant, but to Janie that was just another night out. In the end they decided on a couple of bottles of wine and a Chinese.

With most of the food eaten, they opened the second bottle of wine and toasted their friendship. The wine worked its spell on Lisa's judgement and she decided to see what reaction she would get from Janie concerning the money.

'Janie, can I tell you something?'

'Anything you like,' replied Janie, taking another slug on her wine.

'When I left here four years ago, I entered into a deal and I was told I couldn't tell anybody about it.'

'This sounds intriguing,' said Janie, putting her glass down and settling into the sofa cushions, keen to hear Lisa's story.

'Do you remember that bloke I got from the advert, Jimmy?'

'Well, I never really saw him,' replied Janie, 'but I do remember him, he just talked to you.'

'That was him. Well, he got put away for the murder of two girls.' Janie suddenly sat up straight.

'You're joking ... I remember that case, yeah, it was just after you left.'

'Well, listen, there's more yet. The deal was, he gets put away and I have his money as a kind of safekeeping till he gets out.'

'Sounds dodgy to me,' said Janie, cautiously. 'How much are we talking?'

'Quarter of a million quid.'

'You're fucking winding me up,' said Janie, instantly becoming switched on to the conversation. 'So you're telling me, we're sat here in this flat with a Chinese takeaway and two bottles of cheap wine, while you have a quarter of a million quid in the bank?'

'Well, not exactly,' said Lisa, 'you see I invested it all, well nearly all of it. I kept twenty-five thousand back. I've been living on it ever since.'

'So you...'

'No, listen,' Lisa interrupted her, 'I went to see a financial adviser who invested my money for me. Janie, I'm a millionaire.' Janie fell back in her seat and looked up at the ceiling.

'I can't believe what I'm hearing.' Janie stared at Lisa and it seemed like an age before she spoke. 'Are you sure this isn't a wind up?' asked Janie.

'Absolutely not, straight up.'

'I knew there was something about you the day I meet ya. You had it rough at first girl, but you sure came out smelling of roses.' Lisa laughed at this. 'So what you going to do now?'

'I want to open my own business, a wine bar like the one I work in.' Janie looked at Lisa, a look of uncertainty on her face.

'Do you think that's a good idea? I mean, it's one thing working in a wine bar, but it's something else when you own it.'

'I know it's a gamble, but hey, you don't get many chances in this life.'

'I've got to give it you Lisa, you've got some bottle.'

'Janie, I want to square something with you. I know you must be mad at me for not telling you.' Janie interrupted her.

'Mad at you?' Janie was incredulous. 'I'm not mad at you girl. I think it's the best stroke I've ever heard anybody play. If anything I'm proud of ya. In this line of work we hope for a rich old man to leave everything to us in his will, but you're the first I've ever heard of that actually pulled it off, and without even being touched.'

'I'm glad you feel that way Janie, because I want you to come into business with me.'

'What, wine bars and all that? I don't think so Lisa, that's not for me.'

'Why?' asked Lisa, 'We'd be a great partnership and it will get you out of here.'

Janie looked up, frown lines forming on her forehead. 'What do you mean, out of here? This is my home and it's all paid for.'

'No, I didn't mean it like that,' said Lisa quickly. 'What I meant was away from the men and abuse.' Lisa was getting herself in deeper.

'I think you should quit while you're still in front.'

'I'm sorry Janie, I didn't mean to offend you, just have a think about it.'

'I'm off to bed,' said Janie, 'It's been a long day.'

'OK,' replied Lisa, quietly, 'See you in the morning.'

Lisa lay in bed, deep in thought. She had not intended to offend Janie; it was just the way it came out. For as long as she could remember, Janie was the only person who had really cared for her and she hoped she hadn't jeopardised that friendship.

The following morning Lisa was the first up. She had no sooner made a cup of coffee when Janie came in, yawning and looking very sleepy.

'Morning Janie,' said Lisa, brightly, 'Coffee?'

'Yes please. You know me; I can't get going till I've had a coffee.'

'Janie,'

'Yeah?'

'I'm sorry for last night, I didn't mean to offend you.'

'Don't worry about it, water off a duck's back,' said Janie.

'No really, you've been good to me. I shouldn't have said those things.'

'I know what you meant Lisa, and I do appreciate the thought, but I'm too set in my ways. You've got your whole life in front of you. If that's what you want, go for it.' Janie had a genuine affection for Lisa.

'Thanks Janie. I remember what you said to me when I went down south, I'll always have a home here if I need it. Well I want you to remember the same thing, if you need anything just ask.' It was obvious that Janie was touched by Lisa's words. Janie rarely showed emotion; it was a defence measure she had developed. But what Lisa had said really touched her heartstrings.

'OK girl,' said Janie, 'now where's my coffee and toast?'

They spent the rest of the day quietly, just enjoying each other's company. Lisa had to catch a train at half past seven that evening, which would get her back in time for a good night's sleep before work the following evening. That evening they said their goodbyes and, as usual, Lisa shed a few tears. The journey went without any delays and Lisa was back in the flat for eleven o'clock. A quick shower, she thought, then off to bed. As tired as she was, her mind was running in overdrive; what a great opportunity the money had given her. It was just a matter of choosing what she wanted to do. Her three years of business studies were going to be useful to her in the near future.

The following evening, Lisa turned up at work as normal to find Angie racking the wine and Sue wiping over the tables. Lisa and Sue greeted each other. There was no acknowledgement from Angie, who just carried on racking the wine. Lisa looked over at Sue with an expression which asked 'What's up with her?' Sue raised her eyebrows in an unspoken 'don't know,' and carried on with her job. Lisa went through to the cloakroom, hung up her coat and, without wasting any time, went back into the bar and started work. It was quiet for a few minutes, then Angie suddenly turned round and said, 'Girls, I have to go out this evening for a couple of hours. I'll be as quick as I can, but it's very important, I've been putting it off for a few days now.'

'No problem Angie, take as long as you like,' said Lisa.

'I'll get off now, just in case it gets busy later, just joking.' It had become a standing joke the last couple of months since the two bars had opened on the High Street. The business had really suffered. Angie had already laid off the other two girls who worked in the wine bar and still there was barely enough work for the three of them.

'Couple of hours max. Bye,' called Angie, pulling the door shut behind her. Sue came over to Lisa, 'Am I glad to see you Lisa,' she said.

'Why, what's up?' asked Lisa.

'It's Angie; I think she's going round the twist. I've known her for a long time now but I've never seen her like this before, and I'll tell you something else, she's got it in for you.'

'Why, what have I done?' asked Lisa in amazement.

'You know that really good looking guy, Zak, the one she's been trying to chat up for the last three months.'

Lisa knew exactly who she meant. Zak Wright, twenty-five years old, successful stockbroker, tall, jet-black hair, drop-dead gorgeous. She had trouble keeping her eyes off him herself.

'Anyway,' said Sue, knowingly, 'he's been in here the last couple of nights and all he's said is 'Where's Lisa?' Turns out he only has eyes for you and Angie's had a face on her ever since.' Lisa wanted to smile but resisted.

'How's that my fault?' asked Lisa.

'Just keep your head down Lisa.'

'I will, don't worry.'

By ten o'clock there was still no sign of Angie. The bar had been quiet all night then, out of the blue, voices could be heard down the High Street, coming in the direction of the wine bar. Lisa and Angie looked at each other with raised eyebrows as a crowd of people came in the front door. Within the crowd Lisa instantly spotted Zak Wright; she could see his eyes were searching for her. As soon as he spotted her he came over. The rest of his party found tables and Sue went over to take their orders.

'Hello Lisa,' he said, smiling, 'for a minute I thought you'd left.'

'No, I just needed a few days off,' she replied.

'Good. You see I've wanted to ask you for some time now but didn't know what you would say.'

'What did you want to ask me?' asked Lisa, looking directly at him.

'I'm not normally this shy, it's just...' he hesitated; he was looking at her like a schoolboy with a crush on his teacher. 'Would you like to go out one evening with me?'

'When?' she immediately replied.

'Anytime you like, next time you get an evening off.'

'Yeah, I'd like that.'

'Great, I'm in here most nights. Just let me know when you're off and we'll go out.'

The rest of the evening went really well. Zak had brought a big crowd to the bar and in between serving customers Lisa chatted with him. By closing time they had taken more money in one night than they had all week. Zak was one of the last to leave. He pulled a card from his inside jacket pocket and passed it over to Lisa, 'Don't forget, as soon as you're free, give me a shout. Bye,' he smiled and left.

A short time later Angie arrived. Lisa and Sue had already locked the front door. Angie tried her key but the latch was down. Irate at not being able to get into her own wine bar she began banging on the glass door. Sue came running from the back of the bar, 'Hang on, the latch is down.' She opened the door.

'What do you think you're doing?' shouted Angie.

'We didn't think you were coming back, so we locked up.' Angie had obviously been drinking. 'Well, I'm back now,' she barged her way into the bar, forcing Sue to take a step backwards. 'Where's Lisa?'

'She's out back getting some bottles to rack up.'

'Little miss perfect,' sneered Angie, 'she'd be working in a supermarket if it wasn't for me.'

'That's not very fair Angie, she's worked really hard tonight.' Angie staggered behind the bar, picked up an open bottle of wine and took a huge slug on it, slamming the bottle down onto the bar. Her eye caught sight of the card on the bar; she picked it up and read it out loud, 'Zak Wright, Hennessey & Co., Stock Brokers... Why that little tart.' Sue stood up, unnerved by Angie's behaviour. From the hallway, the sound of bottles chinking in their carrier broke the silence and Lisa came through to the bar with the new stock.

'Hi Angie, we had a good night tonight.'

'I bet you did.' Lisa instantly picked up on the tone of Angie's voice.

'What's wrong, Angie?' she asked, resting the bottles onto the bar.

'What's wrong? You're what's wrong. You think you're so perfect,' she flicked the card in Lisa's direction and Lisa picked it up.

'Oh, he gave me that tonight.'

'I bet he did, and what else is he giving you tonight?'

'What's that supposed to mean?' asked Lisa.

'You're always acting all prim and proper, little miss perfect, but I know what you're really like.'

'I don't have to take that from you,' said Lisa. Angie gulped again from the wine bottle then hurled it to the floor just in front of Lisa's feet, shards of glass flew everywhere and Lisa instinctively turned away covering her face. 'That's it, I'm out of here.' Lisa looked over at Sue. Sue instantly looked down at the floor; she couldn't afford to lose her job and had chosen her side. 'I'll be back tomorrow for my wages,' said Lisa.

'Don't bother,' Angie replied. She opened the till, counted out a hundred pounds and threw it on the bar.

'On second thoughts,' said Lisa, 'you can keep it. I don't need your money.' She went down to the cloakroom, picked up her coat and, without saying a word, walked back through the bar and closed the door behind her. The cool night air hit her face and she gasped for a minute, then began walking up the road in the direction of her flat. Fighting back tears she thought 'I'll have my day with that woman, just wait and see.'

She had been walking a few minutes, still reeling from the encounter with Angie, when a white BMW pulled up beside her; she quickened her pace. She heard the car door open and almost broke into a run when someone called her name. Looking over her shoulder she could see Zak Wright walking around the car and stepping onto the pavement 'I'm going that way, can I give you a lift?'

'I only live a little way down the road,' replied Lisa, relieved that it was someone she knew. He could tell from her voice that she was upset.

'Is everything OK?' He walked towards her and could see that she was close to tears. 'What's happened?'

'Oh nothing, I'm just being silly, I've fallen out with Angie and won't be working there anymore.'

Zak looked down at her legs. 'Lisa, your legs ... you're bleeding. How did this happen?' Tears rolled down Lisa's face and she couldn't speak. 'Please, get in the car and I'll get you home.' He put his arm round her and walked her back to his car. Less than two minutes later he was opening the car door to help her out. 'I don't want to be forward but I'd rather not leave you till I know you are OK.'

'Thanks Zak, but I'll be OK,' said Lisa.

'No, I insist. A couple of those cuts look like they have glass in, and you may need to go to the hospital.' With that, Lisa opened the door; Zak followed her up the stairs, closing the door behind him. 'You sit yourself down. Have you got a first-aid kit?'

'I haven't, it's one of those things I keep saying I'll buy but never do.'

'No problem, I have one in the car.' Zak dashed back down the stairs out to his car and got his first-aid kit. 'Right, let's have a look,' he knelt down in front of Lisa. 'Now tell me, how did this happen?'

'Angie has a bit of a temper,' Lisa replied.

'What, she did this?'

'Well not directly – she threw a bottle on the floor and as it smashed bits of glass flew up.' Zak checked the wounds on Lisa's legs and she winced.

'Sorry,' said Zak, 'I think that's it, just two small pieces. You were lucky. I don't think they'll leave any marks.'

'Thanks Zak, I appreciate your help.'

'Only too pleased. Right, I'll make you a hot drink then let you get some sleep.' Lisa smiled at him. 'Don't you move, I can find my way round a kitchen, I get plenty of practice.' A few minutes later he returned with a cup of coffee. 'I guessed white no sugar.'

'You guessed right,' said Lisa.

'OK,' said Zak, 'I'm not going to intrude on your privacy any longer. If you don't mind, I'll drop in on you tomorrow, just to make sure you're OK.'

'You don't need to Zak.'

'I don't need to, but I want to, if that's OK?'

'Thanks' said Lisa; she did want him to come back.

'I'll see myself out.' As he got to the top of the stairs he turned, 'I'll drop in after work about six.' They smiled affectionately at each other for a moment. 'Bye,' he said. Lisa heard the front door close. It was late and without the daytime traffic and street noise she heard his car starting and listened to the sound of the engine as it disappeared into the distance. She sat back with her coffee. The fiasco at the wine bar was suddenly not so important. All that was on her mind at the moment was the man who had just shown her more true affection than any man had ever done in her entire life.

13

The landlady

The next day, true to his word, Zak turned up at exactly six o'clock. Dressed in a suave Savile Row suit, he looked the epitome of sophistication. Lisa had spent the day pampering herself in preparation for his arrival. A long soak in the bath had taken away the angriness in the cuts on her legs. Zak had left his first-aid kit the night before and Lisa used a few plasters to cover the wounds so that she could wear jeans.

'How are you today, Lisa?'

'Fine thanks, hardly any sign of the cuts,' she replied brightly.

'Good. Do you feel up to going out for a meal this evening?'

'I'd rather stay in,' said Lisa.

'Oh, fine.' Zak looked disappointed.

'Fancy staying in with me? I could make us both a meal.' Zak's face instantly lit up. 'What about if I treat us to a takeaway instead, save you any bother?'

'That sounds even better,' said Lisa.

Zak walked over to the Chinese and picked up a meal. They spent the rest of the evening getting to know each other; they had so much in common it was frightening. Lisa knew that she would always have secrets from him and when he asked her questions about her past she would simply make out all her upbringing had been with Janie. Of course there was never any mention about what she and Janie had done to pay their way; if he had known that, Lisa felt sure it would be the last time she would see him. As far as he was concerned, her parents died when she was young. Zak glanced at his watch, 'It's eleven-thirty – I'll have to make a move – I've got an early meeting in the morning. Thank you.'

'What for?' asked Lisa.

'For your company, it's been the nicest evening I've had in a long time.' He took her hand and gently kissed it. They both stood up. It was one of those uncomfortable silences. As they stood looking into each other's eyes, no words were required. Zak took her in his arms and kissed her. Lisa had never experienced such a feeling of pure passion. Her body wanted him to stay the night, but at the same time she knew it would have spoiled everything; the time wasn't right. He said goodbye and left.

Over the next few weeks they went out on a few occasions. Zak was busy at work and asked Lisa to be patient with him until he had closed a couple of very important deals, after that he would treat her big time. Lisa had been keeping a close eye on Korky's. Every day she would either take a walk down there or, if she was out with Zak, ask him to drive past very slowly so she could have a good look at who was working there. It was obvious that the place was not doing much business; they had stopped opening midweek and at weekends it was virtually empty. Angie had taken back one of the girls she had laid off and Sue was still doing the same old chores. The way it was going it wouldn't be long before it shut down. Angie had clearly given up trying to reinvent the place.

Lisa decided to contact Simon Clark at Craddock & Co.; it was time to make the money work for her. She told him the name of the business and emphasised how important it was to her that if it went up for sale or into receivership, if it was financially viable she wanted to purchase it, but that her name must not be used in correspondence with the owners.

One Friday evening, Lisa had arranged to go out for a drink with Zak. He was a little late, which was unlike him. When he finally arrived he made his apologies and off they went to a pub called The Drum and Monkey, it was one of the first places Zak had taken her to. It was a nice, quiet little pub, just outside of town. Zak looked a little edgy. 'Is everything all right Zak?' Lisa asked.

'Yeah, remember I told you about those deals I had to close?' Lisa nodded. 'Well, I closed them.'

'Well done,' smiled Lisa. Zak went into his inside pocket, pulled out an envelope and placed it on the table.

'What's that?' she asked.

'Have a look.'

Lisa picked up the envelope and pulled out what looked like tickets. She read the attached slip, 'Two return tickets to New York.' She looked up at Zak, 'Does this mean we're actually going to New York?'

'It sure does.' Lisa leapt out of her seat and threw her arms around his neck.

'I said I would treat you,' he laughed.

'I know, but New York! When are we going?'

'Three weeks today, I've got a fortnight off.' Lisa was so excited she couldn't wait. Over the next two weeks she spent a small fortune on her wardrobe. She had entrusted Simon Clark to keep an eye on Korky's and focused solely on the holiday in New York. It was just a week before the flight, and something suddenly crossed Lisa's mind: she hadn't got a passport. How was she going to tell Zak? He would think she was so stupid. That evening he was coming round and she would have to tell him then. Zak arrived just before eight o'clock. 'Hi Lisa, you alright?'

'Yes thanks,' she paused for a split-second, 'Zak, I've messed up.'

'What do you mean?'

'I haven't got a passport.'

He went quiet for what seemed ages; Lisa thought he would be mad at her.

'No problem,' he said calmly, 'we can go to Peterborough. It means we'll have to wait a few hours while it's processed, but we can get it sorted out.' Lisa was visibly relieved.

On the Tuesday before they were due to fly out, Zak managed to swing a day off work. All the necessary forms and documentation had been completed and they set off for Peterborough. Once they had arrived it didn't take long to locate the Passport Control Administration offices. In all, they waited just under four hours, but when the passport was finally passed over the counter Lisa jumped for joy. Now the trip was well and truly on and they could hardly wait.

Jimmy was standing at the serving hatch passing trays of what the institution called food to other inmates. Through good behaviour he had landed himself a nice little number serving up food, which was prepared by outside contractors. As a way of rehabilitating the not so violent inmates, they would give them trivial little jobs that made them feel important. But the truth was that Jimmy didn't give a shit about the job; he was just pretending to show willing to convince the authorities that the rehabilitation plan was working. Dr Phelps appeared to be taking the bait; every now and then he would catch Phelps observing him from a distance. Jimmy would be careful not to make eye contact with him, but would carry on as if he hadn't seen him, hoping to improve the doctor's evaluations.

It was always lights out by ten o'clock. Jimmy had got to like these moments. The first twenty minutes or so were annoying; cries and screams from deranged inmates facing their demons in the dark. But

Jimmy had no such trouble; he would just visualise Lisa in his mind's eye and take every day and night as it came.

Lisa stood at the window waiting. Zak was due to pick her up at eight o'clock prompt and she couldn't believe that by the same time that evening she would be in New York. She glanced at her watch: 7:58. Just then, Zak's white BMW pulled up outside the flat and she ran down the stairs to meet him. 'Hi Lisa, you ready?'

'You bet, I can't wait.'

'We've got plenty of time, but I thought we could check in early and have a good look round the duty-free shops.'

'Sounds good to me.'

Zak carried her case down and put it in the car. Lisa locked up the flat, jumped in the car and they sped off towards the airport. The traffic was quite heavy, normally it would only take about thirty minutes from Lisa's to the airport, but on this occasion it took the best part of an hour. Once they had checked in they went through to the departure lounge. It was the first time Lisa had ever been into an airport and she was so excited. After some time exploring the shops, their flight was called. As they approached the departure gate Lisa started to get a little frightened. She held on to Zak's hand a little tighter than normal. 'You all right Lisa?' he asked, 'You look worried.'

'I'll be all right once we're up,' she replied, nervously. Everything went as scheduled. In just over eight hours they arrived at John F. Kennedy Airport. The thing that stuck in her mind most of all was the sight of the Twin Towers as the plane approached, dominating the New York skyline. The next two weeks were the best of her life. Zak spared no expense when it came to sightseeing: Statue of Liberty, Twin Towers, Madison Square Garden to name just a few. The hotel was first-class, right next to Times Square. Every evening he would take her to the most romantic restaurants then return to the hotel to make love as she had never experienced. She didn't want the holiday to finish, it was all and more than she had ever dreamed of.

They arrived back on a Thursday evening; it was damp and dark and they were both jetlagged. As they pulled up at Lisa's flat, tired and cold, Lisa suggested that Zak should stay the night, an offer he gratefully accepted.

The following morning as Lisa woke she realised Zak wasn't there. 'He didn't have to work today,' she thought to herself.

Just then the door opened and Zak came in with a tray in his hands; he had prepared Lisa a full breakfast, 'Hope you don't mind your eggs fried?'

'How did you do that? There was nothing in the fridge,' said Lisa.

'Mini-market underneath us, very useful store that.' He placed the tray on her lap, leaned down and kissed her, 'Thanks for the last two weeks, it's been brilliant.'

'Thank you,' said Lisa.

'I've put your post on the tray. I'm going to have to go into work for an hour or two, there's a couple of things I have to sort out, but I'll be back by lunchtime.' He leaned down again to kiss her. She put her arms around his neck, kissed him, then held him tight. 'Bye.'

Lisa was eating her breakfast, flicking through the post between mouthfuls. It was mostly junk mail but one letter from Craddock & Co. caught her attention. She tore it open. It was from Simon Clark concerning Korky's. It turned out that Korky's was up for sale and he needed her to contact him as soon as possible. She looked at the postmark on the envelope; it was dated the previous week.

'Shit!' she said out loud. She leaped out of bed and dashed into the bathroom; as soon as she was washed and dressed she would contact him. Lisa went into the mini-market and after a brief chat about the holiday with the lady behind the counter, she left the shop with enough small change for quite a hefty phone call. She dialled the number on the top of the letter; it rang out, 'Good morning, Craddock & Co., Nicky speaking. Can I help you?'

'Hello Nicky, it's Lisa Dean.' They exchanged pleasantries but Lisa was anxious to get down to business. 'I've received a letter from Simon asking me to contact him as soon as possible.'

'Yes Miss Dean, you're hard to get hold of. I'll put you straight through.' Nicky transferred the call to Simon's office.

'Miss Dean, great to hear from you. I must admit I've been panicking a bit. I've been in touch with the owner's solicitors at the wine bar. I think from the sound of things the owners are in financial difficulty, but that's just reading between the lines of course. I think it's ripe for the taking, but there are lots of things to discuss, as it is a substantial amount of money. When can you get into the office?'

Lisa stopped to think. 'How urgent are we talking?' she asked.

'If you really want this, we have to move.' Lisa glanced at her watch; it was just after half past ten.

'I'll be with you after lunch.'

Simon looked at the receiver in amazement. 'You really must want this, Miss Dean. I'll see you after lunch. Bye for now.' Lisa put the receiver down and dashed back to the flat. If she got a cab to Euston station she could be on the 11:30 train.

It was a rush, but by half past eleven Lisa was boarding the train. Provided there were no delays she would be in the offices of Craddock & Co. by two o'clock. The journey seemed to take forever; the excitement was growing with every minute she got closer to her destination. Just to think, in a matter of weeks she could be the proud owner of her own wine bar. With a smile on her face she thought, 'I can't wait to see Angie's face when I take over the keys for Korky's.'

The train pulled into New Street station just before a quarter to two. A ten-minute walk across the city centre and she would arrive right on time. As she walked up to the entrance at Craddock & Co., a voice called out from behind her, it was Simon Clark arriving back from lunch. She looked back just as he reached her. 'Hello Miss Dean, great to see you. I've been trying to contact you for some time now.'

'I've been away on holiday,' said Lisa.

'Somewhere nice I hope?' he stood back and let Lisa enter the building first. They walked up the stairs and into the reception area, where Nicky greeted them.

'You've had quite a few calls over lunch Mr Clark, I've left the messages and contact numbers on your desk.'

'Thanks Nicky, no disruptions for the next couple of hours please, we have a lot of things to discuss.'

They went into Clark's office; he pulled up a chair for Lisa close to the desk and walked over to a filing cabinet.

'You know, Miss Dean...'

'Please call me Lisa,' she always felt uncomfortable when people addressed her formally.

'Lisa, you are the only person I know that doesn't have a telephone at home.'

'I know,' said Lisa, a smile forming on her face, 'I keep meaning to do something about that. In the next few days I'll contact your secretary, just as soon as I have a number.'

'The reason I say that,' said Clark, 'is that I will have to contact you at short notice over the next few weeks, so the sooner the better really.' He walked back over to the desk with a very large file and sat down, 'Right Lisa, Korky's wine bar is on the market for a hundred thousand – that's just the business you understand. With premises, which include a two bedroom flat above, you're looking at two hundred and fifty thousand. The stock, fixtures and fittings will add ten to fifteen thousand extra. I think with the right marketing it could be a viable business. I checked the business name, Korky's, and it is included in the sale.'

'Mr Clark,' Lisa began,

'Please, Simon,' he returned the informality gesture.

'It is absolutely imperative that the owners don't know I am attempting to buy this business. If they find out it's me, they will either put the price up or choose another buyer.'

'You must have had quite a falling out with them,' said Simon.

'Let's just say we don't get on anymore.'

'OK, well, I have a feeling they are looking for a quick sale. I think you should be looking at offering the asking price, to include the stock and fixtures. The price was a little low, and there has been a lot of interest in it, so if you really want it we have to put the offer in ASAP.'

'Simon, it's my dream to own this business,' said Lisa. He could see that she was absolutely serious.

'OK, so now we have to decide how we are going to finance this venture and try to make that dream come true. I have one or two suggestions about how we can do this, but the final decision is yours. Right, let's get down to business.' Over the next two hours Simon showed Lisa various ways to finance the venture from cashing shares to mortgaging, even considering selling other properties they had acquired for her over the last four years. Lisa thought the total asking price was ironic, considering that was how much money she had initially walked into Craddock & Co. with in the first place. The information Lisa was being given would have taken her days if not weeks to evaluate. He hadn't let her down so far, so she again decided to give Simon a free hand with her finances, and do whatever was necessary to secure the deal.

That evening she caught the train back to London; it was time to come straight with Zak. Waiting for him to arrive, she paced from room to room, unable to settle. The doorbell rang and she rushed to the window; Zak's car was parked outside. As she opened the door to let him in, Zak could see that she was worried. 'Is everything all right?' he asked.

'Of course it is, come on up, I have something to tell you.' Zak followed her up the stairs. She offered him a coffee, which he refused. Lisa could see the concern on his face and thought it best to get straight to the point.

'Sorry I wasn't here when you came back earlier, only I had an important letter in the post and had to go to Birmingham this afternoon.'

'Is everything all right?' he asked.

'Yes, in fact it couldn't be better. You see, I haven't told you everything about me.' Zak's look of worry intensified. Lisa knew there were some things that she could never tell him, but at least this was a start. 'The first thing I want to tell you is that I've put in a bid for Korky's.' Zak suddenly sat up straight, eyes wide.

'How the hell are you going to finance that?' he asked in amazement.

'That's something else I want to tell you. When my parents died, some insurance policies automatically matured. Well, the money from them and the rest of their estates was put into a trust fund for me. When I was of age I invested the money. The investments went pretty well, in fact they went exceptionally well, and that's how I'm going to finance Korky's.' Zak let out a sigh of relief.

'Thank God for that, I thought for a minute you were going to tell me there was someone else and dump me.'

Lisa laughed, 'Don't be silly; you're all I want. I just didn't know how to tell you about the money, especially after you spent a fortune on me in New York.'

'That was my treat,' said Zak.

'Yeah, well next time it will be my treat.' Zak stood up, took her in his arms and gently kissed her.

Over the next couple of months everything went to plan and Lisa's relationship with Zak went from strength to strength. They were becoming inseparable and Zak would spend most nights at Lisa's flat. Lisa had decided that when the purchase of the business was finalised, she would move into the flat above Korky's and, fingers crossed, so would Zak. The flat hadn't been used for some time and the girls in the bar used to say it was not in good order. Lisa didn't mind and just hoped that a lick of paint and some new furniture would sort it out. Now that Lisa was looking at the place from a financial point of view, she could see that Angie really had very poor business sense.

It was Monday morning and Lisa and Zak had had a quiet weekend relaxing around the flat. Zak was just about to leave for work when the recently installed phone rang. He picked it up, 'Hello?'

'Could I speak to Miss Dean please?'

'Yeah, who shall I say it is?'

'Simon Clark, Craddock & Co.,' straight away Zak knew how important this call was to Lisa.

'Lisa, it's Simon Clark.'

Lisa came dashing out of the bathroom, wrapping herself in a towel. She had literally jumped out the shower without even turning it off. 'Hello Simon, how are you?' she gasped.

'Very well, thank you Lisa, I've got some good news. I'm pleased to tell you that as soon as you sign the documents I have on my desk you will be the proud owner of Korky's wine bar, in its entirety.'

'YES!' shouted Lisa. She turned and threw her arms around Zak's neck.

'Good news then?' laughed Zak.

'It's mine! It's mine! I've just got to sign the paperwork and it's mine!'

'That's great Lisa, I'm so happy for you,' said Zak, beaming.

Lisa put the phone back to her ear, 'When do you need to see me, Simon?'

'The sooner you sign the sooner the deal goes through.'

'I'll be with you at lunchtime,' said Lisa.

Simon laughed, 'I had an idea you were going to say that. Till lunch then. Bye and congratulations.'

Lisa was overwhelmed with joy. She could not remember being this happy. Everything was coming together.

Later that morning Lisa caught a train to Birmingham and completed the relevant documents. Simon had managed to get the stock included in the asking price, and, as the negotiations had taken place between the solicitors, there was nothing to make Angie suspect that the new owner was Lisa. It was just a matter now of waiting for the money to change hands. Lisa asked Simon if it was possible for him to arrange for her to accept the keys from the previous owner, just in case there were alarm systems and other things she needed to know about the building. Simon knew exactly why she wanted to accept the keys; it was her day of revenge and she was looking forward to it. That evening when Lisa arrived home she took a walk up to Korky's and stood across the road. The bar was all in darkness, as it had been for the last few months, but that was going to change.

One month later to the day, Lisa was sat in the flat eating toast and drinking a large mug of coffee. Zak had gone to work and Lisa was contemplating what to do with herself till he got home when the phone rang. It was Simon Clark. Everything was in place for the bar to be hers by two o'clock that day.

'I've arranged for the previous owner to give you a walk round the premises at two o'clock,' said Clark.

'That's great, Simon,' said Lisa with an enormous smile over her face.

'If you have any problems just call me, OK?'

'I won't have any problems – I've waited a long time for this and I'm going to enjoy every minute of it.'

'OK Lisa, congratulations.'

'Thanks for all you've done, Simon, I really do appreciate it.'

Lisa dressed carefully. When she went in that bar she was going in as the manager and wanted to look the part. She called Zak, who said he was on his way home and wouldn't miss this for the world.

Just after two o'clock, Lisa put on her coat. 'You ready, Zak?'

'You bet I am.' Lisa locked the flat, Zak started the car and they sat there with the engine running.

'OK, darling?' asked Zak. He looked at Lisa and saw an expression on her face he had never seen before. He said nothing, but this was not the gentle face of the girl he had fallen in love with. The cruel act she was about to perform on this poor, probably bankrupt woman, was actually giving her pleasure. They pulled up outside the wine bar. The lights were on but there was no sign of anyone inside. Lisa pushed the door; it opened. As she walked in and looked around memories came flooding back. Not the bad ones but the good memories; the first night she worked there, how proud she felt after that first shift. Just then Angie appeared from the cloakroom passageway. She stood still and stared at Lisa, her bottom jaw agape. 'Woah, what do you want?'

'I think you know,' said Lisa. Angie shook her head from side to side.

'I'm here to show the new owners around. You couldn't afford this place.'

'I could and I have.' They stood in silence.

'Oh I see,' said Angie, after a moment or two, 'you just got me here to gloat.'

Lisa expected to have enjoyed this but she didn't. She remembered Angie as a very strong woman and what she was seeing now was somebody whose pride had been taken from them. It wasn't anything like she expected. Lisa desperately wanted to resolve the situation.

'No, I'm not here to gloat, I just wanted to say I have no hard feelings, even if you did treat me badly on that last evening I worked here.'

Angie's head dropped. 'I can't change the past, but for what it's worth I felt terrible when you'd gone. I wanted to shout after you, but my foolish pride wouldn't let me. Still, what's done is done.' Angie walked over to Lisa and gave her a bunch of keys. 'Good luck Lisa, I hope you have as many happy years here as I did.'

'Good luck to you too. Come in and see us some time,' replied Lisa. Angie smiled and Lisa returned the gesture. Angie walked out quietly closing the door behind her.

Lisa stood in the middle of the bar area scanning the room. Zak stared straight at her. As they had left the flat he had seen a hardness in her that, if the truth were known, he hadn't liked. It was the first time he had ever doubted her nature. But when the time had come for Lisa to unleash the resentment she had for Angie, all the anger had turned to kindness.

'Lisa,' she turned to look at him and smiled, 'I love you,' she felt the emotion building inside her; no man had ever told her that.

'I love you too,' she said and they walked over to each other and embraced for what seemed like hours.

'I was going to ask you to move in with me when I get the flat upstairs sorted,' said Lisa eventually.

'Only on one account,' said Zak.

'Go on then, name it.'

'You marry me.' Lisa took a huge gulp of air and stepped backwards.

'Are you serious?'

'I've never been more serious in my life,' replied Zak.

'Well, in that case, yes I will.' Zak put his arms round her waist, picked her up and spun her round. As he placed her back on her feet, she looked at him inquisitively, 'Lisa Wright, how does that sound?'

'Sounds fine to me,' said Zak, 'just fine.'

14

The family way

As time went by, Korky's became a thriving business. Lisa had to take on staff, one of whom was Sue, the woman who Lisa had worked with the first day she set foot in Korky's. Sue knew the set-up there and Lisa thought it was a good move to take her back on. It turned out to be a very good move. If Lisa needed any time to herself she knew the wine bar was in good hands. The three other girls who worked there were all paying their way through university; again they were very reliable. If they had a really busy night in the week, which was becoming more and more frequent, Lisa knew she could call on them to help. It had been nearly five years now since the bar reopened. It had taken nearly a month from the day she took the keys from Angie to get it up and running again. In the short time the bar had been closed the decoration had deteriorated to the point where if customers had come in they wouldn't have stayed long. But now, five years on, it was a credit to Lisa. People came from all over London to sample the wines. Her knowledge of wines had continued to grow steadily and she insisted that all her staff educated themselves concerning the wines they sold. Usually, after closing at the weekends, Lisa would open a few bottles of wine and let the girls sample them to educate their palates; the staff appreciated it.

The flat above Korky's had taken a little longer to sort out. Lisa had spent over ten thousand pounds refitting it with a new kitchen, bathroom and just about everything had been ripped out and replaced. Lisa and Zak had decided they would get married when the flat was completed; then and only then would they move in together. It took nearly eighteen months to complete the project, but when it was finished it was superb. They married at the local church. Fifty members of Zak's family attended, including uncles, cousins and second cousins. Lisa had six people on her side of the church; Janie, Simon Clark and the four girls from the wine bar. Zak's parents thought it a little strange that Lisa had no family, but that was how it was. It didn't take long to work out where they would have the reception; they had invited some of the regular customers and it went with a bang. Zak arranged the honeymoon and kept the destination secret until the reception; he had arranged another week in New York. He told Lisa that it was in New York that he realised he loved her and wanted to spend the rest of his life with her; it brought tears to her eyes.

On returning from New York, Lisa threw herself into work at Korky's. Zak continued to work at the stockbroker company, Hennessey & Co. Lisa had told him he didn't need to put himself under that sort of stress but Zak said it was all that he knew. Lisa got the feeling he didn't want to be a kept man, not that he ever would be, but she had to respect his feelings.

It was midweek and Lisa was behind the bar. Sue and one of the girls, Holly, a psychology student on her gap year, were clearing tables and engaging in light-hearted banter with the customers. Lisa was deep in thought; Sue had noticed she hadn't been her chatty self all night. Sue collected a few glasses and went back to the bar. 'You all right, Lisa?' she asked. Startled, Lisa looked up.

'Sorry Sue, did you say something?'

'Yeah, are you OK? You're not yourself.'

'I'm fine … just got a few things on my mind.' Lisa carried on working. Not wanting to pry, Sue turned and walked back to the tables. A few minutes later, Lisa called her back over. 'Do you mind if I pop out for ten minutes? I just have to go to the chemist before it closes.'

'No problem, are you sure you are all right?'

'Yeah fine, honestly.' She grabbed her coat and on the way out exchanged friendly conversation with the customers, always trying to be the amiable hostess. She got to the shop just as it was about to close and bought a pregnancy testing kit. 'Good luck,' said the assistant, 'whichever way you want it to be.' Lisa turned and smiled, then went back to Korky's. For the rest of the evening she could think of nothing else but the test kit in her bag. She and Zak had not discussed children but the fact they had not been using any form of contraception perhaps meant Zak had no problem with the prospect, but she couldn't be sure. Lisa loved the idea of having a child. Realistically, the timing was perfect; they were still both young and financially secure. The flat above the wine bar was not an ideal place to bring up a child, but they hadn't intended to stay there forever anyway. At the end of the evening, Lisa sent the girls home as soon as the bulk of the clearing up had been done, telling them that she would finish off. Lisa locked the doors, set the alarm and went up the rear stairs to the flat, clutching her bag with the test kit inside. Zak had fallen asleep watching the television. She left him where he was and went through to the bedroom, quickly changed into her nightgown, picked up the test kit and went to the bathroom. With trembling hands she followed the instructions then put down the toilet lid and sat waiting. The next three minutes felt like three hours. Finally it was time. She peered into the small window on the device: 'Pregnant.' She stood for a couple of minutes looking at it then, with the device in her hand, she went into the living room where Zak was still fast asleep. Standing over him, tapping the device on the palm of her hand, she wondered whether to wake him or leave it until the morning. 'No time like the present,' she thought, and shook his shoulder. 'Zak, wake up, I have something to show you.' Slowly Zak woke.

'Hi darling, what time is it?' he asked, sleepily.

'Just after twelve. I've just locked up. Look.' Lisa passed him the test kit.

He jumped to his feet. 'You, you're telling me you're pre...pregnant?' Lisa nodded. Zak took Lisa round the waist and picked her up in the air. The look on his face said it all. He spun around holding her high in the air. Suddenly, as quickly as he had picked her up he put her back on her feet, 'God what am I doing?! You're pregnant! Quick, sit down, are you OK?'

'Zak, calm down – I'm pregnant not ill!' she laughed, overwhelmed with happiness and relief.

They lay in bed in the darkness, each thinking the other was asleep. It was quite some time later before they finally fell asleep, both wondering what the future held for them.

Jimmy had been incarcerated for ten years. Physically, time had been good to him. His features hadn't changed much – he was greying a little round the temples, but anybody that had been in that place for ten years was lucky to get away with just a little grey hair. Jimmy had sustained a bad cut just in front of his right ear, when a particularly violent inmate had somehow managed to get hold of a plastic knife and, as Jimmy had placed a meal on his tray, he attempted to force the knife down Jimmy's ear. He had missed the ear and stuck the knife in Jimmy's face, just forward of his ear. After several stitches and a day on the hospital wing he was right as rain. But he would always have the scar as a reminder. Dr Phelps knew it was an unprovoked attack and had requested Jimmy be moved to a safer environment. Jimmy had been with them for ten years without so much as saying boo to a goose and Phelps was convinced that with continued counselling and support he could rehabilitate Jimmy. Maybe one day he could even reintroduce him to society.

Phelps arranged for Jimmy to have an evaluation. The timing was planned to coincide with a visit to the hospital by two leading institution governors. After letting them know of his success in rehabilitating Jimmy they just had to sit in on the evaluation. He tipped off Jimmy as to how important these men were, and implied that they could arrange for him to go to a low security hospital, where the threat of violence would be much lower. Jimmy wasn't stupid and his performance was impeccable. A few weeks later he was transferred to Shire Oaks Hospital, a step towards getting back into society. Everything was going to plan.

He lay on his bed daydreaming. Through the ten years of his imprisonment he had not considered that things outside had changed. It hadn't occurred to him that Lisa could have married or even considered having children with somebody else; as far as he was concerned they had a deal, and even if he was in there for twenty-five years, a deal was a deal.

Lisa made an appointment with her doctor the next day and it was confirmed that she was pregnant; it was still early days, so they both decided not to say anything until she was at least three months. It was a long time to keep this sort of thing quiet, but they decided to try. They lasted about a week. Lisa phoned Janie, who was over the moon. Zak phoned his parents; as it was to be their first grandchild they thought if they kept it a secret too long they would never be forgiven. Before long, everyone that came into Korky's was congratulating them, even people they didn't know.

Three months later, Lisa and Zak were at the appointment for her first scan.

'This might be a bit cold at first,' said the midwife applying gel to Lisa's abdomen. She started the scan; the image on the monitor looked nothing more than a blur to Zak but the midwife was smiling broadly. Zak and Lisa looked at each other, then back at he midwife.

'By the look on your face everything is OK, I take it?' said Zak.

'Oh yes, I do love my job, especially at times like this. Tell me, do either of you have twins in your family?' Lisa and Zak looked at each other, stunned. 'Well, you do now. Congratulations both, you're going to be the proud parents of twins.'

That evening they decided it was time to start looking for a house. Zak knew how much Korky's meant to Lisa, and besides, it brought in a lot more money than his job at Hennessey's did. Out of the blue, Zak came up with the idea that he would look after the children. He'd had enough of the constant stress from his job in the city and it made sense; if they were going to build the business, it was the only way. Lisa thought it was a mad idea at first, but soon there would be four of them and money would be much more important.

They sat on the sofa relaxing after a busy night in the bar; they had just locked up, having cleared away all the bottles and washed the glasses. 'I was thinking, Zak,' said Lisa, 'what if we get Simon to look for houses for us?' They had little time for house hunting and were aware that they would not get much for their money if they stayed local to the bar.

'Good idea. There'll be a charge though, it's not really what you pay him to do.'

'Well, it is and it isn't. It's still an investment and at the end of the day that's what he does for me.'

'Give him a call in the morning,' said Zak, 'and see what he says.' The long hours in the city, followed by helping out in the bar, were catching up on him. His eyes were about to close at any moment.

'Zak,' suddenly he was awake again, 'I was thinking, if we got a house outside London, it would be hard for me to come into work every day, so what about giving Sue the position of manageress? She could take care of the everyday running of the bar and I could come in a couple of times a week to sort out all the stock and check everything is OK. I'd only be a phone call away.'

'Now that is a good idea,' said Zak. 'It would give you a little time to relax, because I think over the next few months you're going to need it and I can't imagine what things will be like when the twins are born'

'I'll have a word with her tomorrow lunchtime. Come on Zak, let's go to bed – you look shattered.' Almost as soon as their heads hit the pillows, they were both fast asleep.

Sue had been working in Korky's on and off for nine years. In all the time Lisa had known her she hadn't been late once and was completely reliable. Lisa felt she would be leaving her much loved business in safe hands. Korky's had been opening at lunchtimes for the past two years. It was the same faces most days – people who worked locally – and business was good.

'Can I have a word, Sue?' Lisa called Sue over. 'You know I mentioned that Zak and I were going to move out of the flat and get a house?' Sue nodded. 'Well, we've started looking.'

'That's great,' replied Sue. 'Whereabouts have you been looking?'

'That's the problem. Prices around here for a nice family house with a decent garden are so high, we'll have to go further afield and I'm not going to be able to make it into the bar every day.'

'Oh, I see.' Sue looked disappointed, was she about to hear bad news?

'So I was going to ask if you'd like to become the manageress here at Korky's?' Sue wasn't expecting that and her face was full of excitement.

'Me, in charge?'

'I think you'd be perfect for the job,' replied Lisa.

'You honestly think I could do it?'

'Sue, you know how much Korky's means to me. Do you think I'd offer you this position if I didn't think you could handle it? We can take on another member of staff and then over the next couple of months I'll show you all the things that I do in respect of the general day-to-day running. Before you know what's what, you'll be running the show.'

'I can't believe it,' said Sue, 'manageress – are you sure Lisa?'

'I'm positive, Sue.'

'Then I'd love to.'

Over the next few weeks Sue became a different person. Rather than just doing her general work, she was taking an interest in everything. It was as if suddenly she had a real goal in her life and Lisa was confident that she had made the right decision.

Simon had been hard at work searching for suitable properties; he had found a few that might interest them, but the location was the problem – just how far were they willing to move from London? He decided to put all the property details in the post and see how they reacted. The following day Lisa and Zak received the details; they were all nice, but one stood out from the rest. Although it was little further from London than they had planned to move, it sounded perfect. It was in a small village near Oxford called Stanton Harcourt. Most of the properties in the village were thatched, giving the whole place a lovely quiet and tranquil feeling. It would be a lovely place to bring up children. Simon arranged for them to view the property. Sue said she would look after the bar, so just before lunchtime the following Friday Lisa and Zak drove up to Oxford. It didn't take long to find the village, which was well signposted. As they drove through the village, Lisa was already falling in love with the place: the village green, country pub, children playing in the schoolyard, it was almost like a dream. They stopped outside the house. From the outside it was everything they expected. They were a little early and the estate agent had not yet arrived. As the house had vacant possession, they decided to go round the side of it and take a look at the garden; the details said there was half an acre of land at the rear. The former owners must have had green fingers as the lawns and flowerbeds were in impeccable condition. There were one or two mature trees to the right of the garden and a small copse to the left, which made the garden nice and secluded. They heard a car pull up on the drive; Zak went round to see if it was the estate agent. A blue soft-top BMW was parked on the drive. As Zak approached the door opened and a woman stepped out, dressed in a very smart blue suit and her hair and make-up giving the impression that she had just walked out of a salon. She walked over to Zak, a cat-like grace about her movement.

'Hello there, Mr Wright I presume?'

'Pleased to meet you,' replied Zak. She offered her hand and Zak shook it.

'Helen Cartwright, Banner and Tate Estate Agents. I'm sorry I wasn't here when you arrived.'

'That's OK,' said Zak, 'we thought we'd have a look around the back and very nice it was too.' Lisa appeared from the side of the house and the estate agent introduced herself. She then pulled an envelope from her bag and tore it open,

'Right then, keys. Shall we?' She led the way and opened the front door. 'You've got the details?' Lisa nodded. She took them around the property which was in beautiful decorative order. Being a grade two listed building it had all the original beams on the walls and ceilings and there was a huge inglenook fireplace in the main sitting room; Lisa could imagine them sitting round the open fire on a cold winter evening. It was perfect: four large bedrooms, two of which were en suite, a recently fitted family bathroom and a magnificent oak kitchen. Lisa loved it. She walked over to Zak who was looking out of a rear bedroom window and asked him what he thought. He turned and smiled, 'Perfect,' he said, 'just perfect.'

15

No place like home

Simon Clark had taken control of the negotiations. Lisa had told him 'I want that house.' Simon knew that when Lisa said something like that she meant it. The property was on the market for three hundred thousand pounds. Although the estate agents had told him there was a lot of interest in it, he had a hunch it wasn't completely true. He decided to call their bluff. Against Lisa's wishes, he withdrew from negotiations and informed Banner & Tate Estates that his client was interested but thought the property was overpriced. Three weeks went by and Simon was starting to get a little edgy; had he done the right thing? He began to doubt himself; the last thing he wanted to do was to let Lisa down. Unknowingly, she had paid his wages for the last ten years and the way her assets were growing she would probably pay the next ten too. He decided that if he didn't hear from Banner & Tate that week he would contact them.

On Wednesday of that week Simon returned from lunch and picked up his messages from Nicky. 'You've had a call from Banner & Tate,' she said, 'they said it was important and can you call them as soon as possible.' Simon suddenly felt charged with energy.

'Thank you very much Nicky, you could have just made my day.'

The owners of the property had injected all their available cash into a business venture and now wanted a quick sale on the house. After some haggling, a price of two hundred and seventy thousand pounds was agreed. Simon knew it was an absolute bargain; properties in that area were increasing in price at a phenomenal rate. Lisa and Zak were over the moon. Once Simon had confirmation that all the relevant searches were satisfactory, the paperwork could be completed. He estimated the completion would be in approximately six weeks.

Lisa began stepping up Sue's training. She tried to let Sue have a free hand, especially when it was really busy; if she could cope at those times she would be fine. Lisa remembered the advert in the window at Korky's that had attracted her to the bar, so in addition to an advert in the local newspaper she placed one in the bar window. At first there were just a few enquires, then the second week when the advert was in the paper, the phone didn't stop ringing and they were inundated with applicants. Some were good, some bad and some very bad. Lisa wanted Sue to have a say in who they took on, as they would be working together. After three days of interviews they had a shortlist of four potential applicants. Sue and Lisa were sitting at the bar discussing the applicants when the door opened. Looking up, they saw a young man in the doorway. He was about twenty-five years old, dressed in denim jeans and shirt, with bleached blonde hair, a deep tan and designer stubble. But what really caught their attention were his eyes; he had the most piercing blue eyes they had ever seen.

'Sorry to disturb you ladies, I was wondering if you still had any staff vacancies.' He was so well spoken, although he looked a little rugged; it was a nice combination. The applicants had all been female but it made sense to take on a man; Zak had been doing a lot of the heavy work, but he wasn't going to be here much longer. 'My name's Reece, Reece Townsend,' he added. Lisa snapped out of her stare and looked at Sue. Telepathically, they agreed with each other.

'Hi Reece,' said Lisa, 'come on in and take a seat.' He closed the door behind him, walked over to the counter and pulled up a barstool. It was a rather unorthodox method of recruiting staff, but Lisa thought it was worth giving him five minutes. 'I'm Lisa, and this is Sue.'

'Pleased to meet you both,' he replied. Lisa asked if he had any bar experience and he told them that he had spent some time working in a bar in Tenerife. 'But all good things come to an end and now I'm back here. I'm taking a gap year from university; it was getting me down, so I thought rather than blow it completely I'd take a year out and get myself back on track.'

'Seems a sensible approach,' said Lisa. 'What are you studying at university?'

'Psychology – I plan to go into teaching eventually.'

'Would you be available to help out at short notice, if another member of staff was taken ill for example?'

'At the moment the more money I can earn the better. I took a loan out to get through my degree and it's crippling me financially, so yeah, not a problem.' Lisa thought about the things she had done in the past to get money and was impressed by the way he was trying to sort himself out.

'Do you live locally?' she asked.

'I rent a flat at the top of the High Street with a friend,' he paused, 'well, this week I do anyway. It's getting a bit expensive – that's another reason I need to get work.' Lisa asked for his contact details and he wrote down his address and telephone number.

'That's great,' she said, 'we'll be making our decision over the next couple of days. If you get the job, would you be able to work this weekend?' Lisa wanted to know just how keen he really was.

'No problem. If you give me the chance, I promise you won't be disappointed.' They shook hands and he thanked them for their time before leaving. Lisa put his details with those of the other applicants.

'Well Sue, what do you make of him?'

'On looks he's got the job, the question is how sincere was he?'

'It would be very useful having a man around here. I tell you what, Sue, this is your first managerial decision. They're all good – you choose.'

'Oh don't, Lisa,' said Sue, nervously.

'If they're not up to standard after a trial period you have to sack them, so you can employ them,' replied Lisa.

'I never thought of it like that ... OK.' Sue glanced through the applicants again trying to remember all their good and bad points. After two or three minutes she sat up straight. 'Right, I've decided on Reece.' Lisa smiled. 'And it's not cos I fancy him!'

'Yeah, yeah,' said Lisa, with a big grin on her face.

'I thought about what you said about having a man about the place, especially at closing time.'

'Good decision, Sue. All you have to do now is let him know. I'll put a letter in the post to the others telling them they weren't successful, but we'll keep their details on file.'

That evening Sue called Reece to inform him that he'd got the job. He arranged to drop in and sort out the paperwork the following day. All being well, he could start that weekend.

True to his word, over the next few weeks Reece proved himself to be a very useful member of staff. Lisa tried to keep out the way, letting Sue get the feel of being in charge. In a few weeks' time Lisa wouldn't be there to help. On a couple of occasions, customers had one too many to drink and started to get a little rowdy. Sue was a little intimidated by them and Reece was quick to notice this. His experience of working in the holiday bars in Tenerife had taught him how to deal with this sort of situation and he would quickly calm it down. Sue was very thankful for his presence. Korky's was becoming very popular and was attracting different customers. Sue increased prices, which had the effect of whittling out certain undesirables, but in doing so the takings had doubled in three months. Sue and her team were proving to be very valuable assets for Lisa.

Lisa and Zak finally got into their dream home. It would soon be summer and Lisa was looking forward to lazing around in the garden. Zak had given a month's notice at Hennessey's so that he could be with Lisa as the twins' birth approached. They had kept the flat above Korky's empty so when they went into London, whether it was on business or pleasure, they had somewhere to stay. Every few days they would head down and see how Sue was coping. 'Coping' was the understatement of the year; she was doing marvellously. Lisa had given her a substantial wage rise to reward her efforts and this had made her even more determined. Reece and the girls seemed to be getting on really well and Lisa could tell that as a team they were producing a really great atmosphere; the takings said it all.

Six months passed and it had been a great summer; long hot days relaxing in the garden while the house was being decorated and furnished to Lisa's specifications. She spent hours increasing her knowledge by reading books on wines; never in her wildest dreams did she think she could have been so passionate about such a subject. Janie had stayed for a week mid-summer, which had been a happy time, but Lisa had dreaded Zak asking Janie what she did for a living. Janie didn't make a big issue of what she did, but at the same time she was not ashamed of it. To Lisa's relief, Janie was diplomatic.

Lisa lay back on the sun-lounger, glad to be off her feet. There were just four weeks until her due date. She had mixed feelings. On one hand, the sooner she had the children the better, but at the same time she was worried about going through the labour. Zak had gone into the house to prepare lunch and Lisa relaxed, enjoying the sun on her face. The babies hadn't been particularly active over the last few days and she enjoyed the calm. A sudden tightening of her stomach muscles made her flinch; she had read how these Braxton Hicks contractions were common in the last few weeks. Although relaxed, she felt as if she had lots of energy and decided to go and give Zak a hand in the kitchen. It was a struggle to get up but she managed to sit up straight and turn her legs off the lounger. A sudden surge of liquid alerted her to what was happening; there was still a month to go, but twins were renowned for being early. Within five minutes, Zak had the bag in the car and they were on the road heading for Oxford General Maternity Department. They pulled up at the entrance, 'Stay there Lisa and I'll get help,' said Zak before rushing through the main doors. Lisa tried to concentrate on the breathing methods she had learnt at antenatal classes, but it was becoming more difficult. At last, Zak came rushing out with a midwife pushing a wheelchair.

'OK Lisa, let's get you inside,' said the midwife. After a struggle to get Lisa out of the car, they checked her in, and the midwife confirmed that the two young ones would soon be making their appearance. Zak phoned his parents to let them know what was happening. The contractions had stopped again, which the midwife told them was quite common, but just to be on the safe side the babies' heartbeats were monitored.

It was just after one in the morning and Zak was nodding in the chair next to Lisa's bed.

'Zak.'

'Yeah, yeah what is it?' he was half asleep.

'Get the midwife, something's happening.' Sure enough, something was happening. Over the next hour, Zak was called every name under the sun, but like any good father to be, he took it on the chin. Eleven hours after arriving at the maternity department Lisa gave birth to two healthy babies, a boy and a girl. They had already considered some names and instantly decided on Josh and Jodie. Zak's parents, having insisted on being telephoned, whatever the hour, were absolutely delighted and Janie was equally excited. After a very long and tiring day, Lisa and the babies were sent up to a ward. Zak went home still full of adrenalin but feeling totally exhausted; it was the happiest day of his life.

16

A new routine

Zak woke early. He hadn't been asleep long, the excitement of the day before was still occupying his mind. There were no set visiting hours for fathers, as long as they kept from under the midwives' feet and let them get on with their work. Zak had a quick bowl of cereal, made himself a coffee, showered and dressed, ready to go and see his new family. He arrived at the maternity hospital just after half past ten, bought a bunch of flowers in reception and headed up to the ward. Lisa was sitting up in bed with both babies in her arms. As he approached she smiled and quietly asked for help. Zak laughed and took baby Josh from her.

As he cradled the baby in his arms, Lisa looked up at him, 'Have you done that before?' she asked. 'You look like an old hand at it. It must have been the antenatal classes – some of it must have rubbed off!'

She smiled with a look of contentment, 'Will you stay with the little ones while I get a shower?'

'Take as long as you like,' Zak replied, 'I'll get to know these little monsters.' Lisa was exhausted but had never felt happier. She now had her own family, a thriving business and a beautiful home. What more could a girl ask for? But she was aware that she had even more than that; Zak was going to make a wonderful father and as she knew only too well, you couldn't always be guaranteed a good father.

They spent most of the day bonding with the children. Zak's parents arrived during the afternoon and immediately began fussing over the twins. It was fine for a while, then Zak could see that Lisa was becoming irritable, so he took the parents to the hospital cafeteria for a coffee. Although Lisa appreciated their enthusiasm, she was glad to see them go home. The following morning a doctor and midwife called in to see Lisa and discharged her. 'Home, today?' said Lisa in surprise.

'Don't worry Mrs Wright; we won't just forget about you,' the doctor reassured her, 'but the sooner you get into a routine the better. Will there be someone at home with you for a while?' Lisa confirmed that Zak would be there and the midwife told her that she would arrange for the health visitor to visit at home. By lunchtime Lisa was ready and two midwives had secured the twins into carry car seats. The midwives carried the babies to the car, which Zak had parked at the designated space near the main doors. With a toot of the horn they were away. It felt very strange; suddenly they were on their own, no instruction manual, just two small babies who were completely dependent upon them.

The weeks and months went by and they had their moments, as any new parents do: sleepless nights and all the usual things that come with parenthood. Luckily for them they were both at home, a luxury most families didn't have, but of course they did have twins to contend with.

Over the past six months Sue had managed Korky's without any help from Lisa. There had been one or two anxious moments, but she had coped and had truly established herself in a managerial position. Although Lisa loved being with the children all day, the need to get back to the business she missed so much was intense. Zak was proving to be a great father, never seeming to tire of the twins' constant need for attention. It was amazing that a man could change his job and lifestyle with such ease. However much Lisa wanted to be back in the bar, she realised that Sue was completely in control and doing an excellent job. Lisa didn't want to jeopardise that or the respect they now held for each other. Some time ago she and Zak had considered opening another wine bar, but when the children had come along that idea had taken a back seat. Perhaps this was a good time to start thinking about it again.

It was a Saturday afternoon and Lisa and Zak had taken the children into Oxford on a shopping trip. As they walked down the High Street Lisa noticed a two-story building. It looked as if it had been a bar or a club in the past, but now it was a shell of its former self. A 'to-let' board on the front of the building set Lisa's mind into action; it was a great location, right in the middle of the High Street and the town was full of young, affluent people. She couldn't believe that developers hadn't snapped it up. Maybe there were other underlying reasons as to why it was closed. Zak had noticed that Lisa was focused on the property. She turned to him, 'What do you think Zak?'

'It's certainly a great location,' he said. They looked around; OK, it was a Saturday afternoon, but it was teeming with people, young people at that.

'I'll take the details down and get Simon to do some digging,' said Lisa. Zak knew Lisa was itching to get back to work. They had enjoyed the time they had off together, but in his heart he knew Lisa was career-minded and would soon be back doing what she loved.

Simon had been wondering just how long it would take for Lisa to get back to business, but after receiving the details on her next project, he wondered if maybe this time she was jumping in a little too deep. Over the years, Lisa had proved to be quite a shrewd businesswoman and she was the client, so he had to follow up her hunch. Simon arranged a viewing for Lisa the following week and as she was due for an update on her finances, they could kill two birds with one stone. Simon had become a close family friend, so it was also a great chance for a social visit. That Thursday morning Simon arrived just after ten o'clock. Lisa greeted him looking sharp and professional. As soon as Simon saw her he thought, 'Here we go, she means business.' He couldn't resist a cuddle with the twins, but kept it brief in the hope of avoiding dribble and perhaps worse, which would not have gone down too well at a business meeting. He was amazed how quickly they were growing.

It didn't take long to get into Oxford, which was only about eight miles away. They quickly found a parking space on the High Street. As they walked over to the building a smartly dressed middle-aged man stepped out of a car parked right outside and greeted them. 'Good morning, Mrs Wright is it?' extending his hand in a welcoming gesture, 'I'm Paul Maddock, I represent BTM Leasing.' Lisa shook his hand and he turned to Simon, 'Mr Clark, pleased to finally meet you.' Simon shook his hand. 'You are familiar with the details of the property, so I'll open up and let you have a good look around.'

As he fumbled with the lock, Lisa stood back and took a good look at the property. It was going to be one hell of a challenge; the closer she looked, the more she realised the work that would be involved to get this place up and running. Finally he managed to get the door open, 'There we go,' he said, trying to hide his embarrassment after fumbling with the keys. The ground floor of the property was three times the size of Korky's with an excellent cellar, perfect for wine, and two rooms at the rear, which would make a good staff room and office. On the first floor there was an industrial-sized kitchen. Although Lisa had no experience in the food industry it had always interested her; with good management the profits within the industry could be phenomenal. Simon had been constantly firing questions at Maddock. As far as Lisa could tell he appeared to have all the right answers, but if there was a problem she was sure Simon would quickly identify it. They stepped outside and Maddock again had some difficulty with the lock, which had not been in use for some time. 'Could do with a drop of oil,' he muttered. They thanked him for his time and assistance, assuring him they would be in touch soon. Lisa once again stood back, looking up at the frontage, deep in thought. As Maddock drove off he tooted the horn and waved.

'Well Simon, what do you think?' asked Lisa.

'It's a huge project, but it has a lot going for it. The location is superb; there is another wine bar down the High Street but nothing that could compare to this. I think a restaurant on the first floor, if that's what you choose to do, could be a gold mine,' said Simon.

'That's just what I was thinking. *Korky's Wine Bar and Bistro* sounds catchy, don't you think?' she asked.

'Very,' replied Simon. Lisa had that look on her face, the one that said, 'I want this.' Simon had seen it before, when she had approached him about the bar in Wimbledon. He knew she would jump in with both feet; it was his job to make sure the financial support was available, not just for Lisa's future but for his own. 'Right then,' he said, 'let's go and have some lunch. I'm quite peckish now and we have a lot to discuss.'

As they walked down the High Street they took note of all the bars, restaurants – anything that would be competition. They decided on a small pub, The George, a nice looking place but a little too quiet to have good food Lisa thought; by one o'clock in the afternoon anywhere with a good menu should be busy, even on a week day. Lisa sat down at a table while Simon ordered drinks and picked up two menus. As he placed the glasses on the table he said, 'Your main customers are going to be students, so you have to be careful not to outprice them; most of these kids are up to their eyes in debt.'

'I agree,' replied Lisa, 'but socialising is still a big part of student life.' They scanned the menu. 'I must say it looks nice,' said Lisa, 'two meals for a tenner sounds pretty reasonable too.'

'Not to a student it doesn't,' said Simon. Lisa took the hint and smiled. After a first-class meal they went back out onto the High Street. The place was still heaving with double-parked delivery vehicles trying to drop off their loads and people dodging between cars. 'There's something else Lisa,' said Simon, 'within five years, this will be completely pedestrianised, it's been in the pipeline for some time.' Lisa's face dropped. 'It's not a bad thing or I would have brought it up earlier. Statistics show that people feel safer in traffic-free zones and when people feel safe they tend to stick around a little longer and come back more often.'

'So it will be better for business in the long-term?' The enthusiasm was back in Lisa's face.

'I'd say so.' Simon reassured her.

'Keep talking Simon, you've just about sold it to me.' They both laughed as they headed back to the car. As they pulled away Lisa took one more look at the property. 'How long do you think it would take to get the place up and running?' she asked.

'I suppose it would depend on the level of decoration, manpower and so on. I think three to four months would be a safe bet.'

'Simon, if I take on this project, I want the doors open in ten weeks, not a day longer.'

'That's a tall order, Lisa, what with training staff, getting the kitchens fitted and up to speed and that's just the start,' he replied.

'I want you to do a little more digging and find out why it closed in the first place and what kind of turnover we're looking at to make this place a success.'

'I've got to give it to you, Lisa, you like a challenge.' Lisa smiled at him. 'This is going to put a big hole in your finances,' he added.

'I guess it will – that's why it's got to work. We did it in Korky's, so we can do it again. I tell you what though, we'll have a better menu than that place we've just eaten in.' They both laughed and the car sped out of Oxford in the direction of Stanton Harcourt.

They pulled onto the drive and the front door opened before Lisa had got out of the car. Zak stood on the doorstep with Jodie in his arms. As Lisa smiled lovingly at Jodie, the excitement of seeing her mother spilled over in the baby's actions. 'Calm down little 'un,' said Zak, 'here, you'd better take her before she jumps out of my arms.' Lisa took the baby. 'Josh is flat out. Too much fresh air. How did you get on?'

A big smile appeared on Lisa's face.

'That good was it?' asked Zak. Lisa stood on her tiptoes and kissed him.

'This place is going to make us rich,' she said, still smiling.

'We already are,' said Zak looking at Jodie pulling on the chain around her mother's neck.

'Let's go in,' said Lisa, 'we've got lots to talk about.'

Simon stayed for the rest of the afternoon discussing other areas of Lisa's portfolio and various ways to finance this new project. As always, in this area Lisa allowed herself to be guided by Simon; she knew he would always act in her best interests and get her the best possible deal.

Over the next few weeks Lisa took up another a new challenge. If she was to get to and from Oxford on a daily basis she had to learn to drive. Driving had never appealed to her, but after a few lessons at a local driving school she was hooked. With three lessons each week and countless evenings studying the Highway Code, she progressed quickly and her instructor eventually said she was ready to take her test. Zak was amazed at how well she had picked it up. Occasionally he would let her get behind the wheel of his cherished BMW and, surprisingly, he felt quite safe as her passenger. Three months after taking her first lesson, Lisa passed her driving test. Like everything else in her life, once she put her mind to something, there was no stopping her. The question now, was what car she would get. She told Zak that a woman in her position had to look the part. He thought it was hilarious, but what the hell, she was happy.

Simon made good progress with the new premises. He had struck a good deal with the rent on the property and it was now just a matter of securing the necessary food and drink licences. Once these were granted it would be full steam ahead. Every few days Simon would bring Lisa up to date with the negotiations. She had been busy herself consulting a design firm in relation to the layout of the bar and restaurant. It was becoming very exciting and also expensive. The ideas proposed by the design company were excellent. Simon drew up a budget for fitting out and tactfully asked Lisa to stay within it. Just three months from the first time they had viewed the property it was theirs. The final designs were drawn up and after looking at some of the impressive work from the designer's subcontractor, the contract was signed. A twelve-week deadline was agreed with severe penalties for any overrun and a decent bonus for completion to the agreed specification in a shorter timeframe. The man in charge on site was Danny McClure, a small, stocky man with red hair and a ruddy face. His broad Glaswegian accent could be intimidating, but he was known for getting results and after just a month he was already a week ahead of schedule.

Zak had reluctantly agreed to Lisa using his beloved car two or three times a week to drive into Oxford to see how the work was progressing. Danny would always spend time showing her around, but she had the feeling that he just wanted to get on with his work. That was fine by her; it was what she was paying him for. The next thing she had to organise was staff. It wasn't a problem hiring staff; the problem was hiring good staff. As far as the restaurant was concerned, she planned to leave the staff selection to the chef. Already a first-class chef was interested in the position, but Lisa was unsure as to whether she could afford him. Andy Grigg had first-class credentials, having worked in two top London hotels. They met to discuss some of his ideas, which seemed to fit well with the type of customer Lisa was aiming to attract. As a bonus, he would be able to bring in his own staff. They agreed terms and Grigg immediately began work on the menu.

Lisa planned to open the bar from 11am till late, seven days a week, and needed to get a reliable manager in position quickly to enable her to spend time with Zak and the twins. Sue came up from London for a few days to assist Lisa interview potential bar staff. She had left Reece in charge at Korky's; he had turned out to be an absolute godsend and for his efforts he had been promoted to assistant manager, on a very good salary.

Jimmy sat on a bench, eyes fixed on something in the distance but nothing in particular. He had been there for nearly an hour in one of his transfixed states. In his mind he was lying on a large blanket with the sun beating down on his face. Beside him was Lisa, the love of his life, the most beautiful girl he had ever set eyes on. As she curled up to him pressing her body against his, he felt complete. What else could he possibly want from life? He was financially secure and had a beautiful girl who worshiped the ground he walked on.

'Jimmy, Jimmy, it's time. I've been looking everywhere for you.' The silence was broken by Paul Daws, a Down's syndrome man in his thirties, affectionately known as Pauly. Each day at noon he would turn up at Jimmy's room with a small magnetic draughts game. Before lunch they would play one game. Jimmy always won but Pauly was not deterred, you could set your watch by him. Jimmy snapped out of his dreamscape state, dragged back from lying on a blanket with the most beautiful girl in the world to face the reality of his situation. For the first time in well over a decade the rage inside his body grew. Pauly stared at him. He could see Pauly's mouth moving but couldn't hear him as he repeatedly asked for a game of draughts. Jimmy gritted his teeth trying to control himself then snapped. Grabbing Pauly's throat, his nails sank into his flesh. Jimmy pulled him close to his face, enjoying the shock and fear on Pauly's face. 'Fuck off you little spastic.' He flung Pauly backwards to the ground. Pauly rolled into a ball, clutching at his throat and groaning. Until that moment Jimmy had been the only patient that Pauly had trusted, the only person who had shown any sign of friendship or compassion. That was now destroyed. Pauly got to his feet and backed off. He was the first person in a very long time to have seen the real James Noakes.

17

Open for business

The bar was almost finished. Once the signs for the front of the building were in place and one or two bits of tidying up were finished they would be ready to open. Lisa had placed adverts in local papers announcing a grand opening, complementing the adverts with around ten thousand leaflets saturating the surrounding area. Andy Grigg had devised a classy but affordable menu. All the staff were now in place. Andy had six of his own hand-picked kitchen staff, covering twelve hours a day, seven days a week. Lisa and Sue had chosen the bar staff and restaurant table staff. Lisa didn't want any glitches, so for now she was only taking on experienced staff, aiming for success right from the word go.

The bar was due to open the following Saturday. As a trial run, Lisa decided to hold a private dinner on the Thursday, for everyone who had been involved in getting the place ready so quickly. It would be a small thank you to all the workers and also a great opportunity to iron out any teething problems in the kitchens and bar before the big day. Around forty people turned up and the event was a great success. The kitchen coped with ease. Andy was able to check out the equipment in action and also demonstrate his culinary skills. The guests were appreciative and Lisa now knew she had the right man for the job.

That Friday evening as Lisa and Zak put the children to bed, Zak could see that Lisa was nervous; she hadn't been her usual bright, bubbly self all day. 'Go sit yourself down love, I'll make us both a drink,' he told her. Lisa went into the living room and curled her legs up on the sofa. It was the first time that week she had been able to relax as there had constantly been things to do. After opening the next day it wouldn't get any easier. Zak came in carrying two mugs of coffee. 'Here you are darling,' he said. Lisa took the cup in both hands.

'I hope it all goes well tomorrow, Zak.'

'Hope doesn't come into it, the amount of work you've put in getting that place ready, you deserve every bit of the success you're going to have.'

'I wish I felt as confident as you are,' she replied.

'Lisa,' said Zak turning towards her, 'you're more confident than anybody I've ever met, just wait and see, you'll be having to turn them away by eight o'clock tomorrow night.' Lisa laughed, put her mug down on the floor and slid along the sofa. She put her arms around Zak's neck and kissed him.

'I hope you're right, Mr Wright.'

Zak smiled at her. 'I am. Now lets go to bed and I'll explain why.' A cheeky grin spread over his face.

Lisa woke early. She stretched, still feeling tired and stiff; not a good way to start the day she thought, but it was time to get started. After a light breakfast, Lisa said goodbye to Zak and the twins and headed into Oxford. Zak's BMW may as well have been Lisa's now, as she seemed to be the only one driving it nowadays. Zak didn't mind; although Lisa was a new driver she was certainly competent. Pulling up on the High Street outside the bar, she turned off the engine and took a good look at the front of the building. 'This is it,' she said to herself, 'I've finally made it.' Grinning like a Cheshire cat, she locked the car, opened the main door to the bar and went in. It was still early and the staff were not due in until eleven o'clock. She planned to open the doors on the first day at exactly midday. Fingers crossed, by eight o'clock that evening half the student population of Oxford would be in there. Lisa had arranged for a local security firm to work the front door. If things became a little rowdy she wanted it nipped in the bud but, not wanting to attract the wrong sort of attention, she had asked that the doormen were more pleasing to the eye than the huge henchmen she had seen at some bars. Lisa opened up exactly as planned and by mid-afternoon all was going well, not as busy as she had hoped, but it was still early. The restaurant was ticking over nicely; a constant flow of customers kept Andy and his team on their toes, but the real test was to come that evening, which should be the busiest night of the week.

By seven o'clock it was really filling up. The restaurant was busy and people were booking tables for later that evening, then settling down in the bar. It was all going just as Zak had said it would. By the middle of the evening the staff were working flat out and they had to turn people away. Lisa hadn't stopped all day and was starting to feel the pressure. At midnight, the last customers said goodbye and Lisa dropped the latch on the front door. The sound of music, laughter and lively voices had given way to the clink of glass and amiable banter as the staff cleared the tables and closed the bar. Within an hour they had finished and Andy came through to the bar, his kitchen staff close behind him. Lisa lined the bar with glasses and took out two bottles of the best champagne. 'OK everyone,' Lisa raised her voice to get their attention and they all turned towards her, 'Firstly, I want to say thank you, to each and every one of you. If I'm honest, I have to say I expected a good response, but nothing like what we've had tonight.' Andy uncorked the champagne. As he filled up the glasses, Lisa called for a toast. Once everyone had a charged glass, Lisa raised hers and said, 'To Korky's.' In unison they all raised their glasses and shouted, 'KORKY'S.'

As the weeks and months went by, Korky's became a huge success, with customers responding well to the occasional promotions such as free bottles of house wine with meals and two-for-one nights. Although the business was thriving, it was taking its toll on Lisa; with long hours and lack of sleep, it was grinding her down. Some nights it was two in the morning before Lisa arrived home. Every night, Zak would be waiting for her to come home, as supportive as ever. One Saturday evening, after a particularly busy night, Lisa arrived home just before two o'clock. Zak had fallen asleep in an armchair.

Lisa nudged his shoulder. He opened his eyes slowly, then stretched and sat up. Lisa went into the kitchen and put the kettle on. Zak followed her. 'Lisa,' he said, 'I'm worried about you. You look so tired all the time and the hours you're doing will kill you. Not only that, the kids miss you, I see it in their eyes. It will get to the point where they don't know you any more.' Lisa placed her hands on the edge of the sink and looked through the kitchen window into the darkness.

'I don't know what to do, Zak.' She knew she couldn't go on for much longer.

'Get somebody in, get a manager,' he replied.

'There's nobody I know well enough to trust yet,' said Lisa, 'I could do with another Sue.'

'What about Reece?' Zak had been thinking of a way forward for Lisa for some time. 'He's good and he's got loads of experience. We've got the money. Buy a place in Oxford and include the accommodation in his salary. He deserves the break as much as you do.'

'I'm sorry, Zak,' said Lisa, 'I've been so engrossed with the business I forgot what I was doing it all for.'

Zak walked over to her and put his arms around her. 'I love you Lisa. We'll work this out.'

'What would I do without you?' said Lisa. Gently, Zak kissed her forehead.

'Let's get you to bed. What you need right now is sleep.'

The following day, Lisa phoned Sue explaining her situation and her plans for Reece. Sue said she would miss him, but was pleased for him to have the opportunity to move up, just as she had. Lisa arranged for Reece to come up to Oxford for a few days to cover for her while she took a few days off. It didn't take long for him to settle in and the staff seemed to like him. He stayed with Lisa and Zak, and each night Lisa arranged for a taxi to collect him from the bar. Reece had been in charge for about a week and Lisa decided it was time to make him the offer. The following morning over breakfast, Lisa asked him if he was enjoying managing the Oxford bar.

'It's great,' he said, 'I can't believe how busy it is, it's like going out every night on the town but you get paid for it. I never thought I would be doing something like this for a job.'

'That's one of the reasons I asked you to take over for a few days,' said Lisa. 'How do you fancy doing it full-time?'

'What? You mean running the bar, like, as the manager?'

'Yeah, just like Sue in London. You'll have your own bar.'

Reece couldn't believe his luck and after hearing that Lisa would also help with accommodation, he gratefully accepted her offer.

Lisa phoned Simon and asked him to carry out a further property search. 'Oh no,' he thought, 'what are we getting into this time?' He was relieved when Lisa explained it was only a small flat. It didn't take Simon long to locate a suitable property: a two-bedroom flat, just a short walk from the bar.

Sue quickly filled the position in London. Lisa began to divide her time between the two bars; two days a week in London and two days at the Oxford bar. Zak and the children would travel down to London with her and stay in the flat above the bar. It was a little loud in the evenings for the children, but at least they were all together. It had taken eighteen months to get some stability back into their lives but they had done it. They still had very busy lives, but now they could start to enjoy the fruits of their hard work.

18

As time goes by

Korky's Wine Bar and Bistro had been open for just over nine years. At the end of the second year Lisa had handed over the reins to Reece Townsend. It had become a very successful and well-established business, attracting people from far afield to sample good wines and a menu of the highest quality. Andy Grigg, the chef, had stuck with them right from the start. He enjoyed having the freedom to try out just about anything he chose and this was one of the reasons the restaurant had become so popular. Reece had grown within his role as manager, proving to be a very important link in Lisa's little empire. Lisa had considered opening a third bar on the other side of London, but after a long talk with Zak, they had decided their lives had been stressful enough without another bar to oversee. In addition, the twins were growing up, needing more and more of their attention, especially with their education. They would soon be nine years' old and within another twelve months would be choosing their secondary schools, a decision which would need very careful consideration. But in general, life was good. Lisa could take a day off any time she chose and Zak had no regrets about becoming a househusband; he told Lisa many times it was the best thing he had ever done.

Just over a hundred miles away, north of Birmingham at the Shire Oak Hospital, Doctor Henry Phelps was chairing a meeting. After almost twenty years studying James Noakes, he was completely convinced that Jimmy was now ready to take his place once more in society. What he had to do now was convince the board. Phelps was sure about this one; he was prepared to put his reputation on the line. Although his judgement was highly respected, there were one or two others on the panel who, after reading Jimmy's notes, had doubts about the progress he had made. It was virtually a textbook case, perhaps too good to be true. Could anybody who had carried out such violent attacks ever be truly rehabilitated? If there was even the slightest doubt in their minds after Jimmy's interview he would be refused, that was the way the system worked.

Jimmy sat in his room wondering what he might be asked. Phelps had told him to stay relaxed and just be himself. He had to make them believe he was truly sorry for his actions of twenty years ago. In Jimmy's opinion, he had done society a favour by getting rid of the scum, but he knew that was not what they wanted to hear; they controlled the corrupt establishment that had locked him away. There was a knock on Jimmy's door. The staff were considerate of privacy wherever possible and hoped that a respectful attitude would be reciprocated. 'You ready, Jimmy?' It was Joey Tubbs, a nurse with many years' experience at the hospital. Joey was the type of guy that got on with everyone. Whenever a patient got out of hand Joey was the one they turned to, he had a knack of calming down potentially explosive situations.

'Just coming, Joey.' Jimmy stood up, flattened down his hair with the palms of his hands, took a quick glance at his reflection in the window then went out into the corridor.

'Good luck, mate.'

'Thanks Joey, I appreciate that.' Joey escorted Jimmy down the corridor, through the main reception area and into the administration wing.

'You remember what Dr Phelps said, Jimmy,' said Joey.

'Yeah, just be myself.'

'That's the idea, mate.' Joey stopped outside Phelps' office and gave a fingers crossed gesture to Jimmy before knocking on the door. They were called in.

'Jimmy Noakes to see you, Dr Phelps.'

'Thank you, Joey.' Joey stepped to one side and Jimmy walked into the room, automatically scanning the people in front of him, five in all. He recognised three of them: Phelps, Dr Ian Murray and Professor Colin Woods. The other two he had never seen before.

'Jimmy, please take a seat,' said Phelps, indicating an empty chair, positioned where they would all have a clear view of him. As Jimmy sat down he could feel their eyes burning into his head.

'You know Dr Murray and Professor Woods,' said Phelps, 'this is Dr Carver and Dr Peterson who have kindly offered to sit in on your interview.' Jimmy looked at both of them then nodded. Phelps looked up at Joey who was still standing by the door.

'Thank you, Joey. If you would wait outside for me, please.'

'Right you are, Dr Phelps.' Joey turned and left, closing the door behind him.

'Dr Phelps tells us you're making great headway with your rehabilitation, Jimmy,' said Dr Peterson.

Jimmy looked straight at him. 'I must say I feel good,' he volunteered. 'I enjoy my conversations with Dr Phelps, and Joey likes a chat, but I find it difficult to relate to the patients on my wing.'

'Why is that?' asked Woods. Jimmy made no reply. 'Does that frustrate you, Jimmy?' Woods asked.

'Yes, a little,' replied Jimmy.

'Does it make you angry, Jimmy?' Murray joined in the conversation and Jimmy turned to his left to face him.

'It's been a long time since I've felt angry. Dr Phelps taught me some breathing exercises, but I've not really needed to use them. I think everyone has anger and rage within them, but being able to control it is the key ... well that's my opinion.' Murray nodded his head, and made a note on his pad. 'Karma,' said Jimmy, Murray looked up, 'I think that was the word you used, Dr Phelps.'

'Yes Jimmy, quite right,' said Phelps. For the next hour, the doctors all fired questions at him, some designed to relax him, others to test his patience. Jimmy had waited a long time for this opportunity; if they weren't going to give him back his freedom it wasn't going to be his fault.

'OK Jimmy, is there anything you would like to add to the meeting?' asked Phelps.

'Yes, Dr Phelps. I'd just like to say that never a day goes by without me regretting my actions of twenty years ago. I wish I could turn back the clock, but I can't, so I have to live with my conscience. Hopefully, one day I'll be able to repay society.' Jimmy lowered his head; it had been an excellent performance.

'Thank you, Jimmy. If you would leave us now, Joey will take you back to your room.' Jimmy stood up and acknowledged the doctors with a nod of his head. Closing the door behind him he suppressed a smile. Joey got up from a chair along the hallway and raised both thumbs.

'You were in there a long time, mate. How do you think you got on?'

'Pretty well I thought,' said Jimmy, hesitantly, although his heart was pounding.

'In that case you must have done OK. Come on then, let's get you back.' They set off down the corridor together, Jimmy feeling tremendously pleased with himself.

'Well, gentlemen,' said Phelps, tapping the end of his pen on his notepad, 'comments please.'

'I have to give it to you, Henry,' said Carver, 'after reading his case history, I would never guessed it was the same person, truly remarkable.'

'Yes, I couldn't agree more,' added Peterson, raising his head from his notes.

'There were one or two questions in there that would have provoked even the mildest natured individual. He showed great emotional restraint. I have the feeling he is truly sincere about regretting his past.'

'Gentlemen,' Phelps sat up straight and placed his elbows on the desk, 'I've worked with James Noakes for twenty years. As you know from his notes, he saw things as a child that would have disturbed the best of us. But I can tell you that he has never shown any sign of violence in all the time I have known him, which is quite an achievement in the environment he has to live in. He has been attacked by other patients, but always shows great restraint.'

'Well, Henry,' said Woods, 'I think from what we have seen and your long-term observations, we should give this man an opportunity to start a new life.' One by one they all agreed.

'I'll complete the documentation and arrange to get him straight on the release programme,' said Phelps, adding, 'thank you very much gentlemen. Now, can I interest you all in a spot of lunch?'

'What a good idea,' said Peterson, slapping his hands on his rotund midsection. The others nodded in agreement and they went off down the corridor in the direction of the staff restaurant, still discussing Phelps' latest achievement in rehabilitation.

Over the next few months, Jimmy was taken on days out from the hospital and it was all going to plan. As a condition of his release he had to hold down a job. The authorities had an arrangement with a firm based in Walsall, approximately nine miles from Birmingham. Jimmy's crimes had been committed in Birmingham. It was considered unwise to relocate people close to the area of their crimes and Walsall was agreed on because of the employment opportunity and availability of accommodation. Every Friday morning he had to report to a remand centre; failure to do so would put him in breach of his parole release and the police would be alerted to arrest him. Turning up on Fridays was a small price to pay for his freedom.

Simon Clark was still very much in control of Lisa's finances. He was now a senior partner at Craddock & Co., mostly on the strength of

Lisa's business. The Oxford branch of Korky's had taken Lisa into another league in terms of finance and she was now a well-respected businesswoman. Every few months Simon would meet with Lisa to discuss her finances. On this occasion he had taken a trip down to Oxford and met her for lunch at Korky's. They took a corner table at the back of the restaurant, surrounded by a hive of activity.

'I can't believe how busy this place is,' said Simon.

'Since the High Street was pedestrianised it's been like this constantly,' she told him.

'You're either very lucky Lisa, or very good.'

'I'd like to think it's a little of both,' she replied, smiling, as she sipped a glass of wine.

Simon leaned forward across the table, a serious expression forming on his face. 'Lisa,' he said, 'I want you to spend some money.'

'I like the idea of that,' she said, laughing.

'I'm being serious – if you don't, you'll lose it in tax.'

'How much?' she asked.

'About thirty or thirty-five thousand,' Simon replied. Lisa sat up straight, knocking over her wine glass.

'Are you serious?' she gasped.

'Absolutely. You need to invest, buy a company car, take a working holiday to see how they run these places in Italy, France or wherever. For a wealthy lady, you don't spend much money.' It was a shock to Lisa, who felt that they had all they wanted and certainly didn't hold back on buying anything that the family needed.

'I think I know just the thing,' said Lisa.

After the meeting Simon headed back to Birmingham and Lisa went home. There was something Zak had always wanted – why hadn't she thought of it before?

It was Zak's forty-first birthday and he was expecting a quiet night out with Lisa and the twins. As they drove towards Oxford, Lisa said she needed to call into Korky's. She apologised, 'it'll only take a minute – only Reece said he needed some paperwork signing for the morning.' They pulled up at the end of the public walkway. 'Come on,' she said, 'we might as well all go in, just to say hello.' The twins were reluctant, but eventually gave in. The bar was buzzing, as usual, and one of the girls behind the bar raised a hand in welcome. 'Reece is upstairs Mrs Wright,' she called over the music and laughter.

'It's quiet in here tonight,' said Zak as they climbed the stairs to the restaurant. As they reached the top of the stairs, all the lights came on, 'SURPRISE!' A loud shout rang out from a large group of people. Instantly Zak realised he had been set up and the twins nearly jumped out of their skins. Family and friends gathered around them, shaking Zak's hand and fussing the children.

'Happy birthday, darling,' said Lisa, affectionately placing a kiss on his lips. Josh and Jodie looked very embarrassed at their parents' public show of affection. It was a wonderful night. Andy pulled out all the stops in the kitchen and prepared an exquisite meal. Wine flowed, but Zak, who had hardly taken a drink since becoming a househusband, joined the twins with a juice. Just before eleven o'clock, Reece caught Lisa's eye and gave her a nod and thumbs up sign. Lisa leaned over to Zak, 'I haven't given you your birthday present yet,' she said.

'I was hoping to get that later,' Zak whispered. Lisa gave him a gentle elbow and stood up.

'Everybody listen up, it's time for Zak to open his present.' A hush fell over the room; only Reece knew about this part of the evening. 'It's downstairs, so we all have to go down for a few minutes.' Lisa went first, followed by Zak and the twins.

'You have to close your eyes tight and don't peep.' Zak closed his eyes and Lisa led him through the front door and a little way along the road. The party followed, with Reece indicating to everyone to stay quiet. 'It's just a little way down the road … keep your eyes closed,' said Lisa. 'OK, you can look now.' Zak opened his eyes and parked right in front of him with a huge white bow on the top, was a brand new, soft-top BMW Z4. The black two-seater sports car gleamed and shone in the lights of the High Street. Zak was speechless, having only ever dreamed of owning a car like this. The party cheered, clapped and whistled and swarmed around the car to get a better look. 'Happy birthday darling!' said Lisa.

'It's mine?' said Zak, eyes fixed on the car like a child in a sweet shop. 'To keep?'

'No, it's going back tomorrow,' joked Lisa. 'Of course to keep, you nutter!' He turned to Lisa, amazed.

'I don't know what to say,' he said. Lisa put her arms around his waist.

'Just tell me you love me,' she said; straight away the twins started to cringe.

'Pack it in mum, people are looking,' said Josh.

'Back to the party everyone,' shouted Reece, 'come on twins, let's leave your mum and dad alone for a few minutes.'

'Why don't you take me for a spin,' said Lisa, dangling a key in front of him.

'Now?' asked Zak.

'Why not? Let's go.'

They got into the car and Zak started the engine.

'Seatbelts,' said Lisa.

'You know I don't like seatbelts,' Zak replied.

'Please Zak,' said Lisa, 'it's the law.' Zak rarely used a seatbelt and it really annoyed Lisa.

'OK darling, just for you.' Zak put on his belt, selected first gear and off they went.

When they got back to Korky's it was nearly midnight and the party was ending; the twins looked shattered and people were starting to slope off. Reece drove Lisa and the twins home in their beloved old white BMW while Zak followed in his new car, with a broad grin etched on his face.

Jimmy quickly got into his new routine; the job was boring as hell, but he knew that it would all change once he had made contact with Lisa. She was constantly on his mind. It was difficult for him to move around without attracting attention to himself. He was sure the authorities were having him followed, and in his state of heightened paranoia was certain that every person who glanced in his direction was spying on him. Jimmy decided to visit Lisa at her flat that weekend; surely the authorities could not complain about him contacting an old friend? The week dragged by until, eventually, he was on his way. The city had changed so much that he felt like a stranger in his own town. He got some directions from a public information office as the bus routes and stopping places were unrecognisable to him. But he remembered the flat at number 12A Wellington Road absolutely perfectly. He remembered going up the stairs as if it was yesterday; the sound of the door closing, the feel of the handrail as he climbed each step and the synthetic perfume from spray polish and air freshener. It took a good hour on the bus, but at last he began to recognise familiar parts of the Moseley Road. As he passed Wellington Road, he stood up and moved towards the front of the bus. The bus pulled away and Jimmy stood at the bus stop observing the other passengers who had got off. He waited until they were almost out of sight before starting back towards Wellington Road, glancing back every few yards to check they hadn't doubled back to follow him. He was amazed at how dramatically the road had changed; almost every house had UPVC windows and all the front garden walls and paths had been rebuilt. As Jimmy approached 12A he tucked in his shirt and flattened down the back of his hair. He wanted to look good for her; he had imagined her throwing her arms around him and whispering how much she had missed him. Looking up at the front windows his heart started to race. What would she look like now? Twenty years was a long time. He rang the doorbell and stood back waiting.

Janie was sitting on the sofa, coffee in hand, watching television. She had been retired from the game for a good five years now. Her dreams to retire to a place in the sun had not materialised, but she was comfortable. The house was paid for and she had money saved. She was still in touch with Lisa, albeit not as much as before the twins were born. It tended to be birthdays and Christmas now, but that was OK and they both knew they would always be there for each other if needed. Janie got up, 'Who's that now? Probably someone trying to sell me something I don't want.' She had a habit of thinking out loud, largely due to the amount of time she spent alone. Looking out of the window she could see the figure of a man standing at the door, facing towards the road. She went down the stairs and opened the door. Jimmy turned round and looked at Janie, obviously expecting to see someone else in her place.

'Can I help you?' asked Janie.

'Yes, is Lisa in?'

Instantly taken aback, Janie was stuck for words; it had been over twenty years since Lisa had lived with her. Trying to think on her feet she said, 'Lisa? I'm sorry, there's no Lisa living here.'

'Are you sure?' he persisted, 'Only she's a very good friend of mine, I've been working away for some time and was trying to contact her.'

'I've lived here for years. Nobody by the name of Lisa has ever lived here.' Jimmy stared straight into her eyes; he was absolutely gutted. Janie, as bold as ever, returned the stare. He was searching for the slightest sign of deceit in her eyes, but she stayed strong.

'I'm sorry for bothering you. It may have been a few houses down.'

'That's OK,' said Janie, 'bye.'

She closed the door and went back up to the flat, immediately going straight to the front window to take a look at him. Jimmy looked up just as the net curtains twitched; Janie quickly stood back. 'Something's not right,' thought Jimmy, 'she's hiding something.' Janie sat down and tried to work out who the hell he was.

That evening, Jimmy sat in his flat, deep in thought. It was getting dark, but he didn't notice the gloom descending on the room. 'Bitch,' he said to himself. 'She's just like the rest of them.' He was struggling to control the rage growing inside him. 'You won't outdo me, you bitch. If it's the last thing I do, I'll find you, then you're mine.' He stared into the darkness; a fist clenched in the palm of his other hand, all he could think about was tracking her down. It was after midnight before he fell asleep.

The next morning he woke with a start, still sitting in his living room armchair. He stretched his arms and legs; his back felt stiff. He stood up and again stretched out. After making a coffee he returned to the chair. Lisa was still the only thing on his mind. He was convinced that the woman he spoke to knew Lisa. When he first spoke to her he thought she hesitated. Yes, she was definitely hiding something. If he could get into the flat, he felt sure he would find the information he needed. He decided to go back and watch the flat.

Just after lunch he got off the bus and walked back to Wellington Road. From the end of the street he had a good view of the front door. If anybody came out he would have plenty of time to disappear from view. He had to get into the flat. Two hours passed without anyone going in or out. He considered knocking on the door again, but just then the door opened. Jimmy kept close to the wall. The woman he had spoken to the day before came out and pulled the door shut behind her. Janie checked the door was firmly closed and walked down the road in Jimmy's direction. She had arranged to meet a friend in the city centre for a couple of drinks and a bite to eat. She didn't get out that often now so it was nice when old friends called her up for a drink and a chat. As she approached the corner Jimmy stepped into a front garden a little way down the main road, a large hedge shielding him from her view. He kept very still as she walked past. He waited a minute or two then slowly emerged, looking down the road after her; she was gone. Glancing over his shoulder he walked up Wellington Road. As he approached 12A, he took a pair of tight leather gloves from his pocket, put them on and rang the doorbell. In the inside pocket of coat he had a large-bladed screwdriver. A simple Yale lock could be easily forced; he hadn't seen her put any deadlocks on. Waiting a few moments, just in case there was someone else in the flat, a large terracotta plant pot to the side of the front door caught his attention. 'I wonder,' he said to himself. He grabbed the pot with both hands and rolled it to one side; there on the floor was a key, a Yale key. He picked it up and wiped it, 'Stupid woman.' He smiled to himself. It looked as if the key had been there for some time. He tried it in the lock; it was a little tight so he spat on it and tried it again. This time the key slid in and, with a little jiggling from side to side, the door clicked open. Quickly, he moved inside. Closing the door behind him, he put the key in his inside pocket and pulled out the screwdriver. As he started up the stairs he could feel the adrenalin surging through his body. What if there was somebody else in the flat? What if she came back when he was still in there? His need for answers to Lisa's whereabouts was more important to him than any potential threat. Walking into the living room the flat appeared empty; he had to make it look like a burglary rather than someone looking for something specific. He remembered the flat clearly; the furnishings and décor had changed but he remembered the living room as if it was his own. Randomly he began searching through drawers, turning them out when there was nothing of value or interest. Moving down the hall towards the bedroom his senses sharpened, listening for any sound or movement. He opened the first bedroom door and started sifting through the chest of drawers and bedside cabinets. He turned his attention to the wardrobe. In the very top he noticed two shoeboxes. Reaching up, he pulled them towards himself and threw them onto the bed. The lid came off one, the contents spilling onto the bed. He noticed a passport and picked it up, flicking through to the back page. Jane Coleman. The photo was of the woman he had spoken to, the one he saw leave the flat earlier. The other items were medical cards, library tickets and some old bills, nothing of any interest or value to him. Pulling the lid off the other box, his jaw dropped open; it was full of cash. He flicked through a pile of notes. They were all twenties; there must have been four or five thousand pounds in the box. Quickly, he pushed it into his coat pockets. At the bottom of the box were some letters bound together with an elastic band. He picked them up; they were all addressed to Janie. Pulling the band off, he took out the first letter. It was just general chitchat, nothing of any importance except for the very last part, which read 'yours, Lisa.' He gathered up the rest of the letters, about fifteen in all, and stuffed them in his inside coat pocket. Five minutes later he was heading back down the stairs. He checked that everything he had taken was firmly hidden in his pockets. Very slowly he opened the front door and peered round the edge; there was no sign of anyone in the street. He stepped out and pulled the door closed behind him. Briskly, he walked down the road, turning left at the bottom in the direction of the city centre.

19

The search

Jimmy slammed the door of his flat and emptied his pockets onto the table. He sat down, looking at the mound of cash and letters, adrenalin surging through his body. It had been a long time since he had felt this level of excitement and although it was frightening, he had relished every minute of it. He counted the money; there was just under five thousand pounds. 'Yes!' he said aloud, clenching both his fists in a kind of macho victory gesture, as if to say 'I'm back.'

One by one, he read the letters. They dated back over fifteen years and it was like reading a diary. Lisa had kept this Janie informed of everything she had been up to and it looked as if his money had been well invested. Best of all, he had contact addresses and phone numbers right up to three months ago. A smile appeared on his face, 'Think you can outdo me, you bitch? We'll see. Looks like I'm going on a trip down south next weekend.'

When Janie arrived home it was nearly ten o'clock. It wasn't a late night by her standards, but she had been drinking since mid-afternoon. The cab pulled up outside the house and Janie rummaged through her bag for her purse

'Eight pound fifty, please love' said the driver. Janie found a ten-pound note and told him to keep the change. She stumbled out of the taxi and fumbled with her keys as it drove off. 'Straight to bed for you, miss,' she said to herself as she staggered up the stairs. As soon as she walked into the living room she knew something was wrong and instantly sobered up. The drawers in the wall unit were upside down on the floor, the contents strewn around the room. Rushing to the bedroom she saw the two shoeboxes and the remainder of their contents on the bed. Every draw and cupboard had been ransacked. 'For fuck's sake, I've been robbed.' She checked the rest of the flat; every room had been turned upside down. At first glance it looked like an opportunist, but how had they got in? The door hadn't been forced. Then she thought of the key under the pot. It had been there so long she had almost forgotten about it. She went downstairs and moved the pot to one side; sure enough it was gone. She went back upstairs and phoned the police.

It was a good two hours before the police arrived. On the phone they had told her not to touch anything, but she knew that searching for fingerprints was probably a futile exercise as they rarely caught people for this kind of crime, and if they did, it was usually no more than a slap on the wrist for punishment. The usual format with these things was to get a crime number and make an insurance claim. As the constable took down some details he asked Janie to try and identify what was missing

'Five thousand pounds in cash,' said Janie, 'plus some personal letters.'

The policeman looked up from his paperwork. 'Did I hear you right, Miss? Five thousand pounds?'

'Yes,' replied Janie. There was a look of amazement on his face.

'What on earth were you doing with that kind of money in the house?' She thought about what he had said; it was a crazy amount of money to keep at home. Thinking on her feet she said, 'It was money I'd saved to buy a car ... power of cash and all that.' The officer looked back at his paperwork and shook his head.

'Did anyone know the money was in the house?'

'Not a soul,' said Janie.

'I don't think your insurance will cover you for having that much cash in the house, still, we'll put it all down. Oh, and I'd get these locks changed first thing in the morning,' said the officer. 'If you notice anything else missing over the next few days just give me a call, the number's on the bottom of the statement and I'll add it on for insurance purposes.' Janie thanked him. 'Try not to touch anything, scene of crime officers will drop by in the morning and take some prints. Are you OK on your own this evening or can we call someone for you?' Janie said that she would be fine and the officer told her that a police car would drive by during the night. The officer got to his feet.

'There is one more thing,' said Janie. 'The other day a man knocked the door looking for a friend of mine.'

'Do you know who he was?' the officer asked, opening his notepad.

'No, but the friend he asked for hasn't lived here for nearly twenty years, but he said he knew her well.'

'That is strange,' said the officer. 'Can you give me a description of him?' Janie gave him a full description. 'I'll check him out and see what I can come up with. If he comes by again, give me a call.' Janie nodded her head. The officer put away his notepad and walked towards the stairs. As they stepped out into the street he turned to Janie. 'Make sure you put the bolt on the door till those locks are changed.'

Janie locked the front door and went up the stairs. All she could think about now was the man that knocked the door the other day; it had to be linked with the burglary. If he had her personal letters, he had Lisa's address and phone number. She had to contact her as soon as possible. A feeling of fear and sadness came over her; Lisa's past was catching up with her.

The forensic officers arrived at exactly nine o'clock the next morning. They took Janie's fingerprints for elimination purposes then dusted every drawer, every door handle and every possible surface but found nothing. The officers told Janie that the burglar had known exactly what he was doing and the whole place was clean. Once they had finished, Janie flicked through the Yellow Pages and found a locksmith who would come out that afternoon. The next thing she had to do was tell Lisa – if the burglary was related to the man searching for her she had to know. She replaced the living room drawers and their contents. Her address book was on top of the unit and fortunately he hadn't seen it. Flicking through, she found Lisa's home number, picked up the phone and dialled. It rang out for quite a while. She was just about to hang up when Zak picked the phone up. 'Hi Zak, it's Janie.'

'Hi Janie, how's things?'

'Not bad ... is Lisa about?'

'She's gone into Oxford for the day. They've got a couple of girls off sick at the bar, so she's gone to help Reece out. You should catch her on her mobile; I don't think she ever turns it off. You know what she's like, workaholic and all that.'

'OK Zak,' said Janie, 'I'll give her a call. See you soon.' They said goodbye and Janie flicked back through the pages of her address book, located Lisa's mobile and dialled. The phone rang out.

'Hi Lisa, it's Janie.'

'Hi Janie. It's not like you to call my mobile, is everything OK?'

'I'm not sure,' said Janie.

'You at home?'

'Yeah,' said Janie, shakily.

'Hang up. I'll call you back from the office.'

Lisa shouted across the bar to Reece who immediately looked across. She raised her hand to her ear to signify she had to make a call and he raised a thumb in acknowledgement. It was a typical lunchtime at Korky's, with barely a spare seat in the bar. Lisa went through to the back office where it was quieter and dialled Janie's number. Janie picked the phone up straight away. She told Lisa about the burglary, reassuring her that she was all right. 'I'm fine, but that's not really the problem. Well, it is, but something else happened the day before. A man came to the house and asked for you. I told him I'd never heard of you. Lisa, I think it was that bloke you had the money off all those years ago.'

Lisa froze. Every hair on her body was standing up and she could barely speak. 'What makes you think it was him?' she asked.

'He said he'd been away for a long time and was trying to contact you. I think it was him that broke in. All the letters you sent me over the years were stolen. All the cash I keep in the wardrobe went too. Lisa, you have to tell Zak.'

'How can I tell Zak? He knows nothing of my past and it would destroy his trust in me if he knew I had lied to him all these years. No, I can't tell him. Don't worry Janie, I can deal with this.'

'Lisa, the man was a nutcase.'

'Chance's are he won't find me. If he does, I know what to do.'

'Don't do anything stupid,' pleaded Janie, 'you have too much to lose.'

'Don't worry, Janie. You OK for money?'

'Yeah, you've bailed me out enough over the years. I'll be fine. Please be careful, Lisa, do you hear me?'

'I hear you girl, I'll be careful. Don't worry. Bye for now.' Lisa hung up and sat back in her chair. What should she do? There wasn't a lot really she could do. He had spent twenty years behind bars. The money wasn't a problem; if he wanted his money back she could pay him off easily, without even denting her investments. The problem was, if he wanted more than money, then what? She would have to cross that bridge when she came to it. 'Back to work,' she said to herself. She got up and went back into the bar where Reece looked as if he could do with some help.

Lisa arrived home just after one in the morning. As she locked the car and walked to the front door, every movement in the surrounding bushes alerted her senses. She double-checked all the doors and windows and went upstairs, looking in on the children, before going into the bedroom, where Zak was sleeping soundly. She sat on the bed and looked at him. 'I love you so much, I wish I could tell you about this, but I can't.' Tears ran down her face. 'Sleep tight darling.' She placed her clothes on the dressing table chair and climbed into bed, curling up close to Zak. As she lay there, every sound alerted her senses like electricity: the call of an owl and other night birds, a gust of wind rustling through the trees and bushes, the wings of a moth beating against the window pane. It was a long time before she finally fell asleep.

In the twenty years that Jimmy had been institutionalised, technology had moved on at an incredible rate. He wasn't completely unaware of these advances, but at the same time he had never really had the opportunity to grow with them. Although he may have given the impression of being quite slow, the truth was really quite the opposite. The first thing he decided to buy was a mobile phone – everybody had one and stores selling them were all over the place, so it wasn't hard to get one. He really liked having money again and was confident that it wouldn't be long before he had all his money back. He read the letters over and over again. The thought of Lisa with another man plagued his mind; he had never met this Zak, but he hated him already. He decided that on Friday morning he would sign on at the probation office and then go sick from work for the rest of the day. That would give him three whole days to go down south and sort out what he called outstanding business.

The week dragged, but by the time Friday finally arrived he had developed convincing sore throat and cough symptoms and even the probation officer suggested he should go home to bed. As soon as he got out of the probation office he phoned work on his mobile. By ten o'clock he was at New Street station boarding a train bound for London. A couple of hours later the train pulled into Euston station. Jimmy had studied a map of the London Underground; he knew that Wimbledon was on the District Line, but getting there was something else. He saw an official-looking man with an underground uniform and asked to be pointed in the right direction. The official took him over to a large wall map of the Underground. 'You need to take the Circle Line towards Baker Street. Change at Kensington to the District Line and your stop is right here.' He pointed at Wimbledon station on the map 'The Circle Line is right over there.' He indicated a sign above a passageway. Jimmy thanked him and set off. After some confusion with a ticket machine, Jimmy finally found himself on a train heading towards High Street Kensington. He managed to change lines then, as the train pulled into the next station, a guard stepped on the train and shouted, 'Very sorry ladies and gentlemen, there's a problem on the line and you'll have to take a bus to Wimbledon. The 93 bus outside this station will take you there directly, thank you.' The guard immediately came under verbal abuse from a number of passengers. Jimmy got to his feet and followed the majority of them towards the station exit. All Jimmy knew was that the wine bar was on the High Street in Wimbledon. From the bus he spotted a road sign; Merton High Street. 'This is it,' he thought. Jimmy turned round to the passenger sitting behind him, a man in his twenties. 'Excuse me, do you know if there are any wine bars on this road?'

'Yes mate,' the passenger replied in a broad London accent, 'you've got the Candy Bar, just up here and then there's Korky's, about five minutes up the road.' Jimmy thanked him and got off the bus. He scanned the shops on both sides of the road and saw the sign in big swirled letters, 'Korky's Wine Bar'. He stood opposite the bar for a few moments looking across. It was busy and even if she was in there she probably wouldn't recognise him. He crossed the road, dodging through the traffic, and went in to the bar. Nobody paid him any attention. He sat at the bar looking through the wine list. A woman came over, 'Can I get you a drink, sir?' It was Sue. She had virtually made the bar her own these last few years. One of the best moves Lisa ever made was giving Sue the manager's position; it had transformed her.

'Could I get a coffee?' asked Jimmy.

'Certainly sir, black, white?'

'White, please,' replied Jimmy.

'I haven't seen you in here before,' said Sue, trying to make Jimmy feel welcome.

'No, I'm down visiting a friend,' replied Jimmy. 'Careful,' he thought, 'she might be informing on me.' Sue placed his coffee in front of him.

'There you go, sir. That's two pounds please.'

Jimmy gave her two coins and sat back against the bar on his high chair. Sipping his coffee, Jimmy took in the wine bar atmosphere. He liked what he saw: nice area and upmarket customers. He took out his phone and selected 'Messages'. In the text screen he wrote, 'I LIKE THE LONDON BAR IT LOOKS LIKE YOU HAVE MADE SOME GOOD INVESTMENTS WITH MY MONEY, I HOPE YOU HAVEN'T FORGOTTEN ME. YOURS ALWAYS. He selected Lisa's mobile number, conveniently provided by Janie's letters and pressed 'Send'.

Lisa was being her usual chatty self, making the customers in the Oxford branch feel welcome. Her message tone rang out from her phone and she excused herself from the conversation. Flipping open the phone she pressed 'View message'. As she read it, she felt the colour draining from her face; it was like someone walking on her grave. 'You all right Lisa?' asked one of the customers at the bar, 'you look like you've just seen a ghost.'

'Something like that,' replied Lisa. 'Excuse me gents.' She went into the back office, picked up the phone and dialled Janie's number; it rang out for what seemed an age. Just when she was about to hang up, Janie picked up the phone.

'Hi Janie, it's Lisa.'

'I was in the shower, how's things?'

'Not good, he's got my number. Janie, he's watching me, I just had a text message from him saying he likes the look of the bar.'

'Shit Lisa, you're going to have to tell Zak now.'

'I can't Janie.'

'Lisa, these things happened before you even met Zak. He loves you, he'll understand.' Janie could see just how dangerous the situation was becoming and was pleading with Lisa to tell Zak.

'I'm going to arrange to meet him.'

'Are you mad? If you do, I'm coming with you.'

'No Janie, I got myself into this and I'll get myself out of it. Don't worry; I won't do anything stupid, I'll make sure it's in a public place. I'm going to offer him his money with interest, it's the least I can do when he's been locked up for twenty years.'

'Just remember why he got locked up in the first place, Lisa.' Janie was terrified for her friend.

'Janie, I'll be careful. I'll keep in touch. Bye for now.' Lisa hung up. For the rest of the day Lisa tried to think of a suitable place to meet Jimmy. She didn't want him coming anywhere near the Oxford branch, although for all she knew he might already be in Oxford. 'Wimbledon,' she said to herself. One, it would be on her terms, and two, she would be down there for the whole day on Sunday, but most importantly, Zak and the twins would be staying in Oxford this time. If it all went to plan they would never need to know. She selected Jimmy's text message on her phone and pressed 'Reply'. She wrote, HELLO JIMMY, I HAVE A PROPOSITION FOR YOU. MEET ME AT KORKY'S WINE BAR WIMBLEDON, THIS SUNDAY AT 1PM. I ASSUME BY YOUR TEXT YOU KNOW WHERE IT IS, LISA. She sat down and placed the phone on the table in front of her, nervously staring at it, willing it to ring. 'Come on,' she said under her breath. Almost as if she had commanded it, it rang out. She picked up the phone and selected the message, which said just one word: SUNDAY.

Over the past ten years Lisa had accumulated a considerable fortune. Her personal building society account alone contained in excess of half a million pounds but most of her money was tied up in property and shares. Simon Clark continued to control her finances, but the building society account was completely separate. Early on Saturday morning Lisa drove into Oxford and collected a building society cheque for three hundred thousand pounds made payable to Mr James Noakes. If he wasn't content with fifty thousand interest on his money, then he could crawl back to where he came from. By Saturday evening the nerves were starting to show. Once the kids were off to bed Lisa sat down with a coffee.

'Everything all right, love?' asked Zak.

'Yeah, I'm fine darling, just tired.' It was half true, but her mind was fixed on what might happen at the next day's meeting. Fingers crossed, he would just take the cheque and that would be the end of it, but something in the back of her mind was telling her it wouldn't be that simple.

On Sunday morning Lisa was exhausted; she had tossed and turned all night, sleeping fitfully and going over every conceivable outcome, some good, some bad. She showered and went downstairs for a coffee; Zak and the twins were still flat out and she thought it best to let them have a lie in. She drank two cups of coffee but couldn't face any food. Taking out a pen and paper to leave a note, she heard the sound of footsteps on the stairs. 'Running off without saying goodbye are we?' said Zak, rubbing his ruffled hair.

'Morning, darling,' replied Lisa, 'I thought it would be a nice lie in for you all.'

'What time will you be back? I'll prepare a meal.'

'I won't be late – one of Sue's girls has a christening to go to, but she said she would be in for six o'clock, so seven at the latest. But I'll call if there's a problem. There's a couple of issues Sue wants to discuss, but we'll sort that out before we open.'

'OK,' said Zak, 'but call me on my mobile as I'm taking the twins out for a spin this afternoon.'

'You and that car,' said Lisa, 'just take it easy, and put your seatbelt on.'

'Yeah, yeah,' said Zak, smiling, as he reached in the cupboard for a cereal bowl. It really annoyed Lisa, especially when the twins were in the car.

'See you later,' said Lisa. She grabbed her bag and kissed his cheek. As she walked to the car a feeling of guilt overwhelmed her. She hated keeping secrets from Zak, but this time, it was the way it had to be. As it was early on a Sunday, the roads were almost clear and she arrived at the bar just over an hour later. Midweek it would take at least two hours or more during rush hour. There was an hour to go before the staff were due in and the bar didn't open till midday. Sue said she would get in for eleven o'clock so they could have their meeting before opening time. It was a good chance for Lisa to check the stock levels; if she could get in front of herself she could take a day out in the week to spend some quality time with Zak. She checked the latch was on the door before going down to the cellar. Before putting her bag under the bar she opened it and took out the cheque. Three hundred thousand pounds ... who would have ever thought that she could just go into a building society and ask for a cheque of this amount.

Suddenly, BANG BANG. Lisa jumped up, startled. Sue was staring through the door. Lisa quickly pushed the cheque back into her bag and, with a huge sigh of relief, closed the zip. 'The latch is on,' said Sue pointing at the lock.

'Two ticks,' shouted Lisa. She opened the door and hugged Sue.

'You're bright and early today,' said Sue.

'Yeah, I thought we could have that meeting before opening time.'

'Sounds good to me. I'll get my coat off and we can get straight down to it.' Lisa made coffee and they sat at the bar discussing one or two outstanding issues with suppliers. Over the hour, the rest of the staff arrived and opened up for business.

'Sue,' said Lisa, 'I've got an old friend dropping in to see me later – it won't take long.'

'Somebody I know?'

'No, just a chap I knew years back.'

'A chap, eh?' joked Sue.

'No, nothing like that. Said he was in town. I told him to drop in for a chat.'

The usual Sunday lunchtime regulars began to arrive and Lisa became more and more on edge; every time the door opened she instantly spun round to see who was coming through it.

'I'm just going to get some more chardonnay from the cellar, there's only one bottle left,' said Sue.

'I'll go,' said Lisa, 'I meant to check some stock levels earlier and clean forgot.' She went down the cellar and made a few notes on what she needed to order, picked up a box of chardonnay and came back up to the bar. She hadn't been down there ten minutes, but as she walked down the hall towards the bar she spotted him. He was sitting at the bar on a high stool talking to Sue. A feeling of nausea overwhelmed her. 'Get to grips woman,' she said to herself, but her stomach was in knots. As she walked into the bar he turned and smiled. It was hard, but she returned the smile. 'I didn't know this was a friend of yours Lisa,' said Sue, 'Jimmy's been in the last two days.'

'Hello Lisa,' said Jimmy. Lisa's throat was bone dry.

'Hi Jimmy, can I get you a drink?'

'Sue's getting me a coffee, thank you,' said Jimmy.

'You two go and sit over there,' said Sue, pointing towards an empty corner in the bar, 'I'll bring you both a coffee over.'

'Thanks Sue,' replied Lisa, 'Shall we, Jimmy?' Lisa took her bag from under the bar and they moved across the bar to an empty table.

'You're looking good,' said Jimmy. Lisa thanked him. 'From what I've seen you made some good investments with my money. Seems I was right to choose you.' Sue came over with the coffees then went back to the bar. Jimmy leaned forward.

'You're the only thing that got me through the last twenty years, Lisa – I never once stopped thinking about you.'

'It's been a long time Jimmy, life moves on.'

'Mine didn't,' said Jimmy, his stare sending a shiver down Lisa's spine.

'You have another bar in Oxford. You gambled with my money when you opened that one didn't you?' There was a dreadful silence.

'Why did you break into my friend's flat Jimmy?'

'I had to find you. She told me she'd never heard of you. I knew she was lying.'

'She was only trying to protect me,' said Lisa.

'That didn't help me though did it?' Behind his lips Jimmy's teeth were bared and Lisa sensed he was angry.

'Anyway,' said Lisa, 'what's done is done. I said I had a proposition for you.'

'Excuse me,' Jimmy interrupted, 'you have a proposition for me? Shouldn't it be the other way round?' Lisa opened her bag and pulled out the cheque. She folded it in half and passed it over the table. Jimmy picked up the cheque and opened it out.

'So what's the proposition?' he asked, with a totally blank look on his face.

'That's a cheque for three hundred grand Jimmy, over fifty thousand interest on the money you gave me.'

'But that wasn't the deal was it?' He stared straight at her, his teeth now visibly barred.

'What do you mean?' asked Lisa, barely able to stop herself from visibly shaking with fear.

'This is only part of the deal isn't it?'

'Jimmy, I'm a married woman with two children.'

'Do you think I give a shit about that?' Lisa stared straight back at him; the atmosphere was electric. 'A deal is a deal,' said Jimmy.

'You must be mad if you think I'm going to leave my family for you.'

'Firstly, I'm not mad,' he hissed, 'a board of doctors can confirm that. Secondly, if you think I'm just going to walk away after twenty years of waiting, you're very much mistaken.'

'Is it more money you want?' she asked, desperately.

'You know what I want. I want what you promised me.'

'I never promised you anything Jimmy, you just assumed.' Jimmy raised a finger to his mouth to stop her talking.

'I want you to leave him.' Lisa found it hard to believe what she was hearing.

'You are mad,' she said.

'I'll give you one week to make your decision.' Jimmy continued to stare straight at her.

'Then what?' asked Lisa. She could not believe the audacity of this man. She was a very gentle person at heart, but this man was threatening her family and when loved ones are under threat an inner strength surfaces. Suddenly she stood up, pushing her chair back away from the table, and shouted 'Get out of my bar!' All eyes in the bar were on her and the room fell silent. Jimmy sat still. 'I said get out or I'll call the police.' With that a couple of regulars stood up.

'You OK, Lisa?' they asked.

'Yes thanks,' she said, 'he's just leaving.' Jimmy stood up, slipping the cheque into his inside pocket

'One week,' he said. He walked over to the door and glanced back at Lisa once more, fixing a stare on her. Lisa looked composed, but inside she was terrified. As the door closed, she thanked the two men who had stood up for her.

'Sue,' she called to the bar, 'get these guys a drink on me will you?' Sue acknowledged her with a nod. 'Sorry everyone for disrupting your lunchtime,' she said to the customers, then went down the hall to the office and closed the door behind her. Sitting at the desk her hands were visibly shaking. What had she got herself into? There was a knock at the door and Sue's head appeared.

'You OK, Lisa?'

'Yeah, come in Sue.' She sat at the desk facing Lisa. 'Sorry you had to see that.'

'Don't be silly, so much for old friends.' Lisa stared at the desk.

'Do you want to talk about it?'

'I wish I could, Sue.'

'You can tell me anything and it won't leave this room, anything at all. You've been good to me, Lisa, and I won't forget it, I'll always be here for you.'

'Thanks, Sue, I appreciate it. Just promise me you won't say a word to Zak about what happened.'

'If that's what you want, it's forgotten,' said Sue. 'Why don't you get off home? It's quiet in here. Go and have some quality time with the twins and Zak. We can hold the fort.' They stood up and gave each other a hug. Lisa went out of the back door. Just as she was about to pull it closed she stopped, realising how vulnerable she was. It was a secluded alley with nothing overlooking her. This wasn't paranoia, it was reality. She had to stop taking chances. This maniac had killed before and his victims had been completely innocent; now he had a reason.

20

Revenge

When Lisa arrived home there was no sign of Zak and the twins. Zak had said he would take them out in his car. The BMW Z4 that Zak cherished was purely a two-seater. Lisa didn't like the thought of both of the twins being in the same seat, but they loved it; they thought it was great fun, especially when the roof was down. Lisa decided to prepare a meal for when they came home. From the look of what had been taken out of the freezer, Zak intended to cook sweet and sour chicken with rice and garlic bread, the twins' favourite. She made a coffee and began dicing the chicken. The sound of the BMW pulling onto the drive caught her attention. Opening the front door she could see the twins waving at her through the screen of the car. Waving back she thought how Josh was so like his father; dark hair and eyes, and a very lean yet muscular physique. Jodie's hair was darker than her mother's, but her face had the same beautiful features. Jodie jumped out the car. 'Hi mum, I told him, I told him, put your seatbelt on but he didn't.'

'Jodie's a snitch,' shouted Josh in an annoyingly joyful little tune.

'You tell her, mate,' said Zak. Lisa threw him one of those looks that could kill.

'I've told you about that,' she said, angrily, 'come on, you can help me prepare dinner.' They all went into the house.

After their meal, Lisa and Zak cleared away and the twins got out a board game for them all to join in. It was turning out to be an excellent day. For Lisa it was perfect, and by early evening her annoyance with Zak about the seatbelt had been well and truly pushed to the back of her mind. By eight o'clock the twins were in bed. They had school the following day so, as usual, it would be an early start in the Wright household. Lisa and Zak were sitting on the sofa. The television was on, but like most Sunday evenings, there was nothing worth watching and after about half an hour Zak fell asleep. Lisa had wanted to ring Janie since lunchtime but couldn't get a free second away from Zak and the twins. Now was her opportunity. As gently as she could, she lifted Zak's arm from around her shoulder and replaced it with a cushion. Tip-toeing into the kitchen, she picked up the phone and closed the door behind her. Scanning through the phone's address book, she located Janie's number and selected it. Janie was lying on the sofa when the phone rang.

'Hi Janie, it's Lisa.'

'I was waiting for you to call,' said Janie. 'You haven't done anything stupid with that maniac, have you?'

'I arranged to meet him at the bar in Wimbledon.'

'And?' asked Janie.

'I ended up throwing him out.'

'You're joking!' Janie shuffled around on the sofa, trying to get a little more comfortable. 'Go on tell me more.'

'He said I had a week to leave my family. Well, that was it, I flipped. I told him to get out or else, and the best bit was I had just given him a cheque for three hundred grand.' The phone went quiet; Janie was dumbstruck.

'You still there?' asked Lisa.

'Did you say three hundred thousand pounds?'

'Yeah, well I had two hundred and fifty thousand off him in the first place, so theoretically it was his anyway. I was kind of looking after it for him.'

'Be very careful, Lisa,' said Janie, wishing her friend had not got herself into this.

'That's why I was calling you. When he left here he looked pretty upset, did you get those locks changed?'

'It's like Fort Knox here now, Lisa.'

'Good. I'm hoping he'll just take the money and that will be the end of it.'

'You're playing a very dangerous game, Lisa, just be careful.'

'I will. Listen, I have to go, I think Zak's waking up.' They said goodbye and Lisa hung up. With that, Zak called her.

'What are you doing?' he asked.

'Janie called. I was having a chat.'

'I'm going up to bed,' said Zak, 'I'm shattered.'

'Me too darling, carry on up, I'll be right behind you.' Lisa double-checked every door and window in the house. Subliminally, the meeting with Jimmy had affected her more than she realised. Over the next few days she relaxed a little, but was still vigilant.

Since his meeting with Lisa, Jimmy had become short-tempered and irritable. He had his money back but that wasn't enough. 'If she doesn't leave that bastard,' he said to himself, he would do something about it. He didn't know what, but one thing was for sure, no one was going to make a fool of him.

Jimmy needed transport. He had some driving experience but it had been a long time ago. In his late teens he had a motorbike. He used to spend many hours tinkering with it; at that time in his life it was the only interest he had. He thought about buying a car, but it would have meant taking driving lessons and he couldn't be bothered just now as there were more pressing things on his mind.

Jimmy planned to go down to Oxford the following Saturday and see what else Lisa had been doing with his money. The rest of the week dragged. He had become a virtual outcast amongst the other workers at the warehouse. Somehow they had found out where he had spent the last twenty years and all sorts of rumours were flying around about why he had been there, none of them good. He finished work on Friday at two o'clock; all the orders had been packed so the foreman let them get away early. Jimmy was glad to see the back of the place. He went home and changed his clothes, put a few things in an overnight bag, then headed into Birmingham. The train left New Street station at four o'clock and just over an hour later he was walking out of the station in Oxford. Earlier that week he had paid Lisa's cheque into his bank account, which had startled the cashier, considering he only had a hundred and fifty pounds in his account previously. He pacified the cashier with a cock-and-bull story about being a member of a successful national lottery syndicate; it seemed to work. He also still had the money he had stolen from Janie's flat, so cash wasn't a problem. He jumped in a cab, 'Korky's Wine Bar please,' said Jimmy.

'No problem,' the cabbie replied. He started his meter and pulled out into the traffic. Within fifteen minutes the cab pulled up.

'It's just down the High Street mate, this is as close as I can get, it's pedestrianised you see.'

'Thanks,' said Jimmy. He paid the fare and stood looking down the High Street. It was very busy and groups of young people were preparing themselves for the coming weekend. As he walked along the road he spotted Korky's on the right-hand side. 'Korky's Wine Bar and Bistro,' he read aloud; it looked impressive. 'My, you have done well for us,' said Jimmy to himself. Standing at the main entrance was a smartly dressed doorman in a long black coat; he didn't look like a bouncer but it was obviously one of the reasons he was there. As Jimmy approached he felt the man look him up and down. 'Good evening,' said the doorman. Jimmy nodded and walked into the bar. Although it was not yet six o'clock they were doing a roaring trade. His eyes scanned the bar and surrounding area, half hoping Lisa was in there. It was nearly a week since he had had his little showdown with Lisa and he meant what he had said. 'Can I help you?' asked a barmaid.

'Budweiser please,' replied Jimmy.

'Bottled or draught?'

'Bottled please,' he replied. 'Is Lisa working here this evening?' he asked, as he handed her two pounds.

'Mrs Wright you mean?'

Jimmy thought about what she had said; it didn't click at first. 'Yes,' he replied.

'I think she's in tomorrow evening. Are you a friend of hers?'

'You could call it that, a business acquaintance actually,' said Jimmy.

'Reece is in if you'd like me to get him for you?'

'No, no it's OK. When you see her just say Jimmy was asking after her. You wouldn't know where there's a hotel or B&B locally would you?' She gave him directions to a Travel Lodge, not too far away. Jimmy thanked her then picked up his bag and moved away from the bar. He sat down by the window, deep in thought, watching the world go by. 'This place is worth a fortune,' he thought to himself. 'Three hundred thousand? She's taking me for a ride.' He drank down the rest of his beer and set off for the Travel Lodge.

The room was plain but comfortable and he lay on the bed looking up at the ceiling, contemplating his next move. First, he had to locate Stanton Harcourt. He liked the sound of it; it sounded upper class and expensive. In the morning he would get a cab and see for himself.

On Saturday he had breakfast and went for a walk along the High Street; the whole area looked very affluent. A bike shop caught his attention. Crossing the road for a closer look, he spotted a notice in the window advertising scooters from twelve hundred pounds; he decided to take a look. They had changed a lot since he had owned a bike and even the scooters looked really sporty.

'Interested, sir?' asked a salesman.

'Do I need a licence for one of these scooters?' asked Jimmy.

'Just a provisional initially, and Part 1 of your driving licence, but you can get one of those relatively easily; it's all done on computer now.'

'I'm only here for the weekend,' said Jimmy, 'would I be able to buy one today for cash?' The salesman's eyes lit up.

'I'm sure we can sort something out sir. Come over to the desk and I'll run through the different deals we have on the various models.' Jimmy listened to all the spiel, but at the end of the day he wasn't bothered about this model or that, he just wanted some transport. Just over an hour later, Jimmy was the proud owner of a black Piaggio 125cc scooter. With a helmet and gloves it came to a round figure of sixteen hundred pounds.

'I'll have it ready for you at the end of business today, Mr Noakes.' Jimmy shook hands with the salesman. As he left the shop he decided it would be a good idea to wait till he had his own transport before going to Lisa's village; he would probably look a little conspicuous walking round a small village with no apparent destination. Anyway, there was plenty to see in Oxford and he decided to spend the rest of the day window-shopping.

By half past four he had seen everything he wanted so he collected the cash from his hotel room and headed back to the bike shop. The salesman was true to his word; the gleaming black scooter was parked just inside the showroom door, with the helmet and gloves placed on the seat.

'Good afternoon, Mr Noakes,' said the salesman. 'The scooter's ready. Our engineer's given it a clean bill of health. There's some fuel in it but not a lot, so it's probably best to put some in sooner rather than later. You just have to sort out your tax and insurance.'

'I've already sorted my insurance,' Jimmy butted in. He hadn't, but it got the salesman off his back.

'Excellent. Right then, just the matter of the payment. Shall we go into the office?' Jimmy nodded and followed him through to the office where the paperwork was laid out on the desk. Jimmy pulled out a huge roll of twenty-pound notes and passed them to the salesman who counted the money, placing it in tidy little piles. He then gave Jimmy some documents to sign. 'That's it then, you're the official owner – congratulations. I'll show you round the bike and you can get off.' Ten minutes later Jimmy was sitting on the bike wearing the helmet and gloves. He was a little apprehensive, but at the same time was looking forward to the experience. After a quick stop for fuel, he found a roadsign directing him to Stanton Harcourt. He was surprised how easy it was to get back on a bike and after just half an hour it felt just like the old saying, as easy as riding a bike.

He spotted a sign saying 'Stanton Harcourt 1 mile.' It was a winding road, with blind bend after blind bend. Jimmy slowed right down every now and then, passing a concealed entrance to a farm or field. A large sign welcomed him to Stanton Harcourt and prevailed upon him to drive carefully. It was like driving through a time warp; thatched cottage after thatched cottage. 'Some of these places must be hundreds of years old,' he thought, and obviously worth a small fortune. Which one was Lisa's? He drove round for about ten minutes looking at the houses and hoping to see something or someone to assist him in his search, but to no avail. He would have to follow her. Once he knew what car she drove it would be easy. That evening, he would follow her home when she left the bar. It was about time she realised who she was messing with.

Lisa had just cleared away the dinner plates, 'Can I do the washing up mum?' asked Jodie.

'I'll tell you what,' said Lisa, 'I'll wash, you dry.' The little girl was delighted, pleased as punch that she was helping her mum. She picked up the tea towel and waited anxiously for the plates to be placed on the drainer.

'Mum,' she asked with a puzzled look.

'Yes, love?'

'I know we shouldn't talk to strangers. But if they talk to you and they know your name, is it rude not to answer them, especially if they're really nice as well?' Lisa's heart missed a beat.

'What stranger are we talking about Jodie?'

'The nice man at school.' Lisa took the tea towel from the little girl and dried her hands.

'Come and sit over here darling.' They sat down at the kitchen table.

'He talked to Josh first, called him by his name. I told him not to talk to him but he knew my name too.'

'What did he look like darling?'

'Kind of old. His hair was grey.' Lisa felt a cold shiver up her spine.

'Josh,' she shouted, 'come here.' Josh came running into the kitchen with an Action Man in each hand.

'What's up?' Josh violently banged his Action Men together.

'Stop that and listen,' said Lisa, trying to keep her voice calm, 'both of you stay in the schoolyard till me or daddy arrive. I don't want you waiting by the gate anymore, you got that?' Josh continued to clash his Action Men. 'Josh, are you listening?' Lisa was now raising her voice.

'Yeah, I'm listening, but why?'

Lisa's voice raised at least another forty decibels, 'NEVER MIND WHY!'

The twins fell silent, both staring at their mother with a look of shock on their faces. It wasn't like Lisa to shout.

'Are you two upsetting your mum?' Zak asked as he came through to the kitchen.

'No, it's OK,' said Lisa. 'Sorry kids, I shouldn't have shouted. It's not your fault … just don't talk to strangers. You got that?' The twins nodded and Lisa sent them out to play in the garden. They ran off, Jodie completely forgetting about the washing up.

'Everything all right, Lisa?' asked Zak, a worried look on his face.

'Yeah, just overreacting. Just make sure you're on time for the kids coming out of school.'

'I always am,' he replied.

'Good,' said Lisa irritably as she carried on with the washing up. The thought of him approaching her children infuriated her. How long could she keep this from Zak now?

Lisa had to be in work before seven o'clock as Saturday night at Korky's meant all hands on deck. It was easily the biggest night of the week. It had been a long time since there had been a free table on a Saturday night at Korky's restaurant. Zak and the twins were having a quiet night in with a DVD and popcorn to keep them happy. Lisa always took the old white BMW; it was getting on a bit now and she had considered changing it for a newer model, but it had never let her down, so there seemed little point messing with something that was working fine. 'Don't wait up, Zak,' she said. 'You know what it's like on a Saturday night.'

'OK darling,' he replied, 'don't work too hard.'

She said goodbye to the twins, pulled the front door shut behind her, jumped in the car and set off for Oxford. It didn't take long to get there as she had done the journey so many times she was almost on autopilot. As she parked the car at the end of the High Street her mobile rang out. She searched through her handbag to find the phone.

'Hi Lisa, it's Reece. Just checking you're coming in tonight.'

'I'm just parking the car – I'll be with you in a couple of minutes.'

'Thank God for that,' said Reece, 'two of the girls phoned in sick. It's mad in the bar.'

'See you in a min.' Lisa grabbed her bag and coat, locked the car and started up the road towards Korky's. Jimmy was standing on the opposite corner of the High Street, the collar of his jacket pulled up close around his ears. If she had just looked across the road she would have seen him, but Reece's call had occupied her mind and all she was thinking about was getting to work to help out. Jimmy pulled out a pen and paper and wrote down her car registration. That evening he intended to follow her home and if for any reason she slipped away, there weren't that many places in her village to look.

The night at Korky's was hectic; they tried to contact off-duty staff, but to no avail. By closing time, Lisa was shattered and all she wanted was to be at home in bed. It was after one o'clock by the time they had cleared away and replenished the shelves. 'You get off Lisa,' said Reece, 'I can finish up here.' Lisa thankfully gave in.

'I'll give you a call tomorrow,' said Lisa, 'see if those girls come in.' Placing her hand over her mouth in an attempt to stifle a yawn, she pulled on her coat, picked up her bag and said goodbye. She stepped out into the street. It was now completely silent, not a soul about. The short walk to the car felt longer than normal. Every now and then she glanced over her shoulder. She pressed the alarm button on the key fob and the central locking clicked the doors open. As she got into the car she didn't notice the dark figure sitting on his bike about a hundred metres down the road. As she moved off so did the bike, keeping well back so as not to attract attention. While keeping the glare of the BMW's lights well in front of him, Lisa was completely oblivious to the bike. Jimmy only had to close the distance as they approached the village. They reached Stanton Harcourt with Jimmy approximately two hundred metres behind her, plenty close enough to see which house was hers. He saw the car turn in and the intruder light over the driveway light up. Lisa pushed the door open and stepped out of the car. As she stood up she stretched, thankful to be home. Jimmy slowed the bike and watched as she went inside, then turned the bike and sat watching the house. Lisa locked the door and placed the keys on the kitchen table; her eyes felt as if they would close at any moment. She went straight upstairs and turned on her bedside lamp. Jimmy saw the light and smiled to himself. Lisa slipped out of her clothes and slid into bed. She clicked off the light and almost instantly fell asleep.

'Got ya,' said Jimmy to himself. He put the bike into gear and accelerated away in the direction he had come from.

Lisa woke with the sun shining on her face through the bedroom window. She leaned over to check the time: it was nearly lunchtime. Slipping on her dressing gown she went downstairs. The house was unusually quiet for a Sunday morning. She found Zak was sitting at the kitchen table reading the Sunday papers. 'Morning sleepy head,' he said. Lisa scratched her head.

'Why didn't you wake me?' she asked.

'Thought you needed the rest, darling.' He got up from the table, 'sit yourself down and I'll get the kettle on. Want some toast?'

'Yes please. Where are the twins?'

'Playing in the garden. I told them the first one to find me a four-leaf clover would get a treat, that was just over an hour ago.'

Lisa laughed. 'You're a bad one you are. Go and check on them for me.'

'Lisa, they're in the garden.'

'Please Zak,' Lisa lowered her eyes as if to say just for me.

'OK OK.' Zak stepped out the back door, 'Josh, Jodie,' he shouted. There was no reply. Again he tried, 'Josh, Jodie.' Still nothing. Lisa jumped up from the table and Zak went out into the garden. Just then, two small figures appeared from the copse at the far end of the garden. Lisa stood tensely at the kitchen in a state of obvious anxiety. 'Come on you two,' called Zak as the twins came running over.

'What's up?' asked Josh. He looked as if he had been rolling around in the bushes with leaves and twigs over his pullover and in his hair.

'You'd better ask your mum,' replied Zak. The twins looked at their mother uncertainly.

'Keep out of those woods,' said Lisa.

'But mum...' Josh started.

'Never mind "but mum," just do as you're told.' They both looked down at the floor. It was not often that they were reprimanded, especially when they didn't understand why. But the sun was shining and Josh had a ball at his feet; he suddenly kicked it with all his might over the lawn. Jodie set off in pursuit, a split second later she was being overtaken by Josh.

'Are you sure everything's OK?' said Zak, 'You're acting very strangely just lately.'

'Sorry,' said Lisa, putting her head down on his shoulder, 'I just worry about them that's all. Come on, let's get that tea and toast.' They walked back to the house arm in arm.

Jimmy was sitting in his hotel room, contemplating his next step. He selected 'Messages' on his mobile phone and wrote, 'I TOLD YOU I WOULD GIVE YOU ONE WEEK,' then sent it to Lisa's phone. Lisa was in the bedroom, dressing after a shower, when the message tone on her phone rang out. Wrapping a towel around her hair, she took the phone from her bag and read the message. 'Cheeky bastard,' she said to herself. Infuriated with the audacity of the man she rang his number. Jimmy's phone rang, a rare event, and he was delighted to see from the screen that it was Lisa calling. For one small moment he thought she was ringing to declare her undying love for him. He accepted the call. Lisa went straight on the offensive, her temper reaching a new level. 'Who the fuck do you think you are? I gave you back much more than you gave me in the first place. Now you listen. I'm warning you, if you go anywhere near my children again, I'll have the police on to you faster than you can blink.' Jimmy thought for a moment, 'Near her children?' he said to himself. Lisa continued, 'Now stay the fuck out of my life.' With adrenalin rushing through her body she hung up and, shaking, threw the phone onto the bed. Jimmy still had the phone pressed against his ear. Suddenly, it was as if his whole world had tumbled down around him; every chance of a life with his dream girl was gone. Slowly his hand lowered to his lap. With his bottom lip quivering like that of an upset child, he squeezed the phone in his hand so hard that the plastic casing cracked. 'I'll show you who the fuck I am, bitch.' He put the phone in his pocket and clenched his fist in the palm of his other hand; now he had nothing to lose.

Jimmy drove back home late on the Sunday evening; the last thing he wanted was his parole officer chasing after him for not turning up at work. His temper was becoming harder and harder to control. If he lost control at work he would be back inside the same day. By Wednesday it was unbearable. He had to get out of there. A delivery of large crates had to be moved from the loading bay and Jimmy saw his opportunity. As soon as he attempted to move the first crate he screamed out in pain, dropping to his knees as if the pain was excruciating. The team leader came running over, 'what's happened?'

'It's my back,' groaned Jimmy.

'Can you stand?'

'I'm not sure.'

'Stay there for a second, see if it eases off,' said the team leader. All the commotion attracted the manager who looked out of his office window and saw the crowd standing around Jimmy. Quickly pulling on a high visibility jacket, he went to see what was happening.

'OK everyone, give him some air. What you done, mate?'

'It's my back,' said Jimmy. 'I think I can get up now.' Slowly Jimmy got up, one hand on his lower back and the other on the crate.

'Right,' said the manager to the team leader, 'get it in the accident book, then use the works van to take him up the hospital.'

'No, no,' said Jimmy, 'I'll be OK, I just need to rest. I've only pulled a muscle.' The manager left the team leader to sort things out. Jimmy couldn't be persuaded to go to the hospital.

'If you're sure then,' said the team leader, 'I'll get someone to take you home.' Ten minutes later Jimmy was on his way home. Each time they went over a bump he laid on the agony, 'Ooh, take it easy mate.'

'Sorry pal,' said the driver, 'nearly there.' He slowed down, trying to ease Jimmy's discomfort. The van pulled up at Jimmy's flat and slowly he eased himself out of the passenger seat.

'Thanks mate,' said Jimmy.

'No worries, take it easy.' As the van pulled away Jimmy smiled.

'Time to sort that bitch out,' he said to himself, closing the front door.

Jimmy phoned his parole officer. If he didn't appear on Friday morning there would be a warrant out for him. They were understanding. Jimmy gave the name of the manager who had dealt with his accident and after a quick phone call to verify the facts, the parole officer excused him signing in for a week. But he still had to phone in first thing on Friday morning. Jimmy ate a sandwich then packed an overnight bag and set off on his bike for Oxford. He booked into the Travel Lodge again; it was cheap, comfortable and they didn't want to know his life history.

Jimmy was good at waiting. He had immense patience; being institutionalised for twenty years had given him plenty of practice. He decided to watch Lisa and her family and identify their routine, then, when the time was right, she'd be sorry. Jimmy drove to Stanton Harcourt just before first light, so that he could get into position to watch the house before the family woke. On the second morning, driving into the series of tight bends, he hit a patch of mud and his rear wheel began to skid. The back of the bike flipped towards the long grass on the verge and he pulled up sharply, just short of a ditch and stumpy hawthorn hedge which skirted the fields. Shaken, he put the bike on its stand and flipping up the visor of his helmet, took a moment to steady himself. There was no other traffic around. On the opposite side of the lane, in the breaking light he could just make out a shape, something large but unrecognisable. Curious, he crossed the lane and walked towards it. Just around the bend was a gap in the hedge and a metal gate marked an entrance to the field. The shape became clearer; it was a large tractor with an agricultural rotavator attached. As the darkness lifted further, Jimmy could see that the field on the other side of the lane had been turned in neat rows; the tractor must have been brought over in readiness to begin work in the field on this side. 'Interesting,' he thought.

Jimmy had watched Lisa leave for work at exactly eight o'clock each morning. At half past eight, Zak and the twins would get into the sports car, put the roof down and head towards Oxford, presumably taking the twins to school. Zak was back at the house by nine o'clock. Jimmy had a real loathing for Zak; if Zak hadn't turned up on the scene, Jimmy and Lisa would have been an item, or so he believed.

The following Monday morning, like clockwork, Lisa left at eight o'clock. Half an hour later, Zak and the twins set off in exactly the same routine, but this time followed by Jimmy. Zak sped off towards Oxford. Jimmy followed, but on reaching the gate at the tight bends pulled off the road. He took a good look around; there was no sign of activity in the lane or any of the fields. The tractor was parked on a slight incline. He opened the gate, constantly glancing around in case he was seen. He checked his watch: 8:50. By his reckoning, Zak would pass the gate on his way back in the next five minutes. Climbing onto the tractor he released the brake. It rocked forward then stopped. 'Shit!' He checked the brake was fully off. Why wasn't it moving? He jumped off and looked underneath; a large block of wood had been used to chock the wheel. He kicked it with all his might. The weight of the tractor was now leaning on the block. He kept kicking and little by little, it inched out. Suddenly the tractor lurched forward, narrowly missing Jimmy's foot. It hit the corner post of the gate, snapping it like a twig. The tractor rolled out into the road then the rotavator blades caught on the gate and brought it to a halt, blocking two-thirds of the lane. Jimmy quickly jumped on his bike and drove off towards Oxford. He had not gone more than half a mile when the BMW Z4 passed him going in the opposite direction. The top was down and music was blaring out. Jimmy pulled over and took off his helmet; the cornering ability of the BMW was phenomenal; Zak had always said, 'It corners like it's on rails.' He knew just how much he could give it. As he turned into the fateful bend, the car was touching around 45 mph. Zak's reactions were fast, but not fast enough. He saw the tractor; frantically, he spun the wheel and swerved hard right. The nearside front wheel of the car clipped the tractor. The car flipped up onto its side, instantly activating the roll bar. The car slid at a frightening speed towards the ditch on the other side of the road. Zak's upper body slammed onto the floor, his legs twisted around the steering column. Lisa had told him time and time again to wear his seatbelt. As the front of the vehicle hit the ditch, Zak was thrown forward and with a sickening thud, his head hit the windscreen pillar. The car finally came to rest upside down in the ditch, Zak's broken and lifeless body barely visible from the road. From half a mile away Jimmy heard the vehicle skid and then the loud impact. A slight grin appeared on his face as he calmly put on his helmet and drove off towards Oxford.

21

Retribution

It was just half past ten in the morning, and Lisa and Reece were sitting at the bar; they always got into work early on Mondays to discuss stock and accept the week's deliveries. A knock at the front door attracted their attention and through the glass they could see two police officers. 'What have you been up to then?' asked Reece, jokingly.

'You, ya mean,' replied Lisa, returning the banter. Lisa got up and opened the front door.

'Morning, madam, I'm trying to locate a Mrs Wright.'

'I'm Mrs Wright, what's wrong?'

'I'm PC Crawthorne and this is WPC Berrow, can we go inside?' The officers followed Lisa into the bar, where Reece was already standing up, inquisitively wondering what they wanted.

'Please, take a seat Mrs Wright,' said Crawthorne. Lisa did as he asked. 'Does your husband drive a Black BMW Z4, registration PB05 NSW?'

'Yes ... is he all right?' Gripped with anxiety, Lisa stood up.

'Mrs Wright, there's been an accident.'

'Where is he, has he been hurt?'

'I'm sorry to inform you, Mrs Wright, the accident was fatal.' Reece's mouth fell open. A wave of nausea swept over Lisa and without warning, she fainted.

'Lisa, Lisa, can you hear me?' Slowly, Lisa regained consciousness. Reece and the two police officers were standing over her, Crawthorne supporting her head.

'I'll get some water,' said Reece, as Lisa sat up.

'Careful, Mrs Wright. Don't get up too quickly, you've had a bad shock,' said Crawthorne.

'The children,' said Lisa, 'my God, are they OK?'

'He was the only person in the vehicle,' said Berrow. Reece came back with a glass of water, which he carefully passed to Lisa, her hands visibly shaking. She sipped some water then they helped her up onto a chair.

'It appears to be a freak accident,' said Crawthorne. 'He swerved to miss a farm vehicle that had slipped its brake and ended up in the middle of the road.' Lisa's head dropped, she was completely devastated and silent. Crawthorne looked at Reece, 'Can you stay with her?'

'Of course,' replied Reece. 'I'll get her home, then we'll take it from there.'

'There will have to be a formal identification,' said Crawthorne, 'I'll give you a call later today concerning that.' Reece took out his wallet and gave him a business card with his mobile number on it.

'I'll stay with her today. You can contact me anytime on that number.'

'Right you are sir,' said Crawthorne. 'Once again, Mrs Wright, I'm very sorry.' As soon as the officers had left Reece made some calls. Within a short time three girls arrived – members of Reece's staff he knew he could trust to take over.

'Come on Lisa, let's get you home,' he said, helping her on with her coat.

'Don't worry about this place, it's all taken care of,' said one of the girls. Reece thanked them then put his arm around Lisa and walked her to the door. Lisa's car was parked just off the High Street. Reece opened the passenger door and Lisa got in, then he went around to the driver's side. Lisa hadn't moved; she was obviously in shock. Reaching over, he fastened her seatbelt.

As they approached Stanton Harcourt they passed the scene of the accident. Reece immediately recognised Zak's car upside down in the ditch, with a large 'POLICE AWARE' notice taped to the side. Lisa's head was down and she was still silent. There was no other way into the village from here, so Reece passed the scene as quickly as he could. Back at the house everything was so quiet and still, there was an eerie feeling about the place. Reece made a cup of tea and handed it to Lisa. 'Who would you like me to call Lisa?' She shook her head. She couldn't believe what was happening. It was at times like this that people turned to their families, but that was not an option for Lisa.

'Janie,' she replied.

'Janie?' asked Reece. 'That's your friend from Birmingham isn't it?'

'Yes, pass me the phone, I'll call her.'

'If you're sure you're up to it,' said Reece. Lisa took the phone from him and dialled Janie's number.

'Hi Lisa, I'm honoured, twice in the last two weeks.'

'Janie, there's been an accident.' Tears began to roll down Lisa's face. 'It's Zak. He's been killed.' She could barely get the words out.

'Lisa are you at home?'

'Yes.'

'I'm on my way darlin'.' Dependable as ever, Janie immediately called a cab, explaining that there was an emergency and she needed driving to Stanton Harcourt as quickly as possible. She quickly put a few things in an overnight bag. When the cab arrived ten minutes later, Janie was already waiting at the front door. The driver knew Janie from years ago; he used to take her on jobs around the city. Since she retired from all that they hadn't seen much of each other. When he heard about her situation he volunteered to take the job right away.

Reece phoned the school and informed the headmaster of the situation. There was no point in rushing to the school and collecting the twins; they would have to cope with their grief soon enough. Just an hour and a half later the cab pulled up at the house. As Janie was an old friend, the driver only charged her for the fuel, but she gave him fifty pounds anyway, as a kind of thank you. Reece saw the car pull onto the drive and went straight to the front door; as he opened it, Janie was already on the steps.

'Hi, where is she?'

'In the living room.'

Janie dropped her bag in the hall and went straight through. As she reached the living room she stopped. Lisa was sitting on the sofa, her hands clenched together. The last time Janie had seen her looking this vulnerable was the day she found her all those years ago, being set upon by that waster in the bus shelter. Lisa looked up, her eyes brimming with grief and face stained with mascara; she looked dreadful. Janie walked over to her.

'I'm here now girl.'

Lisa stood up and as Janie put her arms around her she cried, all her emotions spilling from her body.

'Let it all out,' said Janie. 'Let it all out.' She held her tightly.

Reece went into the kitchen feeling completely helpless. What else could he do for her? He didn't know. By mid-afternoon, Janie had contacted Zak's parents and Sue at the Wimbledon bar. Janie said she would collect the twins from school in a cab while Reece stayed with Lisa. It was something Janie wasn't looking forward to, but Lisa was in no fit state to tell them what had happened. The cab pulled up at the school and Janie could see Jodie and Josh waiting at the entrance with the form teacher and the headmaster.

'Auntie Janie!' the twins shouted, smiles beaming across their little faces. Janie forced a smile and waved back. Janie introduced herself to their teacher and headmaster, trying not to let the twins pick up on the situation.

'We're all thinking of them,' said the headmaster.

'Thanks,' replied Janie. 'Come on kids, let's get you home.'

'Bye miss. Bye sir,' said the twins and they walked towards the cab, unaware of what waited for them at home. The twins were so excited to see Janie; she had never collected them from school before.

'You're the second person that's come to see us today,' said Jodie.

'The second?' asked Janie.

'The man came again; he was waving at us from the gate. Mum told us we're not to talk to any strangers, even if they know who we are, so we just waved and stayed away. I don't think he's a bad man. He only ever asks about mummy anyway.'

'How many times has he been at the school?' she asked.

'How many times, Josh?' asked Jodie. Josh was busy watching the driver changing gear. 'Josh!' Jodie barked at him.

'About five ... something like that,' he said. Janie was worried; Lisa hadn't said anything about this to her.

'Does your mummy know you've spoken to him?' asked Janie.

'Yes,' replied Josh, keen to get back to watching the driver, 'she knows.'

Lisa had washed her face; she didn't want the twins to see her like that, she had to be strong for them. They both came bursting into the living room.

'Mummy, auntie Janie collected us from school!' They both searched around the room with their eyes.

'Where's daddy?' asked Jodie.

'Come here kids, sit down with me,' said Lisa. The next fifteen minutes were to be amongst the hardest in Lisa's life. The pain in the eyes of her children was more than she could bear. She wasn't sure how long they held onto her, but it felt like a lifetime. Zak was everything to the children; he had brought them up, playing a motherly role since they were six months old. It would be a long time before any form of normality returned to their young lives.

Over the next few days, Janie was a rock to the family; if anything needed doing, she was there. The hardest moment for Lisa was identifying the body of her husband and without Janie she could not have coped. The police had eliminated foul play, but the farmer who owned the tractor had been taken in for questioning. He could not explain the brake failing or the block of wood missing from the wheel; he assured the police they were all in place the day before. It appeared to be just a tragic accident.

Meanwhile, Jimmy had returned to Birmingham. He knew that Zak's car had crashed, but didn't know the severity of the accident. As far as he was concerned, he had dealt out a short sharp shock.

The funeral had been arranged two weeks to the day of the accident. Both of Zak's parents had been ill. The stress of it all had taken its toll on them, but they soldiered on for Lisa and the twins. Family, close friends and all the staff from both bars attended the service as a mark of respect; it was a terribly sad occasion. That evening, once Lisa and Janie had got the twins off to bed, they sat in the living room both with a coffee in their hands.

'Why did it all go wrong, Janie?' Lisa asked.

'I wish I could answer that one. Life can be a real bitch sometimes.' There was a long silence, 'I know one thing, Lisa, he wouldn't have wanted you to give up anything. That's why he stayed at home looking after the kids all these years. He knew how much your business life meant to you.'

'How long can you stay, Janie?'

'As long as you need me, I'll be here.' It warmed Lisa's heart and reassured her to know she had such a good friend.

Jimmy had returned to his normal routine. He loathed his job, especially now that he didn't need the money, but he had to stay as a condition of his release. It was Wednesday lunchtime; Jimmy was on his break playing with his phone. He had been writing text messages to Lisa then deleting them, unable to find the right words. If he had known Zak had been killed in the crash he would probably have chosen a different message. He wrote, 'HELLO LISA, HOPE YOU ARE ALL WELL HA HA, SEE YOU SOON.' He sent the message.

Reece had taken the twins out for the day to give Lisa and Janie a break. They had not yet gone back to school, but inevitably life goes on and they would have to do it some time soon. Janie and Lisa were sitting at the kitchen table when the message tone rang out. Lisa got up, took the phone from her bag and selected 'Messages'. At first she thought it was some kind of sick joke, but then it started to sink in. She dropped the phone.

'What's wrong?' asked Janie, jumping to her feet and picking up the phone. Lisa stared into space. Janie read the message, 'Which sick bastard sent that?'

Something inside Lisa clicked; it was like switching on a light in a room which had been dark for a long time. She turned to look at Janie.

'It's Jimmy. I think he murdered Zak.' Janie felt a shiver go down her spine.

'I'll call the police.'

'Don't,' said Lisa, her tone had changed. 'If I'm right, there's nothing that will stop that bastard. If he gets put away again he'll only turn up some time in the future when I least expect it.'

'Listen to me, Lisa, you have to go to the police. Tell them the whole story. Show them the text. They'll believe you.'

'I can't do that, Janie.' Jimmy had taken away one of the three most important things in her life. If he thought he was going to get away with that he was wrong. All she wanted now was revenge. 'I'm going for a lie down.'

'Are you all right?' asked Janie, 'You can't just leave this.'

'I'm OK. I have a lot to think about,' Lisa replied. 'See you later.' She went upstairs but her mind wasn't yet ready for sleep; all she could think about was Jimmy. She would have her day, for Zak's sake.

Lisa woke; how long she had been asleep she didn't know. She rolled off the bed and went into the bathroom, splashed her face with water and took a good look at her face in the mirror. Janie heard her getting up and put the kettle on. As Lisa walked into the kitchen, there was already a coffee waiting for her.

'Are you all right?' asked Janie. 'Did you sleep OK?'

'So, so. It gave me a good chance to work some things out.' She hesitated, 'Janie, you know people...'

'Yes, one or two.'

'You know what I mean, from the old days.'

'Where's this going?' Janie felt uncomfortable.

'Janie, I've decided. I'm going to get that bastard sorted out once and for all.' Janie walked over to the kitchen door and closed it firmly.

'Can you hear yourself?' asked Janie.

'I can do this with your help or without it,' said Lisa. 'I'd much sooner have it, but one way or another, I'm going to get it sorted out.' With that, Lisa went off to the living room. Janie sat down at the kitchen table, hardly able to believe what she had just heard, and concerned because she knew that Lisa was usually true to her word. Janie thought she had finally escaped her past. The people Lisa had referred to were pimps, drug pushers, people who took payment for harming people as if it was an ordinary, nine-to-five job; these were all manner of criminals. If she had to categorise them it would probably be as the scum of the earth. But like everyone, they played a role in society whether it was for good or for bad. It had been a long time since she had had any contact with any old associates, for all she knew they could be dead and for Lisa's sake, she hoped they were.

They said little to each other for the rest of the afternoon, each deep in their own thoughts. It was dark when Reece returned. The twins were tired so Lisa made them both some hot milk and took them up to bed, staying with them until they fell asleep. When she came down, Janie was standing looking out of the kitchen window, the darkness reflecting her image like a mirror.

'I'll help you,' said Janie. Lisa looked at Janie in the reflection.

'Thank you,' she said.

'I still think you're wrong, but if I don't help you, you'll only do something stupid.'

Lisa smiled, 'You're probably right.' Whatever they decided to do, it would be dangerous. First, they had to find out where he lived. That meant arranging another meeting with him, then following him home. Once they had an address, Janie would have to make contact with some of her less desirable acquaintances. Janie tried not to think further ahead. She shivered and pulled her cardigan tightly around herself.

The next day Lisa sent a text message to Jimmy. She kept it brief, saying she had another proposition for him and could he make it that Saturday at the Oxford bar.

Lisa wanted to make him think she was offering him a partnership in the bars. She knew that if the plan was to work she had to control her emotions. For the sake of Zak's memory, she had to make it work. Jimmy sent a text message back agreeing to meet at one o'clock. After the meeting, Janie would follow him at a safe distance. If he so much as caught a glance of Janie, that would be it. They had to make him relax, actually believe what she was offering him. The prey was now hunting the predator.

On Friday night, Zak's parents came to collect the twins. Lisa had arranged for them to stay with their grandparents, not returning until late on Sunday evening. She had told Reece that she would be working all day on Saturday. By Saturday morning Lisa was agitated, questioning whether she could pull it off, but not willing to abandon the plan. She told herself that there would be too many people around for him to try anything and once he left the bar, it would be out of her hands.

Jimmy had driven down early that morning. As before, he booked into the Travel Lodge, planning to go back home on Sunday morning. Lisa arrived at work just after midday, dropping Janie off before parking the car, just in case Jimmy saw them together. Although Janie had only seen him once she felt sure she would recognise him, but he would probably recognise her too. Janie got into position opposite the bar, making out that she was window-shopping, going into a shop for a brief look every now and then. Just before one o'clock she spotted him walking straight towards her. Quickly, she ducked into a clothing store and hoped that she would fade into the group of women absorbed in looking through the garment rails. Jimmy stood right outside the store. In his usual state of paranoia, he scanned the street for a good five minutes, wondering if it was a set-up and whether or not to go in. Eventually, he crossed the road and went into the bar. Janie sighed with relief and left the shop. Lisa was behind the bar and saw Jimmy come through the door. Under her breath, she told herself to stay in control.

Jimmy walked straight up to the bar, 'Hello Lisa.'

She could have hit him with anything and everything on the bar, but knew it was control that was going to win the day.

'Hello Jimmy,' she forced herself to say, 'would you like a drink?'

'No thanks,' he replied. 'You have something to talk to me about,' he was giving her that stare that unsettled her.

'I'll just get someone to take over behind the bar and we'll go into the office.' Mistake; Janie had told her to stay in full view of everyone in the bar. Lisa got one of the girls to take over and went through to the office at the back of the bar. She sat down at the desk and Jimmy pulled up a chair.

'I won't beat around the bush,' said Lisa, 'I want to offer you a business proposition.'

'Go on,' said Jimmy.

'Fifty fifty, straight down the middle of the business, equal shares in both bars; you can be a sleeping partner. You won't even have to get out of bed, your future will be secure.' Lisa's throat was tightening as she spoke.

'Does that include leaving your husband?' Lisa was suddenly stumped; he didn't know Zak was dead! Had she got it all wrong? Was it just a tragic accident after all? She had to think on her feet, and fast.

'We're having a trial separation.'

Jimmy masked a smile. 'So, his little accident made you both see sense then?' In one sentence he sealed his own fate. Now she knew that he was behind the accident, he just didn't know the outcome. Every muscle, every ounce of strength in her body wanted to fly at him, but somehow she managed to control herself.

'I'll get a contract drawn up for you to sign, then we can stop this nonsense,' she said. Jimmy thought for a moment, it was a step in the right direction. He was getting close to his goal now with Zak out of the frame.

'OK,' said Jimmy. Lisa stood up and with all her strength and courage, held her right hand out to him. Jimmy took her hand in his and slowly shook it. The physical contact with him made her skin crawl.

'I'll be in touch,' said Lisa.

'Can't wait,' replied Jimmy. The grin on his face repulsed her, but she managed a thin smile. As Jimmy left the bar, Janie stepped back into the shop doorway. He set off in the direction of the Travel Lodge. Janie came out of the shop and followed, keeping a safe distance between them. As Janie walked along she sent a text message to Lisa, letting her know in which direction she was going. Lisa read the message and told Reece she had to pop out. She rushed to her car and jumped in. By driving down the road parallel to the High Street she could meet up with Janie. If he changed direction Janie would call her. Jimmy turned left at the top of the High Street and went straight back to the Travel Lodge. Janie carried on straight past and a minute later Lisa's car came round the corner. Janie flagged her down and got in the car.

'He's gone into the Travel Lodge,' said Janie.

'He must have booked in there this morning,' said Lisa. 'Looks like we could have a bit of a wait on our hands.' They sat back in their seats and waited, constantly watching the main entrance.

Jimmy was sitting in his room smiling. To say that he was pleased with himself was an understatement. To him everything looked as if it was going to plan: he was going to have more money than he had ever dreamed of and to top it off he might just get the girl. He decided not to stay for the night; there was nothing more he could do just now. He packed his things and went down to reception where the now familiar receptionist was sitting behind the desk reading a newspaper.

'I'm sorry,' said Jimmy, 'I've just had a call – my fiancé has been taken very ill. I'm going to have to go back home.'

'I'm very sorry to hear that, Mr Noakes, let me have a word with the manager about the bill.' She went into the office behind the desk and returned a few minutes later accompanied by the manager.

'Mr Noakes, I'm very sorry to hear about your fiancé, I hope it's not too serious,' said the manager. 'There won't be a charge on this occasion, I'm sure we'll be seeing you again very soon.'

'Thank you,' Jimmy replied. 'Yes, I have quite a lot of business to attend to in town. Thanks again. Bye for now.' Jimmy left the Travel Lodge with his bag in one hand and crash helmet in the other. As he turned right to head for the car park Janie spotted him.

'Lisa it's him, I think he's leaving. Shit, he's on a motorbike, we'll never keep up with him.' Jimmy's bike stood just inside the entrance to the car park, out of sight from the road. Lisa started the car and waited.

'We'll just have to try and keep up, I've got plenty of fuel,' said Lisa. With that, Jimmy turned out onto the road on his bike.

'It's a fuckin' moped! I should have guessed, he's a right arsehole,' said Janie.

'Never mind what he's on, just keep an eye on him,' Lisa replied. Jimmy picked up a sign for Stratford upon Avon. From there he headed towards Birmingham, and finally through to Walsall. Lisa kept him well within her sights but not close enough to attract his attention. He pulled up outside his flat and pushed his bike into the side alley. Lisa parked a safe distance down the road and waited for him to go indoors. Once the door closed, they slowly drove past.

'7A,' said Janie, 'Banford Road, Walsall, that's all we need, Lisa.'

'What about a photo of him?' asked Lisa.

'I think we can give a good enough description of him, don't you?'

'Yeah, let's go home. We can get something to eat on the way back.' They drove home via the M40, pulling in at the motorway services for a meal and a well-deserved coffee.

The following day Janie called an old girlfriend, Naomi Hicks. She hadn't seen Naomi for nearly twelve months, one of the reasons being the company she kept. At twenty-five years old, Naomi had been on the game since leaving school and, if the truth were known, probably before that. She had got herself into a protection racket run by Denton Fraser, a six foot two inch, powerfully built West Indian with a history of drug dealing and grievous bodily harm. The word on the street was that for a price he would hurt people; a few had disappeared all together. The police would have loved to get him off the streets, but he was so feared that nobody would come forward and give evidence against him. Janie asked Naomi if she still knew him.

'Unfortunately, yes,' she replied. He usually hung around in the Handsworth area of Birmingham at a pub called The Golden Cross, a favourite haunt of local prostitutes and drug dealers. Janie asked her to give him her number, saying that she had some work for him if he was interested. Naomi agreed.

Three days later, Janie was in the living room at Lisa's house reading a newspaper when her mobile sounded out. Janie took the call and heard a strong West Indian accent.

'Dis is Denton. Ya got some business far me.'

'A friend of mine has. Can we meet to discuss it?' asked Janie.

'Friday, eight o'clock, Golden Cross car park, Black BMW.' He hung up. Janie looked at her phone and then put it back to her ear,

'Hello?' she realised he had hung up. 'Ignorant bastard,' she said out loud.

Later that day she told Lisa what had been arranged and they decided to go together for safety.

On Friday evening Lisa arranged for one of the girls from the bar to baby-sit for her. She did it on an overtime basis and there were always one or two girls who would jump at the opportunity; it was a lot easier than working behind a bar all night and there was a guaranteed paid cab home. They arrived at the Golden Cross car park just before eight o'clock. There was no sign of a Black BMW so they waited, nervously. After another fifteen minutes they were beginning to wonder if he was coming.

'We'll give him five more minutes,' said Lisa.

'Wait,' said Janie. A Black BMW rolled into the car park and stopped right in front of them. Polished alloy wheels, blacked out windows, the vehicle's body visibly vibrating from the bass produced by the sound system. The driver's window dropped down half-way so that the top half of the occupant's face could just be seen. He was wearing strip sunglasses and had short dreadlocks, pulled back and tied together. The glint of a gold tooth caught Lisa's eye. He looked straight towards them.

'Stay here, Janie,' said Lisa, 'you've done enough for me already.'

'Be careful, Lisa, I don't like the look of him one bit.'

'Don't worry, I will.' Lisa got out the car and walked over to the waiting BMW. The driver looked her up and down. In a deep West Indian accent he said, 'Ya lookin' far I woman?'

'Are you Denton?' asked Lisa.

'Tis I.'

'Then, yes,' Lisa replied.

'Gettin da back, ya tract'in too much attention wid dem legs.' Lisa turned and looked at Janie, signalling her to stay put, then took a deep breath and got into the car.

'Lisa you idiot,' said Janie to herself. The BMW reversed out of the car park and Lisa felt her heartbeat quicken.

'What are you doing?' asked Lisa.

'Too many eyes round 'ere,' said Fraser. He pulled around the corner and parked along the roadside; he kept looking forwards so that Lisa couldn't see his face.

'Wot kinda bizness we talkin'?'

'I want you to sort someone out for me.' Lisa could hardly believe she was speaking the words.

'Dis person messing wid ya?'

'He ... he killed my husband.'

'A bad man den. Bad men cost more.'

'I want him killed,' said Lisa.

'A lot more,' replied Fraser. 'Tree grand up front, an' two more when 'im dead.' Lisa thought for a few seconds; she couldn't believe what she was getting herself into.

'OK,' she said, 'it's a deal.'

'Gimme a name, description an' address.' Lisa had anticipated this and had written it all down on a piece of paper, which she took from her pocket and passed forward. He read it then put it in his pocket.

'I be in da car park Monday at eight. Be dare wid da cash.'

'OK,' said Lisa. He reversed back down the road to the entrance of the car park and stopped. He said nothing, just sat there.

'Monday then,' said Lisa, wondering what was to happen next. She opened the door and got out. As soon as the door closed, he drove off, leaving Lisa standing by the edge of the curb. She turned and walked back into the car park, where Janie released the central locking so that Lisa could get into the car. Janie looked almost in a state of panic.

'Thank fuckin' God!' said Janie.

'Exactly what I was thinking,' said Lisa.

'Don't do that again girl, I thought I'd lost you for a minute.'

'Me too,' replied Lisa. 'Anyway, it's sorted. I pay him three thousand on Monday then another two thousand when the job's done. Fingers crossed, that bastard will be out of my life for ever.'

Lisa arranged to collect the money from the building society. The weekend dragged and all she could think about was handing the cash over. Once she did that she would be an accessory to murder. It terrified her, but the stakes were too high; Jimmy had killed more than once and it was only a matter of time before she and the twins were on that list too.

On Monday evening she made the trip up to Birmingham. Just as before, she got into the rear of the BMW, then passed the cash forward. He didn't count it, just flicked through it, like some kind of casino high-roller and then slipped it in his inside pocket. Again, he reversed back to the car park. All he said was, 'I'll be in touch,' in that deep West Indian accent. Lisa got out of the car, pleased it was all over and done with. All she had to do now was sit tight.

Jimmy was still working in the warehouse, far from happy with it, but at least Lisa was coming round to his way of thinking. He was sure that any day now he would get the call he had been waiting for. It was all fitting nicely into place, or so he thought. For the last few days everywhere he had been, somewhere nearby was a black BMW, watching, waiting, for the right time and place. Although Jimmy hated his job, at least he was around people, and occasionally someone would make conversation with him, albeit rarely. Most of his evenings were spent watching television. When the weather was fine he liked to go into Walsall town centre and take a walk around the market area, checking out the people more than what they were selling. On this particular occasion, Jimmy himself was being watched. Jimmy hadn't noticed Fraser, at times no more than a metre away from him. Walking down a subway just off the High Street, Jimmy desperately needed the toilet and knew there was one down there. Fraser saw his chance. Inside his coat a large meat knife was neatly stored in an adapted pocket. He wanted it to look like a robbery. Jimmy went into the toilet, checked the cubicle for paper and closed the door. Fraser came in, stealthily quiet, his hand inside his coat holding the knife. The toilet was empty except for the one closed cubicle door. Fraser stopped, broad daylight, town centre, lots of blood, 'Too messy,' he thought. He slid the blade back into its pocket and pulled out a thick piece of wire, about eighteen inches long, with a toggle on each end, perfectly designed for garrotting his victim. Fraser slowly moved towards the cubicle and silently stood inside the one next to it. A few minutes later, he heard Jimmy fastening his clothes and then the toilet flushed. Fraser wrapped the wire round both his hands. He heard the bolt on the door open and Jimmy left the cubicle, moving towards the exit, suspecting nothing. Fraser came out from the other cubicle door. In a flash, the wire was around Jimmy's neck. Fraser's power was immense. He dragged Jimmy backwards into a cubicle kicking the door shut. Jimmy frantically struggled, clutching at the cable as it cut into his throat. He could feel the life being squeezed from his body. He tried to twist free but Fraser was just too strong. Jimmy tried hitting out over his shoulder, but to no avail. In a last desperate attempt to save himself, Jimmy fumbled to reach his inside coat pocket where he always kept his trusty screwdriver. Jimmy clasped the handle of the screwdriver and wrenched it from his coat. As his legs buckled under him he lunged over his shoulder. Fraser didn't see it coming. By pure luck rather than judgement, the screwdriver found its target, hitting Fraser in the corner of his left eye. Buried up to the hilt, six inches of steel rod were thrust through Fraser's eye socket into his brain. They both went down in a heap, Fraser's body twitching spasmodically. He was dead before he hit the floor. The cable loosened around Jimmy's neck and as he breathed in, it felt as though his windpipe had been crushed. For the first few seconds all he could muster was a whistling sound, then he gulped at the air in an attempt to replenish his body with oxygen. He struggled to his feet and pulled the door open. Stepping out of the cubicle, he looked down at the spread-eagled body of the huge man. He pulled the screwdriver from Fraser's eye socket, wiped it on the dead man's trousers, then returned it to its special pocket. As he turned to walk away the anger within him took over. He felt the old, familiar, burning rush of rage surging through his body. Turning back, his teeth gritted, he raised his boot and stamped on the dead man's head. Again and again he stamped until his head was deformed beyond recognition. 'Fuckin' black bastard!' he shouted. One more sickening stamp, then he turned and walked away. As he reached the exit he scanned the subway, making sure no one saw him leave the toilet. He darted along the passageway, then turned the corner and started walking back towards the main shopping area, quickly becoming just another face in the crowd.

22

Double-crossed

An unsuspecting member of the public walked into the toilets and found, to his horror, Fraser's lifeless body. After the initial shock, he called the police. Two officers quickly responded to the call, arriving on the scene within minutes. What they saw physically shook them. Concealing their feelings of nausea, their training took over and they proceeded to cordon off the area. It wasn't hard to work out that an emergency ambulance wasn't really necessary. What was important was that any forensic evidence was preserved. When the scene of crime officers arrived they got straight to work. Shortly afterwards, two CID officers arrived, Detective Inspector Jack Gillman with his sidekick, as the rest of the department liked to put it, Detective Constable Phil Kent. Gillman was a veteran of these situations. With over twenty years of CID experience he was fast approaching his fiftieth birthday. Fingers crossed, within a couple of years he would be offered an early retirement package. The stress of the job was beginning to wear him down; the lines on his face were a testament to many late-night stakeouts and a few too many scuffles. Why he had never made it to Detective Superintendent was a mystery. It was true to say that over the years he had taken a few chances, but usually he came out on top. Some of his policing methods had been questioned, but when you're trying to nail pimps, drug dealers and self-confessed gangsters, you have to bend the rules slightly. He was getting results and, ultimately, he felt that was what counted. DC Kent was referred to by the rest of the department as Gillman's lap dog, following him around everywhere, day in, day out. Kent didn't really care what the others said behind his back; Gillman was the best there was, and if that's what it took to follow in his footsteps, so be it.

Gillman stood over the body while a forensic officer took photos from every conceivable angle.

'Phil, I want you to radio in, do a check on known and suspected hit men.'

'Hit men, sir?' replied Kent.

'What's that in his left hand?' asked Gillman.

'Looks like a piece of wire, sir.'

'I think this is a hit that's gone wrong. The question is, who was he hitting? Whoever it was, looking at this guy, he was either very big or very good.' Gillman knelt down, 'Look at this, Phil.' Kent got down on one knee beside the body and looked towards the area Gillman was pointing at with his pen. 'See the puncture hole in the corner of the eye?'

Kent was amazed at Gillman's observational skills; with the amount of blood and God knows what other fluids coming from the man's head, how he had spotted the wound he didn't know. 'Yes,' said Gillman, the expression on his face was like a child finding the right piece in a jigsaw, 'see the blood on the wire? I'll bet you that's not the victim's. Let's get it bagged.' For the next few hours the forensic officers combed the entire toilet block. Eventually, the body was removed to the local hospital mortuary for autopsy and the toilets were locked, pending further investigations.

Gillman and Kent went back to the police station to see if the computer could put a name to their victim. It didn't take long until they had a full profile on him. 'Looks like someone just done society a favour, sir,' said Kent. 'Look at this: GBH, ABH, dealing Class A drugs, as if that's not enough he was also a goddamned pimp. The guy that took him out needs a medal.'

'Steady, Phil,' said Gillman, 'it's not our job to judge old Denton here, just catch the person that put him on the slab.'

'Sorry, sir,' said Kent.

'That's OK, Phil; I know exactly how you feel. I'm sure there's a lot of people out there who'd want him dead, but we have to find out who *he* wanted dead. When we find that person we have our murderer. It says here he frequents the Handsworth area.'

'The Golden Cross, sir,' Kent laughed, 'really nice place for a quiet drink.'

'Tell me, Phil,' asked Gillman, 'when was the last time we saw our dear friend Squiggy?' Squiggy was a twenty-five year-old, mixed race, down and out, who lived in and around Handsworth. His real name was Mark Squires and if anything was happening on the streets, Squiggy knew about it. If certain people knew he was a police informant he wouldn't last five minutes.

'Must be six months since we've been in touch,' replied Kent.

'I think it's time he earned his corn,' said Gillman. 'Let's go and have a word in his ear.' They spent most of the evening cruising around Soho Road, a popular haunt for Squiggy, as there were plenty of opportunities to beg some change. Just after ten o'clock they spotted him trying to get some change from a middle-aged couple outside the Kentucky Fried Chicken fast food bar. 'Squiggy,' shouted Kent. Squiggy glanced in their direction, obviously realising who they were, but pretending not to hear them. Suddenly, his attention moved away from the couple and he quickly disappeared around the corner.

'Oh dear,' said Gillman, 'he's got his hearing problem back again.' Kent quickly accelerated down the road and around the corner. They pulled up by an alley behind a row of shops and both got out of the car. Squiggy wasn't the sharpest tool in the box. 'Come out, Squiggy,' shouted Gillman. There was no sound. 'I won't say it again, Squiggy.' Suddenly, from beneath a pile of bin bags, a head popped up.

'Is that you, Mr Gillman sir?' came a thready voice.

'What do you think?' replied Gillman.

'Thank God for that, I thought it was a couple of boneheads from the Black Horse. They've been giving me some trouble lately.' Squiggy's voice was now steadier.

'What do you know about Denton Fraser?' asked Gillman.

Squiggy's face said it all. 'You know I always help you when I can, Mr Gillman sir, but Denton Fraser, sir, he's a bad man.'

'He's a dead man,' said Gillman. Squiggy looked shocked. 'Found him earlier today, in Walsall,' continued Gillman. 'Are there any heavies moving into this patch that we haven't heard about?'

'Nobody I've seen or heard of, Mr Gillman sir, but I can tell you something. About a week ago, outside the Golden Cross, Fraser was talking to some posh bird. Seen it with me own eyes, Mr Gillman sir, a blonde bird, she was in a smart, old, white Beamer. There was two of them in the car. The reg caught me eye, 888 somethin.' Kent made a note while Gillman took out his wallet, pulled out a crisp ten-pound note and handed it to Squiggy. 'Thank you very much, Mr Gillman sir, only too pleased to help ya.'

'Take it easy, Squiggy,' said Gillman as he walked back to the car. 'I think we'll call it a night, Phil. Don't eat too much,' he added, 'we've got that autopsy at ten in the morning.'

'I'm really looking forward to that,' said Kent, already looking grey around the gills just thinking about it.

'It's all part of the job, Phil, all part of the job.'

The next day, the pathologist confirmed Gillman's thoughts. 'As you can see,' he said, 'the puncture wound to the left eye shows where an object has entered the brain on the left frontal lobe.' The top of Fraser's head had been removed, exposing his brain and the pathologist was holding it in such a way that the puncture wound could be easily seen. 'A trauma such as this would have caused death instantaneously.' It was all a little too much for Kent, who excused himself. The pathologist continued. 'All the rest of the damage to his head was caused after his heart had stopped. He was already dead before someone jumped up and down on his head. Looking at the puncture wound I would say you're looking for a screwdriver, something like that, approximately seven inches long with a flat end. The mark found on his trousers showed that the murderer removed the weapon and wiped it on his victim's leg.'

'I think I'll leave you to it now Doc, if that's OK,' said Gillman.

'Sure, anything else you need just give us a call. Oh, don't forget your friend on the way out.' Gillman laughed and went out into the corridor, where Phil was leaning against the wall. As he saw Gillman, he stood up.

'I was just coming back in, sir.'

'Come on, Phil, we've got some cars to check out.'

Kent was leaning over a young police constable who was logging himself into a computer. 'There can't be many BMWs with 888 in the registration,' said Kent.

'You'd be surprised,' said the young constable. 'Here we go ... it can take a few minutes.' They both watched the screen. The monitor changed to a new window showing the search results. 'Twenty four, that's not bad at all,' said the constable.

'Too many,' said Kent, 'what's that there?' he asked, pointing to another area on the screen.

'You can narrow the search. Got anything else on the vehicle?'

'It's white,' replied Kent. The young PC turned and looked at him as if to say, why didn't you say that in the first place. He turned back to the screen, typed in 'white' and the screen quickly changed.

'Four – that's more like it,' said Kent. 'Can you give me a printout of that?' The PC pressed a key and the printer on the desk burst into life. Kent sat reading the results, which were listed according to their distance from the police station, giving the furthest first; Ayrshire, Cornwall, Oxfordshire and West Midlands. 'Bingo!' he said aloud. Mr Alan Bullock, 72 Foxton Road, Acocks Green, 5 series Reg D888 VOV. He took out his mobile and selected Gillman's number; the phone rang out. 'Hello sir, I've got a couple of matches on that BMW and one's local.'

'Well done Phil, I'll be at the station in twenty minutes; we'll pay him a visit.' Half an hour later they were on their way to Acocks Green. Kent's portable satellite navigation system made these little excursions so much easier. They pulled up at the house.

'Looks like he's got a few bob,' said Kent as they got out the car. Gillman walked up to the front door and knocked. Kent glanced up the side of the house before coming to the front door. Gillman knocked again. 'Looks like he's out, sir.' Then, through the glass in the front door they could see someone approaching, albeit very slowly. The door opened and an elderly man, supported by two sticks, stood in front of them. Gillman held up his identity card and introduced himself and Kent.

'Are you Mr Alan Bullock?' he asked.

'Yes,' the man replied, 'what's happened?'

'Don't worry sir,' replied Gillman, 'we are just making some enquiries about a vehicle, a white BMW registration D888 VOV.'

'That's my car.' The elderly man looked concerned.

'Do you know where it is at the moment?' asked Gillman.

'It was in the garage last time I looked.'

'Does anybody else have access to it?' asked Kent.

'Not since my son moved out a couple of years back,' Bullock replied.

'Could we take a look at it?' asked Gillman.

'Of course, no problem at all, but if you don't mind me asking,' the old man looked a little bewildered, 'why would you want to look at it?'

'Just to eliminate it from our enquiries, sir, nothing more.' He turned and very slowly shuffled down the hall, through the kitchen into a passageway leading to the garage.

'You'll have to excuse me, I had a hip replacement operation three weeks ago and I'm still a little unstable.'

'That's OK, Mr Bullock, take your time.' As they reached the garage, Kent turned away and scratched his head; the BMW looked like a huge, disassembled jigsaw puzzle. Gillman stared at Kent.

'I'll finish it one day,' said Bullock. The BMW was literally, all over the garage. In healthier days he had been a keen car enthusiast but his intentions to renovate this particular vehicle had not materialised.

'Thank you very much, Mr Bullock, we won't trouble you any longer,' said Gillman. After a further lengthy journey, shuffling to the front door, they thanked him for his assistance and left. On the way back to the station Gillman said, 'Phil, just out of curiosity, did you check the last time it was MOT'd or taxed?'

'No sir,' replied Kent, in a low voice. Gillman looked out the window and shook his head. 'Sorry sir.' It was quiet all the way back to the station.

Kent selected the next vehicle on the list and read it out to himself, 'B888 DXT, Mr Zak Wright, 4 Oak View, Stanton Harcourt, Oxfordshire. That's all I need; this one's older than the last one.' Lisa had not yet got around to transferring the name on the logbook from Zak's to hers; Zak had always taken care of everything to do with the cars. Kent did a check on the vehicle and everything appeared to be up to date. He went into Gillman's office, 'This one looks a little more promising sir.'

'Go on,' said Gillman.

'Well, it's a little way out; Oxfordshire.'

'And it's all in order I take it?'

'Yes sir.'

'I could do with a trip out into the country,' said Gillman. 'We'll go after lunch.'

Earlier that morning, Lisa was getting the twins ready for school when Josh asked if he could run to the village shop to get some sweets for break time. Lisa told him to hurry or they would be late. Josh grabbed his coat and dashed out of the door. Lisa finished putting on her make-up then glanced up at the kitchen clock; it was almost nine o'clock. 'Shit,' she said to herself. 'Jodie, get your coat and Josh's bag; we'll pick him up on the way along the road. Bye Janie,' she called up the stairs. They rushed out and climbed into the car.

Lisa drove down the road and pulled up opposite the village shop. She could see Josh standing in the open doorway of the shop, happily talking away to someone just inside. She wound the window down and called him. 'Josh, come on, we're late,' she shouted, 'watch the road.' Josh waved at the person inside the shop, then came running out, bouncing along without a care in the world. 'Come on,' said Lisa, 'we're late.' Josh checked that the road was clear and ran across. He jumped into the back of the car and, as soon as his seatbelt clicked, Lisa drove off. A man came out of the shop and watched the car disappear down the lane.

'There you go, Jodie.' Josh passed a large chocolate bar towards his sister, 'he said it's for you.' Jodie, wide-eyed, took the chocolate.

'Who said that?' asked Lisa.

'The man from school. He was in the shop.' Lisa hit the brakes hard and the car screeched to a halt.

'Who was in the shop?' she shouted, turning to face the twins.

'The man from school,' said Josh, as if she should know exactly who he meant, 'he bought us both a chocolate bar.' Lisa spun the car round like a maniac.

'Take it easy mum,' said Jodie. The BMW roared back down the lane towards the village shop. Lisa pulled up, turned off the engine and got out of the car.

'You two, stay right there, don't move.' She ran into the shop and the woman behind the counter greeted her. 'Mrs Church, the man who was just in here, who was he?'

'Oh, not one of our regulars, you've just missed him.'

'Was he in a car or on foot?' asked Lisa.

'In a car I think, yes a red one, it was parked just past the shop pointing towards the village. Is everything all right?' Lisa ran from the shop, started the car and drove back into the centre of the village. Nothing had passed her on the way back to the shop, so he must have driven into the village. Slowly, she drove past the green looking out for a red car, but to no avail; he had gone. She pulled up.

'What's wrong, mum?' asked Jodie. Lisa was almost in tears.

'Promise me something, both of you, if you ever see that man again, run and tell someone he's bothering you, straight away.'

'But,' started Josh.

'No buts, Josh. Promise me.' They both promised. After dropping them off at school, Lisa drove home and told Janie of the incident. Why was Jimmy still hanging around after all she had said to him? It didn't make sense. Janie could see that Lisa was shaken and they decided to go together to collect the twins at the end of the school day, in case Jimmy was there.

Kent's satellite navigation system was again foolproof. They set off just after two o'clock and were cruising around the Oxfordshire countryside an hour and a half later.

'It's nice to get out of the city occasionally,' said Gillman. 'I could quite easily retire to some place like this.'

'I think you'd miss all the hassle, sir,' said Kent.

'Trust me, Phil, I wouldn't.' They saw a sign for Stanton Harcourt, Kent's trusty machine told him to turn left at the next junction.

'Very clever these things,' said Gillman staring at the machine in amazement.

'Take you anywhere in Europe this will, sir,' said Kent, enthusiastically.

'This will do fine for today, thank you, Phil.' After a few further turns the machine announced that they had arrived at their destination. A brass plaque on the wall said '4 Oak View'. There was no sign of a white BMW on the drive. Gillman and Kent walked up the drive to the front door. The house looked still. Gillman rang the bell and they waited for a reply.

'It's a long way to come for a wasted journey,' said Gillman. 'Let's wait in the car.' It had already been a long day. Kent reclined his seat, closed his eyes and nodded off to sleep. A while later, Gillman, as alert as ever, saw the BMW approaching in his door mirror. It turned into the drive behind them. 'Phil,' Gillman nudged Kent; instantly he woke. 'The car's arrived.'

As they walked up the drive they could see Lisa getting out of the car. Kent quietly said to Gillman, 'Posh blonde bird in a white Beamer, well done Squiggy.'

'Absolutely,' replied Gillman. Lisa turned and looked at them. 'Good afternoon, madam. I'm Detective Inspector Gillman and this is Detective Constable Kent, West Midlands Police, could we have a word?' He held out his identity card.

'Is something wrong?' asked Lisa.

'Just a routine inquiry,' said Gillman. Janie and the twins got out of the car.

'Shall we go inside?' said Lisa. Gillman took a long look at Lisa and Janie, immediately he recognised them, but where from? Lisa showed them into the sitting room and went to the kitchen to make coffee. Janie was already there, putting the kettle on.

'What shall I do?' whispered Lisa.

'You've done nothing, and you know nothing, got it?' Lisa looked frightened. 'Listen, pull yourself together, finish making the coffee and get back in there.'

Lisa put the drinks onto a tray and carried them into the living room.

'Is Mr Wright about?' asked Gillman. Lisa stood silently, unable to speak or put the tray down. Gillman and Kent glanced at each other.

'Mr Wright died in a car accident a few weeks ago,' said Janie from the doorway.

'I'm so sorry, I wasn't aware. Please accept my sincere apologies,' said Gillman, looking directly at Janie.

'That's Mrs Wright,' said Janie, nodding towards Lisa. Gillman hastily turned to acknowledge her.

'I'm very, very sorry, Mrs Wright.' Gillman apologised. The twins were standing at the doorway, obviously concerned about the situation.

'What's wrong, mum?' asked Jodie.

Lisa turned to them. 'Nothing, kids, go and play in your room.' They turned, uncertainly, and then went off through the kitchen and upstairs.

'Mrs Wright, have you been to Birmingham recently?' asked Gillman.

'No,' replied Lisa, hoping that he would not detect that she was lying, 'not in ages.'

'A car very similar to yours was seen in the Handsworth area of the city. The occupant was seen talking to a gentleman by the name of

Denton Fraser.' Gillman watched very closely for a reaction. Lisa stared straight back at him.

'No, I'm sorry,' said Lisa. 'Never heard of him.' Gillman picked up his coffee and drank some.

'Oh, I needed that,' he said with a look of satisfaction on his face. He put his cup down. 'Only yesterday he was found murdered in a public toilet.' As Gillman maintained his gaze on her, Lisa battled furiously to control her emotions. Gillman turned to Janie, 'I feel sure I know you,' he said.

'I don't think so,' replied Janie.

'Have you ever lived in the Midlands?' he asked.

'On and off, yes,' replied Janie, 'but I've lived here for some time.' Gillman racked his brains; every case he had ever worked on was filed somewhere in his head and his recall methods were usually spot on. Then it came to him, it was when that nutcase taking it out on prostitutes in the mid to late eighties. What was his name? Think, think, think, he said to himself. Noakes, that was it, James Noakes. She was one of the call girls he made an appointment with when they were trying to nail him. He turned to Janie.

'Moseley, 85, 86ish, did you live up that way?'

'No,' said Janie, 'I think you've got me mixed up with someone else.'

'Sorry,' said Gillman. He turned to Lisa, 'Mrs Wright, have you ever lived in the Midlands?'

Observing Gillman's face, recognition dawned on Lisa. 'No,' she said, and hoped her decisive answer would hide the realisation that she knew exactly who he was.

'Well thanks for your help,' said Gillman. 'If we need to ask any more questions we know where to find you.' Kent quickly drank down the rest of his coffee and stood up. 'Goodbye ladies and once again, Mrs Wright, please accept my sincere apologies.' Lisa nodded an understanding gesture and showed them out.

'Well Phil, I don't think we need to look any further for our vehicle or its occupants,' said Gillman.

'Do you think that's definitely it then, sir?'

Gillman looked straight at Kent and shook his head.

'You do make me wonder sometimes, Phil, you really do.' Kent still wasn't sure what he had said.

Back in the house, Janie watched the detectives walk down the driveway to their car and within a couple of minutes they drove off. She turned and went over to sit next to Lisa on the sofa.

'Did you realise who that was, Janie?' said Lisa. 'It may have been the best part of twenty years, but you never forget a decent copper in our line of work anyway, and he knows something.'

'OK, so Fraser's dead,' replied Janie.

'Janie, Jimmy's killed him.'

'You don't know that,' said Janie. 'Fraser's got a lot of enemies ... it could have been anyone.'

'I just know it, Janie. If Jimmy knows I put Fraser up to it, I'm next.'

Later that evening, Gillman was at his desk. In front of him was a notepad on which he had drawn a triangle: at the top point he wrote the name 'Denton Fraser'; at the second point he wrote 'Mrs Wright, White BMW'; and at the third point 'Call girl, 1986ish'. What was the common denominator? There was a link; he just couldn't see it yet. But he knew that when he found the answer to that question, he would find his murderer.

Jimmy was sitting in his armchair in front of the television as the local ten o'clock news came on. It had been a long day and his eyelids felt heavy. He had to be in work early the following morning as a big order had to be on the road before eight o'clock. 'Best go to bed,' he thought. He stood up and stretched, then walked over to turn off the television. The newsreader's opening headlines stopped him. 'Police are investigating the death of a Midlands man. Thirty-five year-old Denton Fraser of Handsworth, Birmingham, was found dead yesterday afternoon in a public toilet in Walsall town centre.' Jimmy stood listening. 'Mr Fraser had multiple convictions for grievous and actual bodily harm. Police believe it was a contract killing that had gone terribly wrong. Police are appealing for witnesses who saw anybody hanging around or entering the Warren underpass or public conveniences between twelve and two o'clock yesterday afternoon. All calls will be treated in strict confidence.' The newsreader gave out a telephone number and went on to the rest of the day's news. Jimmy clicked the television off, incredulous as to what he had just heard. 'So that's what the bitch was up to. Playing games are we?' he said out loud. Just like the flick of a switch, his mood turned from pleasantly relaxed to raging anger. Infuriated, he threw himself back down in his armchair, fists clenched tight and teeth bared. 'Double-cross me will ya? Fucking whore!' Saliva foamed at the corners of his mouth as he spat out the threat. 'You had your chance bitch. Now you'll get what you deserve.' As he stared at the wall in front of him, a small bead of saliva traced a route down his chin. He didn't care about anyone or anything now, just revenge.

23

Revelations

Gillman was in work early, all night he had racked his brain trying to find the missing piece of the puzzle. As Kent walked through the station he could see the light on in Gillman's office; it was very unusual for the DI to get into work before him. He stuck his head around the door and saw Gillman sitting at his desk, deep in thought.

'Morning sir, bright and early today aren't we?' said Kent in a jovial voice.

'Morning Phil, come in, I've got a job for you.' Kent closed the door behind him and sat down. 'I want you to do some digging for me. Mrs Wright, I think there's more to that lady than meets the eye. I want to know everything about her, right down to her shoe size. Oh and get all the details you can on her husband's death.' If there was one thing Phil Kent was good at it was digging up information. He had an uncanny talent for finding things out. Where and how Gillman didn't know, but he was a very useful asset.

'I'll get straight on it, sir.' Kent loved the idea that the DI really needed him. It was an opportunity to shine in the eyes of his mentor; he would stop at nothing to prove his worth. Kent got up and hastily headed for the door.

'Phil,' Gillman stopped him in his tracks. 'I didn't mean it about the shoe size.' Kent returned a large grin and went about his business.

Jimmy arrived at work that morning a little late. He had hardly slept and all he could think about was Lisa. 'The double-crossing bitch,' he repeated to himself, over and over again. As he parked his bike, the foreman came over. The one day the foreman had asked him to be early and he had let him down. 'Pleased you could make it, Noakes,' said the foreman with a look of displeasure. 'Have you seen the time?' Jimmy took off his helmet and looked straight at the man, his eyes cold and menacing. The foreman was taken aback by Jimmy's threatening stance, 'Is everything all right, Jimmy?' Jimmy held the stare for what seemed like an age with the foreman visibly shrinking before his eyes. Then, without saying a word, Jimmy stepped forward, brushing the man's shoulder as he passed him. The foreman swallowed hard and took a deep breath as he turned to watch Jimmy walk through the loading bay and disappear into the changing rooms.

By lunchtime, the aggression in Jimmy was close to boiling point. Sooner or later he was going to explode and when that happened, the person nearest to him was going to take the full brunt of it. He visualised himself taking Lisa by the throat and squeezing the life out of her. It was like a temporary pressure relief valve, but temporary it was, for as soon as the image was gone the pressure came back. He avoided contact with his fellow workers as much as he could, not wanting to give the foreman any reason to send him home, which he felt sure would please him no end. Jimmy was sitting on the end of the loading bay, as he always did at lunchtime, with a cup of extra sweet coffee in one hand and a Mars bar in the other. He tried to resist the urge to call Lisa and tell her he knew she had arranged for him to be attacked, but letting her think she had one over him was more than he could take. Throwing the dregs of his coffee onto the loading bay floor he put the cup down beside him. Taking out his phone he selected 'Messages'. In the text box he wrote, 'I KNOW IT WAS YOU BITCH. SEE YOU SOON'. Then he selected Lisa's number and pressed 'Send'. If she had set him up, which he was sure she had, she wouldn't respond to the text. Not only that, she wouldn't go to the police, because what she had attempted to do would undoubtedly have carried a prison sentence in itself. Again he started to feel that he had the edge. A grin spread over his face, for now he was pacified; he would have his day very soon.

Lisa was working in London at the Wimbledon bar. She had left Janie with the twins. It meant taking them to school in a cab, but it was only for one day. Sue could cope very well on her own but when Lisa had spoken to her on the phone she got the feeling Sue was a little down in the dumps. Lisa wondered if Sue was feeling a little isolated, being such a long way from what had become the centre of the company. The last thing she needed was Sue handing in her notice; it would almost certainly be the end of Korky's in London. Lisa was behind the bar putting clean glasses onto the shelves when the message alert sounded on her phone. She reached under the bar and rummaged through her handbag for the phone. She selected 'Messages' and read Jimmy's text. It felt as if somebody had walked over her grave; every hair on the back of her neck was standing up. She called out to Sue, who was over by the window having a laugh and joke with some punters, customer relations, as Lisa liked to call it. Sue excused herself and came over to the bar.

'You OK Lisa? You look as if you've just seen a ghost.'

'Something like that,' said Lisa, 'Sue, I have to go home.'

'Sure, are the twins OK?'

'Yeah, just a couple of things I have to sort out that can't wait.' All Lisa wanted to do was get to her children; nothing else mattered as long as they were safe.

The journey back to Oxford was slow with traffic jam after traffic jam. She couldn't remember it ever being this bad. School finished at half past three; for all she knew he could already be there waiting for them. The thoughts going through her head were causing her to make silly mistakes at the wheel; if she didn't compose herself she wouldn't get there at all.

She finally arrived at the school with fifteen minutes to spare. Turning off the engine she sat back in the seat, rubbing the back of her neck in an attempt to relieve the pent-up stress. Suddenly she felt very emotional and a surge of tears welled up in her eyes. 'Keep it together,' she said to herself, 'the kids will be out soon.' Suddenly, a loud tap on the passenger door glass startled her and she turned sharply. Janie was peering through the glass. 'What are you doing here? I've got a taxi waiting over there.' Lisa dropped the window down.

'Sorry Janie, I didn't have time to call.' Lisa went into her bag and passed Janie a ten-pound note, 'Pay him off, something's happened.' Janie went over to the taxi, apologised and gave him the money. She came back and got into the passenger seat. Lisa already had her phone out with the message selected, 'Read this.' Lisa passed the phone to Janie.

'For fuck's sake, Lisa, now we have to go to the police.'

'What, and tell them I tried to have him killed but it never worked? Sorry, can you lock him up for me now please?' The sarcasm was obvious in Lisa's tone and on her face. 'Janie, if I go to the police I'll get five years minimum.'

'I told you this was a fuckin' bad idea from the start. Now we're right in the shit!' Janie turned and looked out the window; in all the time they had known each other, it was the first time they had had a cross word. Both of them realised it at virtually at the same time.

'I'm sorry Janie,' said Lisa. Janie turned back and looked straight at her.

'Me too' she replied. 'What's done is done. Let's get the kids and go home, then we can try and decide what the friggin' hell we're going to do.' They both got out of the car and, keeping a cautious watch on everything around them, went over and stood by the school gate.

Kent had spent the whole day scanning the computer, searching for anything that could tell them a little more about Mrs Wright. Being a police officer he could obtain access to restricted areas and some of the areas he accessed he knew he shouldn't, but he needed results and fast. After nearly eight hours with his eyes fixed on the computer monitor, he had more information on Mrs Lisa Wright than Gillman could have ever imagined. Kent flipped open his phone and selected Gillman's mobile number. It rang two or three times before Gillman answered it. 'Hi Phil, what you got?'

'Some very interesting stuff, sir. I think we have another couple of pieces of the puzzle.'

'Brilliant – I've been clearing up some outstanding paperwork. I should be back at the station in about an hour.'

'OK sir, I'm just going to get a bite to eat; it's been a long day.'

'Well done, Phil, see you in a while.' Gillman rang off. Kent looked over the notes he had made on Mrs Wright and, pleased with himself, he headed to the canteen for a well-earned meal.

Gillman arrived back at the station and seeing no sign of Kent around the offices, took a stroll up to the canteen. Half a dozen officers coming off duty were drinking coffee, laughing between themselves about a particular incident they had been involved with earlier that day. Kent was sitting on the far side of the canteen reading through some of his notes. 'Phil,' shouted Gillman. Kent instantly looked in his direction. 'In the office,' mouthed Gillman, pointing down towards the floor. Kent raised a hand to acknowledge him and Gillman went back down the stairs. Kent gathered his paperwork and started walking towards the stairs. As he passed the other officers, one shouted, 'Woof, woof, come on boy.' They all laughed. Kent simply raised his middle finger in the air and carried on walking. 'Oooh,' came a harmonious reply from all of them.

Gillman was at his desk when Kent came into the office. 'So, what have you got for me then?'

Kent sat down and placed a folder on the desk. 'Well sir, it's been a very enlightening day, to say the least. Firstly it's Mrs Lisa Wright, formerly Miss Lisa Dean. For the last fifteen years she's been the owner of Korky's Wine Bar's, based in Wimbledon, London and Oxford, and very successful she is. On paper, a self-made millionaire.'

'Interesting,' said Gillman.

'But what went on prior to that is going to interest you more,' said Kent, 'Miss Lisa Dean was claiming benefits in the mid to late eighties from an address in Birmingham. Moseley to be precise, 12A Wellington Road.' Gillman raised a hand to his forehead and closed his eyes; the address instantly rang a bell. 'You OK, sir?' asked Kent.

'Yes, sorry Phil, go on.'

'The property belonged to and still does, a certain Jane Coleman.'

'Yes!' said Gillman, 'that's the name I was looking for, Janie, that's what she called herself, the woman with Mrs Wright. I met her in the eighties. I was trying to catch a right psycho, a serial killer taking it out on the local prostitutes.' Gillman again closed his eyes and put his hand to his head. 'Noakes, that was his name, James Noakes.'

'There's more, sir,' Kent continued. 'Previously to living in Moseley our Lisa was a missing person, disappeared from her parent's flat one weekend, turned up twelve months later.'

'Yes,' said Gillman, everything Kent said jogged his memory – the beating Janie had received at the Victoria Hotel, collecting Lisa from the flat in Moseley, taking her to the hospital to get a statement from Janie. It was all coming together.

'Sounds like she stayed away long enough to prevent them taking her back home. Obviously having problems with her parents,' said Gillman.

'You can say that again, sir, she hadn't been gone long when mother and father had a domestic and Mrs Dean ended up dead. Young Lisa didn't have a home to go back to, even if she wanted to.' Gillman sat back in his chair.

'What a fuckin' life. You think you have problems then you hear a story like that. She probably saw a TV or newspaper report about her parents, that's when Janie Coleman came into the picture.'

'Not really a great role model, sir.'

'No, she was probably on the game before she was sixteen. What I want to know is how the fuckin' hell she turned it all around.'

'Beats me, sir,' said Kent.

'One more thing, Phil, did you find out anything about her husband's death?'

'Oh yes, sir,' Kent flicked through his folder and pulled out a sheet of paper. 'Here it is. Looks like it was a complete accident, agricultural vehicle, blind bend, no seatbelt on, never stood a chance. Open and shut case as far as the attending officers were concerned.'

'As if she hadn't had enough shit in her life, we still have to find the connection between these two women and the dead man in Walsall.' Gillman again looked in deep thought; suddenly he banged both palms of his hands on the desk, 'Good job, Phil. That's given me a lot to think about. Fancy a drink? It's on me.'

'Cheers, sir. I could do with one.' Both detectives grabbed their jackets and left the station heading in the direction of the local pub, Kent feeling particularly pleased with himself.

That evening after the twins were settled in bed, Lisa checked that all the windows and doors were locked. She went into the sitting room, where Janie was watching TV. 'They both in bed now?' asked Janie.

'Yeah, fast asleep.' Lisa sat down in an armchair, 'I think I'm going to give Zak's mum and dad a ring, see if they'll have the twins for a few days. At least I'll know they're safe there.'

'Good idea,' said Janie. 'I tell you what, while they're away we can get the security on this place beefed up a bit.'

'If it's OK with their nan and grandad, I'll take them over after school on Friday. It shouldn't be a problem, they haven't seen them for a couple of weeks.' They both sat in an uncomfortable silence, listening for the slightest sound.

'Lisa, we can't go on like this, something has to be done.'

'What, Janie?' Lisa sounded exasperated. 'What can I do?' Again, silence fell on the room. Lisa knew that Janie was right, but at this moment she didn't have an answer.

Jimmy had spent the last two evenings in his flat sat in silence, planning his revenge. He was still unaware of Zak's death, but in his current state of mind, Zak was irrelevant. He was planning to launch his attack when they would least expect it. If Zak got in the way he would deal with him too. He would visit them on the following weekend; it would be his last visit and all scores would be settled.

24

Salvation

That Friday morning Jimmy was up bright and early; he had arranged to start work earlier than usual so he could leave at lunchtime. He still wasn't on good terms with the foreman, but the arrangement suited both of them on this occasion, as there were a couple of early deliveries to get on the road. Jimmy had called the probation officer and explained he was in work early. Not wanting to upset his employer, they allowed him to sign in at lunchtime after his shift had finished. Everything was going to plan and once he had signed in he was away – the weekend was his.

It was a similar story at the police station where, for the second time in just over a week, Gillman was in work before Kent. The missing piece of his puzzle was intriguing him. As he sat at his desk sipping coffee from a plastic vending machine cup a thought suddenly jumped into his mind, 'I wonder...' he said speaking to himself out loud. He slugged back the remains of the coffee and dropped the cup in the bin. Getting up from his desk he made his way through to the station main desk, hoping to find an operator for the main computer. He could work it himself but found it frustrating; what took him half an hour took these youngsters two minutes.

'Morning sir, you're early again.' It was Kent, coming in through the main entrance.

'Morning Phil, just the man I was looking for. I'd like the use of your keyboard skills again.' Gillman was relieved to see him.

'No problem, sir, what do you want me to check out?' Kent followed Gillman to the main computer room and sat down in front of a screen, Gillman leaned on the back of the chair peering over his shoulder.

'I need you to do a check on James Noakes,' said Gillman.

'Wasn't he that bloke you helped put away in the eighties?' replied Kent.

'Yep, the very same.'

Kent logged in, 'Right then, let's have a look ... searching for sex male, surname Noakes, forename James...' He moved through half a dozen screens in a matter of seconds while Gillman continued to peer over his shoulder, shaking his head from side to side, still partially baffled by the the technological age.

'There we go ... search.' He clicked 'Enter' and sat back in his seat, 'Just a minute or two, sir.' The status bar loading the information shot across the bottom of the screen, within seconds displaying the information they required. Kent read out the information, 'James Noakes, convicted of the murder of a Miss Michelle Summers, a known prostitute of 22 Belfort Road, Edgbaston, and Miss Sunli Chun of Flat 44, Compton Towers, Bristol Road, Birmingham, a Chinese girl, student, also suspected of being on the game. He pleaded not guilty on the grounds of diminished responsibility.'

'I know,' said Gillman, 'I was there. He got away with it. There was too much press coverage; the judge wanted a quick decision before the defence claimed an unfair hearing due to the media influence.'

'Anyway, he was sent to a high-security psychiatric hospital at Brockton, just outside Leeds.' Kent continued, 'Ah, after ten years he was transferred to a low-security hospital. Says here he went on a rehabilitation programme.'

'It's called working the system, Phil.'

'The Shire Oak Institution, just north of Birmingham.' Kent suddenly went very quiet. He turned to Gillman, 'Released May 2005. He's back on the fuckin' streets.' Kent looked absolutely amazed.

'I think they refer to it nowadays as care in the community,' said Gillman wearily. 'Fingers crossed, we may have just found the missing piece in our puzzle. First thing we have to do is find out where he's living. They'll have kept close tabs on him; part of his parole will include signing on once or twice a week. A support team will have arranged accommodation for him and found some form of employment; after all, he'll have been out of society for twenty years.'

'I can't imagine that,' said Kent.

'Don't kill anyone and you won't have to,' said Gillman.

'Sir, it says here that this Doctor Phelps claims he's completely rehabilitated.'

Gillman sighed. 'Phil, I don't give a shit what the doctors say, I saw the remains of those poor women and if we hadn't reacted the way we did he would have killed more.' Gillman paused, 'Trust me on this one. He can't be rehabilitated.' For a second or two Gillman appeared to be in deep thought. 'Right, let's make a few phone calls. We need to find out who his parole officer is, from there we'll get an address, then we'll give him a tug.' Once again, Kent's keyboard skills proved very useful in locating Noakes' probation office, which was on the Birmingham Road, just outside Walsall. It was no more than a fifteen-minute drive from the station; they couldn't believe that on his release he had been relocated so close to the area in which he had committed his crimes. Still, the authorities must have had their reasons. Gillman decided to pay them a personal visit.

Jimmy's parole officer was a woman in her forties by the name of Gillian Maclaire, slightly built with bright red hair and a very soft yet obvious Scottish accent. Gillman called first to confirm that Noakes was still under their authority and by a stroke of luck, Mrs Maclaire answered the phone. Gillman explained who he was and, as he wanted to discuss confidential information, he arranged a meeting with her at one o'clock that same day.

Jimmy finished work at noon. As quickly as he could, he gathered up his things, clocked out and headed down to the probation office. The sooner he signed in, the sooner he could get away. Normally he was in and out in ten minutes but for some reason, today she was asking lots of questions about his job and social life. It was beginning to frustrate him, but he knew he just had to grin and bear it. Forty-five minutes later, just before one o'clock, Jimmy left the office. He put on his crash helmet and secured the clip around his chin. He had prepared his overnight bag as usual, but this time had included a couple of little extras – things he might need to get his point across. Slipping his arms through the shoulder straps, he pulled the bag onto his back and was quickly on his way.

As Gillman and Kent turned into the probation office's car park, Jimmy's bike exited and disappeared down the road. It was two minutes to one. They waited a short time for a car to reverse out of a space, then parked and walked round to the front entrance. Gillman knew these people were sticklers for punctuality and as they approached the desk the receptionist's eyes raised from her paperwork.

'Good afternoon,' said Gillman, introducing himself and Kent, 'we have an appointment to see Mrs Maclaire at one o'clock.'

The receptionist glanced at the clock. It was two minutes past, but from the look on her face you would have thought they had the wrong day. 'Take a seat and I'll see if she's still available.'

As they sat down Kent whispered, 'Snotty bitch.'

'My sentiments exactly,' replied Gillman, 'but keep your voice down.'

A few minutes later a door directly opposite them opened and Mrs Maclaire appeared. 'Good afternoon gentlemen,' her soft voice not befitting her position. The officers introduced themselves, holding up their ID cards, which she took from them and scrutinised carefully, before handing them back. 'That's fine gentleman, now what can I do for you exactly?'

'We are making enquires concerning a murder that took place in Walsall town centre,' said Gillman, 'We'd like to ask a Mr James Noakes a few questions about the incident.' She looked baffled and invited them into her office.

'I don't know how Jimmy can help you,' she said. 'He's such a nice man, a completely reformed character. I can't say a bad word about him. He's usually on time and if there is a problem he always calls. Only today he finished work early, came here straight away to sign in.'

'You mean he was here this morning?' asked Gillman.

'Not this morning – I was talking to him only fifteen minutes ago. You probably passed him in the car park.'

Gillman took a deep breath. 'If you could give me his home address, we can eliminate him from our enquires.'

'Of course, Detective Inspector Gillman, but I really think you're wasting your time.' She got up and went over to a filling cabinet. 'Here we are,' she pulled out a file, turned and went back to the desk. 'You know, Inspector Gillman, I see many people come and go in this job and the unfortunate thing for a lot of them is that society never really forgives them,' she shook her head, 'I'm not surprised that they reoffend.' Gillman was starting to lose his patience with the woman; all she seemed to do was sing the praises of, as far as he was concerned, the scum of society. He'd had enough.

'What about the families, Mrs Maclaire? What about the people they kill and maim, lives that are irreparably damaged, could we have a little thought for them?' Gillman suddenly went quiet. Kent looked at the floor and the atmosphere could have been cut with a knife. Mrs Maclaire copied the address onto a sheet of paper and passed it across the desk.

Five minutes later they were getting into the car. 'Good for you, sir,' said Kent. Until that point they had been silent.

'People like that get right up my fucking nose,' said Gillman, 'Come on, let's give Mr Perfect a wake-up call.' Kent entered the address into his satellite system. 7A, Banford Road, Walsall. Precise addresses were always better than postcodes. Within seconds they were on their way, Kent's trusty machine instantly providing them with directions.

As they pulled into Banford Road, Kent slowed down, allowing Gillman to scan the door numbers. 'That's it, Phil, 7A.' Kent found the first available parking space and pulled in. They both got out of the car and walked back to the flat, where Kent vigorously banged the doorknocker. 'Steady Phil, you'll have the door off.' A large grin appeared on Gillman's face. Kent cupped his hands and attempted to peer through the front window, but the thick and grubby net curtains obscured his view.

'I don't think he's home, sir,' said Kent.

'No,' replied Gillman, 'if he was, I'm sure he would have heard you knock that door. Come on, we'll get a sandwich then come back later.' As they walked back towards the car, they used their peripheral vision to observe for any slight movement from the net curtains. Gillman wasn't going to let this lie; his instinct and experience told him that somehow this man was an integral part of his puzzle.

Earlier that day, as Lisa dropped the twins at school, she didn't notice the red Vauxhall Cavalier. The driver had watched her every move since she had opened the front door, and was now staying at a safe distance so as not to attract her attention. As the twins chased each other in the playground, appearing not to have a care in the world, Lisa watched, waiting for the school bell to announce that it was time to go in. She had endured so much tragedy in such a short life. Jodie and Josh were all she cared about now. After the events of the last few months, all the material things, the house, the business, had suddenly become insignificant.

Not fifty yards away, leaning against the school railings, Alex Dean, Lisa's father, stood watching both Lisa and the children. He had been released from prison just over twelve months ago, at first not even considering trying to find Lisa. However, prison had made him a very humble man, and he realised that the things he had done all those years ago could never be forgotten or forgiven. Since the day he had been arrested, not a drop of alcohol had passed his lips, at first through enforced abstinence in prison, but as time went by he realised what it had cost him. He had made peace with his God and hoped that one day, before he died, he could do the same with his family. Although now past retirement age he was a fit and strong man, his short but stocky, muscular build not diminishing with age and only the grey hair and deep lines on his face giving away his years. He hoped one day to be able to talk to Lisa, but even now, a year after his release, he felt too ashamed to approach her. He had spent many late evenings watching her house from a distance, wondering what she was talking about with her family. He had seen the funeral procession when her husband died, and the urge to go and hold her and tell her it would all be OK was almost overwhelming, but he knew that could never happen. As the school bell sounded, the children waved to their mother and ran towards the main entrance. Alex glanced over at Lisa, the love for her children absolutely clear on her face. Alex smiled sadly, turned and disappeared into the crowd of parents.

By mid-afternoon, Jimmy had arrived in Oxford and after filling his bike with fuel, he went straight to the Travel Lodge and booked himself in. He told the receptionist he would only be staying for one night. After closing the door of his room behind him, he placed his bag on the bed, took out his toothbrush and razor and put them on the shelf above the sink. From the bottom of his bag he took out his trusty screwdriver; it had helped him in one or two sticky situations. Next, he took out a pair of skin-tight black leather gloves and, finally, an eight-inch filleting knife. He held the blade close to his face, turning it towards the light, admiring the razor sharp edge; before she died he planned to have a little fun.

At the same time as Jimmy arrived in Oxford, Lisa and Janie pulled up at the school. They parked the car and stood by the gates. Already it was getting busy with small groups of mothers taking up their usual positions.

'You know what,' said Janie, 'we haven't had a girly night in for ages. What do you say, after we drop the twins off, we get a Chinese and sample a couple of bottles of your wine and just curl up in front of the telly?'

'That doesn't mean you're going to get completely off your face does it?' asked Lisa.

'Me?' replied Janie, a look of mock offence giving way to a broad grin, 'would I do that?' The school bell sounded and, like ants, children came swarming from the main doors. Jodie and Josh ran across the playground, quickly spotting Lisa in the crowd, they raised their hands and waved in unison.

'Hi mum, hi auntie Janie,' said Jodie, 'are we still going to nan and grandad's?'

'Yeah, we're having some work done on the house and it'll be really boring for you guys.'

'Yay!' shouted Josh, who liked spending time with his grandfather; he reminded him of his father, and always found time to play with him.

They arrived an hour and a half later with Zak's parents looking as excited as the twins. Lisa had always got on well with Zak's parents, but since his death they had felt closer than her own parents ever did. Lisa and Janie didn't stay long, just long enough not to be rude. After a coffee and half an hour's chat, Lisa could see that the twins were already being spoiled rotten so they said their goodbyes and started back.

'Right, come on then girl, let's let our hair down for a few hours,' said Janie.

Gillman and Kent had spent the remainder of the afternoon clearing outstanding paperwork from their desks; the present case was taking up so much of their time that everything else was suffering. By half past five Gillman had had enough, he got up and went into the main office where Kent was busy trying to file away a particularly large tower of folders. 'Come on Phil, let's get some fresh air, we can have another drive down to Noakes' place and see if he's home yet.'

'Sounds good to me, sir, I don't feel like I'm going anywhere with this lot.' Kent grabbed his jacket and fifteen minutes later they arrived at Jimmy's flat. After more banging on the door and peering through the window, it was safe to say he wasn't at home.

'I need a look round in there,' said Gillman, 'I'm sure he's linked to this case; we need a warrant. Let's put the case over to the Old Man.' The Old Man was Detective Superintendent Chris Long. DS Long was closer to retirement than Gillman; at fifty-five years of age he had literally a few months before he retired.

When they arrived back at the station, DS Long had already gone home. Not to be beaten, Gillman rang his mobile number, which he knew he was obliged to keep on at all times. He knew he wouldn't be pleased at being contacted after hours but Gillman had a gut feeling it was important. Long was driving when the phone rang out; he answered it on his hands-free system. 'Sorry to bother you, sir,' said Gillman, 'but something urgent has come up.' Gillman explained that he thought he had a suspect for the Fraser case.

'Go on,' said Long.

'Back in the eighties I locked up a man for a double murder, James Noakes. Well, he was released recently, he's living not fifteen minutes from where the body was found and...'

'Wait a minute, Jack,' Long interrupted. 'You put him away twenty years ago, he's been released back on your patch, and now you want a warrant to search his house. Have you got any hard evidence?'

'Well, if I can...' started Gillman.

'Jack, have you got any hard evidence?'

'Well, no sir.'

'Listen, put your case together on my desk at nine o'clock tomorrow morning and I'll consider it. But if you think I'm going to issue you a warrant to go on what will look like a witch-hunt, you're wrong. Jack, off the record, you're fifty years old, I'm fifty-five. I don't think taking risks is a particularly good idea at this stage of our careers. Now go home and I'll see you tomorrow.' Long hung up.

'Bollocks,' said Gillman. 'Turned us down flat. I remember when he would have took that gamble. Trouble is he's too worried about his pension.'

'So, what's the next step, sir?' asked Kent.

'We go home. I'll put the facts on paper and present it in the morning. Go on Phil, you get off and I'll finish up.'

'If you're sure, sir?'

'Yeah, go on, I'll see you in the morning.'

Back in Oxford, after picking up a Chinese take-away, Lisa and Janie arrived home. Janie took the food through to the kitchen as Lisa locked and bolted the front door. 'I'll plate it up, you pour us both a drink,' said Janie.

'Any preference on the wine, or is that a silly question?' asked Lisa. Lisa's expensive wines were wasted on Janie, who appreciated the effect rather than the flavour. They sat down on the sofa, meals on trays and each with a large glass of wine.

'This is the life,' said Janie, raising her glass towards Lisa. Lisa smiled back at her. Briefly, her mind flashed back to all those years ago in Janie's flat when the girls' nights in were so comforting; so many good memories, but at the same time bad. Lisa shivered. She wasn't proud of what she had done, no doubt neither was Janie, but at the time survival had been the name of the game. Lisa drank deeply from her glass. Three bottles of wine later, they had talked and laughed a lot, but Janie now looked worse for wear, having drunk the lion's share herself. In a drowsy but very happy state, Janie climbed the stairs with Lisa following her, just to make sure she didn't topple over backwards. Janie flopped onto her bed and within seconds was snoring. She hadn't undressed, but Lisa thought it best to let her sleep. She covered her with a blanket, wished her a good night and partially closed the door on her way out. Yawning aloud and a little light-headed herself, Lisa decided to call it a night. She quickly changed into her nightclothes and climbed into bed. Just like Janie, within a few minutes she was fast asleep.

Jack Gillman sat in his living room, in front of him an unopened bottle of scotch. He was so tempted to unscrew the lid, pour himself a large one and forget the case. As DS Long had said, 'Jack, it's too late in your career to take chances.' He stared at the bottle. 'Bollocks it is!' He picked up the bottle, took it into the kitchen and put it in the cupboard. Snatching up his mobile from the breakfast bar, he selected Kent's number. 'Listen Phil, how do you fancy breaking into a flat?'

Twenty minutes later Kent pulled up outside Gillman's house. Gillman was waiting for him and quickly got into the car. 'Thanks Phil,' he said, 'I know this sounds a little crazy, but I'm sure we're going to get a result.' He passed Kent a pair of black leather gloves, 'Don't want to leave any prints now, do we?' Gillman wiggled his own leather-clad fingers in an almost comical fashion. Kent pulled on the gloves and drove off in the direction of Jimmy's flat. When they arrived, the flat was still in darkness. They knocked, but there was again no reply. 'Keep your eyes open, Phil.' Kent stood by the front wall. From inside his coat Gillman pulled out a short spade-ended crowbar. He looked at Kent; Kent's eyes were wide with surprise. 'I knew this would come in handy one day,' said Gillman. He pressed the crowbar in between the door and the frame, close to the lock, and gave an almighty yank. As the door sprang open, small shards of wood flicked up into Gillman's face. 'Let's go,' he whispered, flicking the splinters from his face. Quickly, they dodged through the door, closing it behind them. 'OK Phil, anything that could connect him to Fraser. You start in the bedroom, I'll look in the living room.'

'OK, sir.' Cautiously, they both went about their business. They planned to make it look like a burglary and not worry about messing the place up a little. After a good half an hour they had found nothing and Gillman was beginning to think he had got it wrong. Then, from the bedroom, Kent called out, 'Sir, come and take a look at this.' Gillman went into the room where Kent was sitting on the bed reading a letter. 'It's a letter from Lisa Wright to that Janie.' Gillman took the letter from him and started reading.

'Well done Phil, this is the connection we've been looking for.'

'There's a pile of them, sir, they were under his mattress.' Kent collected up all the letters and after a quick glance up and down the road, they were on their way.

'OK Phil,' said Gillman, 'back to my house, we've got some reading to do.'

It was fast approaching midnight. Gillman and Kent had been reading for a good hour, and had seen the last twenty years of Lisa's life documented in the letters, right down to how she had acquired the money from Jimmy in the first place. Theoretically, she had done nothing wrong; at the end of the day he had gifted her the money. What she hadn't considered was what would happen if he ever got out of prison. It seemed that her worst nightmare had come true. They could only speculate about the link with Fraser, but whatever it was, she was in serious danger. 'Phil,' said Gillman, 'I know it's late, but Noakes has disappeared. I think we need to take a drive and quickly.'

It was just midnight and Jimmy was on his bike, driving towards Stanton Harcourt. As he approached the village he slowed down, lowering the revs to reduce engine noise. He turned off his lights and slowly made his way towards Lisa's house. Unknown to Jimmy, in a car parked further along the road, Alex Dean sat thinking about what he had lost and whether his family would ever accept any contact with him; for now, watching from a distance was as much as he could have. Then, a movement caught his eye. Even without street lighting the moon was bright enough to provide a good view along the road. Alex had sat there for so long that his eyes had adjusted to the dark. It was unusual for anyone to be walking around in the village at that time of night. Sitting perfectly still, he could see a figure, Jimmy, pushing a bike into a small opening at the end of Lisa's garden. Alex watched as Jimmy glanced up and down the road, then hopped over the small fence, keeping himself as low and close to the hedges as he could. Alex's senses sharpened; what was going on? Was this man breaking in? Should he intervene? A dozen thoughts flooded into his head; he needed to think straight.

Jimmy checked the downstairs windows; they were all securely locked. As he approached the back door he took his screwdriver from inside his jacket. First he just tried the latch; it was locked. Undeterred, he gouged the screwdriver into the edge of the door, damaging both the frame and the door. Placing his shoulder against the door he pushed, gently but firmly. As the screwdriver loosened off he forced it in a little further then, without any warning, the latch broke and Jimmy fell inside the door, struggling to stay on his feet. He stood still for a few seconds, his ears straining for the slightest sound; nothing. He smiled to himself. He attempted to close the door behind him but the wood around the latch was split, so he left it ajar. Quietly, Jimmy went through the kitchen and stealthily climbed the stairs, slipping the filleting knife from his jacket as he went. Still unaware of the outcome of Zak's accident, he intended him to be his first target. At the top of the stairs he hesitated; it was dark and he didn't know the layout of the house. Turning left, he crept along the landing wielding the knife in front of him. The first door he came to was slightly ajar. Looking through the opening, in a shaft of moonlight he could see Janie lying on the bed, gently snoring and obviously sleeping soundly. Moving along the landing, the next door he came to was closed. He readied himself; this could be the one. Slowly and carefully turning the handle, trying to avoid even the slightest sound, he felt the catch release, then opened the door. It was obviously the twins' room, but neither of the beds had been slept in. Making his way back along the landing he passed the bathroom, the door standing wide open. There was only one door left; this had to be the one. Slowly, he opened the door and saw at once that a light was on. He caught his breath and stood perfectly still. Nothing. Checking his grip on the knife, he gently pushed the door further open. Before him lay his prize. The bedside lamp was on and in the soft glow he could see Lisa, lying alone in bed, her legs tucked up in a foetal position. His eyes rapidly scanned the room in search of her husband, but he was nowhere to be seen. A sadistic smile spread across his face and silently he walked over to the bed, knife still in his hand. He sat down on the bed behind Lisa. Her eyes opened almost instantly, her senses reacting to the sensation on the mattress. It was like one of those dreams when there is someone behind you but you can't look, like being in a state of paralysis. In a flash the memories of her childhood came flooding back, those terrifying late-night visits that had haunted her for so many years. She knew she had to turn and look but the fear was overwhelming. As if countering a huge magnetic field she summoned all her strength and turned, willing herself to look behind. Before she was even halfway round, Jimmy's hand was across her mouth forcing her head back into the pillow. 'Payback time, bitch,' he snarled at her. Lisa struggled to pull his hand from her face, then Jimmy raised the knife and she became very still. He pressed the flat of the knife against her cheek just below her eye and she began to shake uncontrollably. 'Now listen, bitch, we're going to have some fun, you got that?' Lisa could see the madness in his eyes and knew she had no choice but to do exactly as he said. Nodding submissively, she tried to stay calm. 'When I take my hand off your mouth, if you make the slightest noise, I'll cut your throat. You got that?' Lisa knew he meant it and again she nodded. Keeping the knife close to her throat, he released his hold on her mouth. Lisa drew in a huge breath. With his eyes remaining fixed on Lisa's face, Jimmy pulled back the duvet. He straddled her, running the point of the knife from her neck down the middle of her body to her navel.

Suddenly, Janie woke, her bladder informing her that she needed to relieve herself. Drowsily, she rolled out of bed, opened the door and went down the hall towards the bathroom. Her senses slowly returned. How did she get into bed, fully clothed as well? She realised she must have had one drink too many, then remembered Lisa had also had several glasses, but they'd had a good time. She could see that a light was on in Lisa's room and went along the landing to check on her. As she approached, the sound of a voice stopped her in her tracks; it sounded male. Lisa's door was slightly ajar. Peering through the gap Janie was instantly wide awake, senses in overdrive. She could see Lisa lying on her back with a man sitting on top of her. The light from the bedside lamp showed the fear on Lisa's face. It wasn't hard to work out who the man was. Janie quickly looked around the landing for something to arm herself with. Pulling the flowers from a vase on a small landing table, she tiptoed back to Lisa's door. Janie couldn't hear what he was saying to her, nor could she see that he was wielding a knife. Praying that the door would not creak, she pushed it open and quietly walked up behind him, the vase raised ready to strike. As she pulled the vase back to swing at him the water inside it spilled out onto the floor. In a millisecond Jimmy spun round and, still sitting on Lisa, slashed the knife through the air, narrowly missing Janie's throat. Janie brought the vase crashing down onto Jimmy's shoulder and, wincing with pain, he leapt off the bed to his feet. On seeing the knife Janie froze. Jimmy's right fist hit her just below her left eye, knocking her out cold. Before she hit the ground Jimmy kicked her at least twice. Lisa saw her chance. Not wanting to leave her friend, but realising that the only way to save her was to get help, she ran out the bedroom door bouncing off the landing wall in a bid to reach the stairs. Jimmy was momentarily preoccupied; kick after kick slammed into Janie's body. He heard Lisa running down the stairs; one more sickening blow, then Jimmy gave chase.

Alex Dean couldn't contain himself any longer and slammed both hands on the steering wheel. 'Fuck the consequences,' he said to himself. He jumped out the car and ran towards Lisa's house. The deep gravel on the drive impeded his progress but he finally reached the side of the house and saw the back door standing ajar. He pushed the door open and stepped inside. At that moment Lisa came frantically running down the last few stairs. As she turned into the kitchen she felt she was living her worst nightmare. Although he was over twenty years older she recognised him straight away. She couldn't believe her eyes, her father was standing in front of her not five yards away. It seemed as if everything had slipped into slow motion. As he raised his hands as if to say come to me she froze, almost falling over backwards. Behind her, Jimmy came running down the stairs with the knife held high like an ice pick ready to strike. Alex's face turned to one of pure anger. As he darted forwards Lisa thought he was aiming for her, but he ran straight past. Jimmy and Alex clashed like two charging bulls. Alex, being the more powerful, drove Jimmy back before they both fell down in a heap in the corner of the kitchen. Alex was doing his best to hold on to the wrist wielding the knife, but already blood was on the floor; one of them had been cut as they fell to the ground. Cowering in a corner at the far side of the table, unable to take in the madness that was unravelling before her, Lisa watched as Alex and Jimmy reigned blows on each other, both trying to control the blade in Jimmy's hand. As they rolled over and over, blood flowed onto the kitchen floor; Lisa was still unable to tell which one of them was bleeding. Both men, now covered in blood, were tiring. Jimmy gave a last almighty thrust. Again both men rolled over, then they lay very still, Alex slumped on top of Jimmy. Lisa could hear her own heart pounding. Suddenly, Jimmy pushed with all his might, rolling Alex onto his back and exposing the handle of the knife, which had been plunged deep into Alex's lower chest, right up to its hilt. Jimmy got to his knees, blood staining his hands and face. His breathing was rapid and laboured. Taking hold of the knife handle, he pulled the blade from Alex's chest and watched as a pool of blood quickly formed and spread across the floor. Slowly he got to his feet and turned towards Lisa, baring his teeth and squeezing the handle of the knife as he walked towards her. Jimmy's focus on Lisa was so intense that he didn't hear Janie stagger down the stairs. She stood at the kitchen doorway trying to make some sense of the ghastly scene which lay before her. As Jimmy raised the knife above Lisa, Janie's basic instincts took over. Snatching a knife from the wooden block to her right she lunged towards Jimmy. He tried to swing round to defend himself but it was too late. Janie plunged the blade into his back just below his neck. The strike was lethal, instantly severing his spinal column. Jimmy dropped the knife and fell face down in front of Lisa, dead before he hit the ground. Lisa pulled her knees in close to her chest, expecting him to resume his assault. Cautiously, Janie approached his lifeless body, stepping slowly around the side of him. 'Come on, Lisa,' she whispered, extending her arm and beckoning Lisa from her safety zone. Lisa stood up keeping her back firmly pinned to the wall, her eyes fixed on Jimmy's body. Trembling, she sidestepped round him, grasping Janie's hand. 'Who's that?' asked Janie, pointing in the direction of Alex.

'It's my father,' replied Lisa. Janie's mouth dropped.

'Your father?'

Lisa nodded. They both stared at Alex and the blood congealing around his body. Suddenly, he took a deep, rasping breath.

'Fuck's sake, Lisa, he's still alive,' shouted Janie. Lisa quickly ran towards him, grabbing a tea towel as she dropped to her knees to attempt to stop the flow of blood from the chest wound.

'Janie, ambulance, quickly.' yelled Lisa. Janie had already gone. Darting through the carnage into the living room, she grabbed the phone and dialled 999.

Alex Dean lay on the kitchen floor mortally wounded; Lisa pushed her knees into the nape of his neck to support his head and slowly his eyes opened.

'Lisa, I'm sorry,' he could barely speak.

'Don't talk, an ambulance is on its way.'

'Too late for that,' he gasped. 'I don't expect forgiveness, just hoped one day to prove I was sorry.' Lisa didn't know what to say; the shock of Jimmy's attack had been too much to take in, let alone having her father, who she hadn't seen for twenty years, turning up and attempting to defend her. 'Your mum's death was a terrible accident, I never meant to hurt her, it was the drink. I've lived with the guilt every waking moment since that day. His eyes were heavy and his breathing shallow. Lisa was desperate.

'Hold on dad, they're coming, I can hear the sirens.' She pressed harder on the wound. In the distance, the sound of the emergency sirens got louder.

'I'm not proud of the things I've done in my life; if I could change it, I would. Bye Lisa.'

'Dad, hold on, hold on,' Lisa begged him. He looked into her eyes and she could see that he had found peace with himself.

'Sweet Lisa,' he whispered. Slowly, his eyes closed and Lisa wept, another chapter of her life had come to an end.

Outside the house an ambulance pulled onto the drive. Janie was waiting outside to direct them. Two paramedics, in their green uniforms with reflective jackets, grabbed their medical bags and ran in Janie's direction. They rushed through the back door then stopped dead in their tracks; the sight in front of them was like a scene from a horror movie. Quickly regaining their composure, they each went to work on the two casualties, realising within moments that their efforts were futile.

'Nothing I can do here, Paul,' said one of the paramedics to his colleague.

'Likewise mate,' his colleague replied. Instantly they turned their attention to Lisa and Janie.

'Are you injured or is all the blood theirs?'

'It's all theirs,' Janie replied. With a loud, crunching noise, Gillman and Kent pulled up on the gravelled drive, having broken every traffic regulation in the book to get there in such a short time. Gillman stepped through the back door and surveyed the scene, with Kent close behind him. Taking out his badge, Gillman introduced himself to the paramedics. His first thought was that they had arrived too late, but then, from the corner of his eye, he noticed two figures huddled in the corner. 'Mrs Wright, I thought for a minute that it was you.' He stepped around the carnage and placed his hands on their shoulders; they were both trembling. 'Are the children in the house?'

'No,' said Lisa, 'they're staying with their nan and grandad.'

'Thank God for that. Come on ladies, let's get you out of here.'

'Excuse me,' said one of the paramedics, 'these ladies need to be checked over at the hospital, especially you, madam,' looking directly at Janie, 'that cheek looks very sore.' His colleague went out to the ambulance and came back with two blankets; he placed them round the girls' shoulders and walked them out.

Gillman turned to Kent, 'Phil, I want you to secure the scene, get on the phone and get the ball rolling. I'll go with the ladies and get a statement when they've been given the all clear. There's quite a few questions still to be answered.'

'No problem, sir.' Gillman climbed into the ambulance. As they drove off, Kent was already on the phone. Quickly, the house was cordoned off and scene of crime officers arrived to secure every possible piece of evidence.

The ambulance arrived at Oxford General Accident & Emergency; it was surprisingly quiet for a Friday night. Gillman had so much he wanted to ask them, it wasn't hard to work out who the one dead man was, but the other one baffled him. The girls were checked out and cleaned up. Janie had severe bruising to her cheek and ribs, but considering the beating she had sustained, she was very fortunate. Lisa had not sustained any physical injuries, but it was plain to see she was in deep shock. The doctor prescribed tranquillisers for Lisa and painkillers for Janie. Once the nurse had collected their medication from the pharmacy, the doctor said they could go. Lisa and Janie sat in a cubicle, both in deep thought. A face appeared around the curtain, it was Gillman. 'Alright ladies, can I get you a drink?'

'No thanks,' said Lisa.

'Sorry I didn't suss him out sooner,' said Gillman, coming into the cubicle, 'but you know, if you'd been straight with me right from the start, it may not have come to this.' Both the girls dropped their heads. 'Who was the other man?' asked Gillman.

'It was my father,' replied Lisa.

'Your father, I thought he got life?'

'He did, now he's dead thanks to that bastard.' Lisa still wasn't sure how to feel about the death of her father.

'I want you to tell me everything you can,' said Gillman, 'I know all about your background so just give it me straight and we'll see what we can do.'

Weary from living with lies and hiding the past, she told Gillman everything: how she was sure Jimmy murdered Zak, right back to the day she first set eyes on Jimmy. They talked for well over an hour. Gillman listened attentively; it was quite some story, the jigsaw pieces were finally falling into place.

'So that's it,' said Lisa, 'what happens now?'

'Well,' said Gillman, 'there'll be an inquiry, statements to be written,'

'I mean about Fraser,' said Lisa.

'Ah, Fraser. Theoretically, that's the only illegal thing you've done and he's dead. Noakes is also dead. Looks to me like a mugging that went seriously wrong.'

'Are you saying you're not going to say anything about what I just told you?'

'That would be illegal, Mrs Wright,' again, Lisa's head dropped. 'Do you mind if I call you Lisa?' She shook her head. 'I've been a police officer for a long time, Lisa. I don't think putting you behind bars is going to do anybody any good, especially those kids of yours. Let's just say I have selective hearing. Of course, there's going to be a lot of questioning at the station. But as for Fraser and Noakes, their secrets died with them.' Janie wanted to smile but resisted the urge. 'Have you both got somewhere to stay tonight? Your house will be swarming with officers.'

'We can stay at Reece's flat,' said Lisa, 'it's only ten minutes from here.'

'OK,' said Gillman, 'I'll drop you there and collect you in the morning. The sooner we get those statements written the better. I'll give my colleague a call, I won't be long.' Gillman turned to leave the cubicle.

'Mr Gillman,' said Lisa; he stopped and turned, 'thank you.'

He smiled at her, 'All in a day's work. Oh, don't you remember, it's Jack.'

It was the early hours of the morning before they arrived at Reece's flat and he was only too happy to put them up for as long as necessary. Gillman left them to get some rest. It was some time before they finally settled down and attempted to sleep.

Gillman arrived, as arranged, right on time the next morning. Lisa and Janie spent most of the day at Oxford Central Police Station. Finally, when all the 'i's were dotted and the 't's crossed, they were allowed to go home. Or at least to Zak's parents. It was an emotional reunion for Lisa and the children. The twins couldn't understand why their mother should be so tearful; they had only been away for the weekend. Zak's parents and Lisa thought it best not to mention the events of that weekend, at least not till they were older and able to understand.

25

Epilogue

A month passed and life started to return to some kind of normality. Lisa had not been to work at the bar since that terrible weekend. Although the house showed no physical signs of the ghastly events, the homely atmosphere Lisa felt the day she first moved in was now gone. Lisa could tell Janie felt the same and although they didn't speak about it, neither of them liked to be in the house alone; there were too many fearful memories.

Lisa and Janie were sitting at the garden table, watching the twins playing with their toys further down the lawn. The sun was shining and to the uninformed observer it was an idyllic scene of English village life. A voice called out from the side of the house, 'Hello, anyone home?' Lisa and Janie turned to see Jack Gillman's face peering over the hedge. 'Afternoon ladies.'

'Come on in, Jack,' shouted Lisa, 'great to see you.'

'Likewise,' said Gillman, as he came along the path, 'how are you both?' They smiled at him.

'Still got a lot on our minds,' said Lisa.

'Time's a great healer,' Gillman ventured, 'but I think you already know that.' He looked directly at Lisa and she returned a gentle, understanding smile. Lisa made coffee and they spent the next hour or so talking and occasionally laughing, but deliberately avoiding any reference to the previous month's events.

Eventually, Gillman stood up and stretched his legs, 'I'd best be making tracks,' he said, 'it's a long drive home.'

'It was great to see you,' said Lisa, 'you know you're always welcome here.'

'Before I go,' Gillman raised a finger to his mouth, 'I have something, it's for you actually, Janie.' Janie looked surprised. 'It's in the car.'

'We'll walk out with you,' said Lisa. Gillman shouted goodbye and waved to the twins, still both happily playing further down the garden. Gillman opened the boot of the car and took out a parcel, about the same size as a shoebox.

'This belongs to you, Janie.' It was wrapped in brown paper and tied with string.

'What is it?' asked Janie.

'Open it,' Gillman encouraged her. She pulled off the string and paper then, placing the box on the boot lid, she took off the lid. It contained every letter Lisa had ever sent to Janie. 'I thought you should have them back,' said Gillman. Janie smiled,

'Thank you, Jack,' turning to Gillman she put her arms round his neck and hugged him, then placed a gentle kiss on his cheek.

'Have a good life, ladies,' he said, walking round to the driver's door. Lisa felt he was attempting to give them some kind of closure on their terrible ordeal and it was working. Gillman smiled, 'Bye now.' He was just about to get into the car when Lisa walked up to him and stopped him; a simple goodbye was insufficient. Putting her arms around him, she too kissed his cheek. 'You're a good man, Jack Gillman.' His face flushed

'Well, I've been called many other things,' he stammered, 'take care.' He got into the car; the engine burst into life and as he drove off he tooted the horn. Lisa and Janie waved as he disappeared down the road.

Walking back into the garden and on to the lawn, Lisa turned to Janie, 'I think I'm going to sell the house,' she said.

'That sounds like a good idea,' replied Janie.

'How do you fancy living by the coast?'

Janie turned and smiled, 'Now that's a really good idea. You know something, Lisa?'

'What?'

'You could write a book about your life.'

'Not yet Janie, not yet.'

Lightning Source UK Ltd.
Milton Keynes UK
02 September 2009

143274UK00001BA/22/A